Experiencing God in
Everything and Nothingness

Experiencing God in Everything and Nothingness

Negativity, Embodiment, and Spirituality—
South African Perspectives

EDITED BY
ANNETTE POTGIETER AND
KHEGAN M. DELPORT

◆PICKWICK *Publications* · Eugene, Oregon

EXPERIENCING GOD IN EVERYTHING AND NOTHINGNESS
Negativity, Embodiment, and Spirituality—South African Perspectives

Copyright © 2024 Wipf and Stock Publishers. All rights reserved. Except for brief quotations in critical publications or reviews, no part of this book may be reproduced in any manner without prior written permission from the publisher. Write: Permissions, Wipf and Stock Publishers, 199 W. 8th Ave., Suite 3, Eugene, OR 97401.

Pickwick Publications
An Imprint of Wipf and Stock Publishers
199 W. 8th Ave., Suite 3
Eugene, OR 97401

www.wipfandstock.com

PAPERBACK ISBN: 978-1-6667-6435-2
HARDCOVER ISBN: 978-1-6667-6436-9
EBOOK ISBN: 978-1-6667-6437-6

Cataloguing-in-Publication data:

Names: Potgieter, Annette, editor. | Delport, Khegan M., editor.

Title: Experiencing God in everything and nothingness : negativity, embodiment, and spirituality—South African perspectives / edited by Annette Potgieter and Khegan M. Delport.

Description: Eugene, OR : Pickwick Publications, 2024 | Includes bibliographical references and index(es).

Identifiers: ISBN 978-1-6667-6435-2 (paperback) | ISBN 978-1-6667-6436-9 (hardcover) | ISBN 978-1-6667-6437-6 (ebook)

Subjects: LCSH: Spiritual life. | Spiritual life—Christianity—History of doctrines.

Classification: BV5021 .E88 2024 (paperback) | BV5021 .E88 (ebook)

05/01/24

Unless otherwise noted, Scripture quotations are taken from the New Revised Standard Version Updated Edition. Copyright © 2021 National Council of Churches of Christ in the United States of America. Used by permission. All rights reserved worldwide.

Where noted, Scripture quotations are from the ESV®Bible (The Holy Bible, English Standard Version®), copyright© 2001 by Crossway Bibles, a publishing ministry of Good News Publishers. Used by permission. All rights reserved.

Contents

List of Contributors | vii

Introduction: Spirituality between Everything and Nothingness
—Annette Potgieter and Khegan M. Delport | 1

Chapter 1: Navigating Nothingness: Spirituality amidst Upheaval
—Lisel Joubert | 10

Chapter 2: The Spirituality of Space: Locating the Spiritual Body through the Lens of Romans 8:18–30—Annette Potgieter | 27

Chapter 3: The Attention Assemblage and the Machines of Acedia: On Evagrian Practice in the Age of Hyperattention—Khegan M. Delport | 44

Chapter 4: Beyond the Totality of Religion: Memories of Violence, Finitude, and the Organic Body—Calvin D. Ullrich | 63

Chapter 5: "Wash me, and I shall be whiter than snow": Exploring the Potential of Purgation for Racialized Spirituality—Louis van der Riet | 78

Chapter 6: Youth and Environmental Consciousness: Do Religion, Faith, and Spirituality Matter?—Jacques Beukes | 95

Chapter 7: Characterizing Pharaoh's Self-Destructive Politics alongside the Plagues and Politics of South Africa—Gavin Fernandes | 109

Chapter 8: Spirituality, Poverty, and the Problem of Evil in the Book of Qoheleth: A Comparative Religious-Philosophical Supplement
—Jaco Gericke | 132

Chapter 9: The Tension between Experiences of Nothingness and Hope in the Metaphorical Meaning of the Names of the Children (Isa 7–8) from a Perspective of Generational Imprinted Trauma and Resilience
—Elizabeth Esterhuizen and Alphonso Groenewald | 148

Chapter 10: Using Biblical Trauma-Texts to Help Pain-Bearers Find Hope —June F. Dickie | 172

Chapter 11: Hope in the Midst of Death? A Reading of the Book of Job in the Time of Despair—Hassan Musa | 190

Chapter 12: Bible, Spirituality, and Method: Continuing the Debate —Christo Lombaard | 204

Author Index | 221

Scripture Index | 227

List of Contributors

JACQUES BEUKES has a PhD in practical theology and is currently a senior lecturer in the Department of Practical Theology and Mission Studies at the University of Pretoria's Faculty of Theology and Religion. His research foci are theology and development, religion and development, community development, congregational studies, diaconal (*Diakonia*) studies, youth, youthwork, youth ministry, and children's ministry.

KHEGAN M. DELPORT (PhD, Stellenbosch University) is a postdoctoral fellow at the University of Pretoria and a lecturer at Huguenot College. He is also an incoming postdoctoral fellow of the Alexander von Humboldt Stiftung at the Otto-Friedrich-Universität Bamberg, and the author of *On Tragedy and Transcendence: An Essay on the Metaphysics of Donald MacKinnon and Rowan Williams* (2021).

JUNE F. DICKIE (PhD, University of KwaZulu-Natal, South Africa) is a Bible translator and researcher with particular interests in the Psalms, performance, and psychological hermeneutics. She has worked in various communities since 1994, mainly in Africa.

ELIZABETH ESTERHUIZEN (PhD, University of Pretoria) is a research associate at the University of Pretoria. She is an Old Testament and psychology scholar with a special interest in the prophetic books of Isaiah and Nahum.

GAVIN FERNANDES leads *The Philip Project*, a biblical studies training course in Cambridge, UK. He is a tutor of hermeneutics and Old Testament at London School of Theology (University of Middlesex, UK) and a research associate of the University of Pretoria (South Africa).

JACO GERICKE (DLitt, Semitic Languages; PhD, Old Testament) studied theology and philosophy at the University of Pretoria (1994–2004). Since 2013 he has been associate research professor of ancient texts, contexts and reception in the Faculty of Theology, North West University, South Africa.

LIST OF CONTRIBUTORS

ALPHONSO GROENEWALD is professor in Old Testament and Hebrew Scriptures at the University of Pretoria. He holds a DTh from Radboud University Nijmegen.

LISEL JOUBERT is lecturer in church history in the Department of Systematic Theology and Ecclesiology at the Faculty of Theology, Stellenbosch University. She is also an ordained minister in the Dutch Reformed Church in Gansbaai.

CHRISTO LOMBAARD is professor and head of department: Practical Theology and Mission Studies, Faculty of Theology and Religion, University of Pretoria. He holds two doctorates: a PhD in communication studies (North-West University, Potchefstroom campus, specializing in religious communications) and a DD in theology (University of Pretoria, specializing in Old Testament studies).

HASSAN MUSA is a Nigerian who obtained his PhD at Stellenbosch University South Africa. He has been engaged in teaching biblical theology and spirituality courses at ECWA Theological Seminary Kagoro and ECWA Theological Seminary Jos, both in Nigeria. He has also been a research conversation partner with the Center for Youth and Culture at Yale Divinity School, Yale University. He is a research fellow at Stellenbosch University, South Africa.

ANNETTE POTGIETER is a senior lecturer in the Department of New Testament and Related Texts at the University of Pretoria since September 2023. She was a lecturer and programme coordinator for Huguenot College 2020–2023. She completed her DTh at Humboldt Universität zu Berlin (2019).

CALVIN D. ULLRICH (PhD, Dr theol University of Stellenbosch, South Africa) is a senior lecturer at the Department of Historical and Constructive Theology, at the Faculty of Theology and Religion, University of the Free State. He was formerly a research fellow at the Ecumenical Institute of the Ruhr University Bochum, Germany. His recent book, *Sovereignty and Event* (Mohr Siebeck, 2021) was the recipient of the Manfred Lautenschläger Award for Theological Promise (2022).

LOUIS VAN DER RIET is a research associate in the Department of Systematic Theology and Ecclesiology in the Faculty of Theology, Stellenbosch University. He holds a PhD in systematic theology from Stellenbosch University and Vrije University Amsterdam.

Introduction

Spirituality between Everything and Nothingness

Annette Potgieter and Khegan M. Delport

Spirituality has garnered an increasing amount of interest. A significant strain of the discussion around "spirituality" in latter part of the twentieth century has concerned its discursive and disciplinary porousness. Where should the field of "spirituality studies" be situated? Should it be subordinated to the regimens of theological science or the descriptive parameters of religious studies? Is its relationship to theology analogous to the similar distinction made between theory and praxis, or are such distinctions insufficient for the lived hybridity of spiritual experience? Part of the reason for this indeterminacy is the ongoing debate regarding how spirituality is to be defined.[1] And indeed definitions, despite their inherent slippage and instability, are important. Some of the conceptual problems and nebulousness surrounding the term "spirituality" point to one of its central concerns, namely the holistic nature of human experience. "Spirituality studies" indeed recognizes the complexity of being human.[2] This is raised especially as our culture advances beyond the rate of our biological evolution. Just think of the impact of social media, AI, Chat GPT—just to name a few. On the one hand, the adventures and advances we have made are significant, but on the other hand, we have not developed fast enough to keep up with the impact of our advancements. We have become more aware of the harmful effect we as human beings have on the planet and also on each other.[3] Although we live in the most advanced time, we have an increase in mental health problems, among many other spiritual crises. Life is complex, and ever vacillating between states of everything and nothingness; that is, we are faced with

---

1. Schneiders, "Study of Christian Spirituality."
2. Kourie and Kretzschmar, *Christian Spirituality*, 3.
3. Joubert and Lombaard, "Theology and Spirituality," 4.

the fecundity of experiences, the totality of entangled challenges, as well as an awareness of our finitude and limits, of the fact that we live our spiritual lives within contingencies of embodiment and the threat of non-being.

In academic study, and spirituality studies specifically, disciplinary boundaries are important for the development of specialization; and yet, as we have just said, we do not live within such divisions. Our lives are entangled. Our experience is lived, material, and embodied, and so transgresses any abstracted or rigid divisions we develop for describing experiences. We create distinctions, necessarily so, for the ordering of thought and research, even as our daily lived experience continually crosses these domains. Nevertheless, we need working definitions, and so—as has become common in the field—we will offer one as well. Following Schneiders,[4] and for the purposes of this volume, we define "spirituality" as concerning those practices and experiences related to the integrating and orientating of lived experience towards transcendent values. This definition provides an orientation point for this collection of essays; however, it seems worthwhile to further specify the semantic range of "spirituality" for this volume. We are aware of course that the resurgence of interest in spirituality is within a postmodern society, as well as a global and interreligious context; however, the contributors to this book, for the most part, are Christian theologians and biblical scholars; and so some further definitions may be required here.[5] As regards *biblical spirituality*, a recurring theme of this volume, we indicate the plurality of spiritual visions within both Testaments and how they imagine, describe, and prescribe the relationship of created beings to the God of the biblical texts. Related to this, though conceptually distinctive, is the phenomenon of *Christian spirituality*; for us, this concerns both *what* the Christian church has taught about the practice of Christian living throughout the ages, here drawing upon the authoritative sources of Scripture and tradition, as well as the study of *how* those values have been historically and culturally expressed in time. Echoing Joubert and Lombaard, Christian spirituality may also be summarized as "the experience of faith,"[6] even as it remains continually informed from interactions from other relevant fields. Such experience, as we have already suggested, should be grasped holistically. In the words of Rowan Williams, Christian spirituality should be "far more than a science of interpreting exceptional private experiences" and should rather be understood as relating to "every area of human experience," so that "the goal of a

---

4. Schneiders, "Study of Christian Spirituality," 5–6.

5. It is unfortunately not possible within this volume to study other religions and their spiritualities, but we are aware of the wealth of wisdom and enrichment that cross-cultural dialogue brings; see Kourie and Kretzschmar, *Christian Spirituality*, 9.

6. Joubert and Lombaard, "Theology and Spirituality," 2.

Christian life becomes not enlightenment but wholeness—an acceptance of this complicated and muddled bundle of experiences as a possible theatre for God's creative work."[7]

Regarding the title and subtitle of this book, a few words are also required. The human body is the location where religion and spirituality occur, as it is the space that transmits, embodies, and transforms religious ideas and spiritual experiences.[8] Our bodies move through time and space. They become the sites where culture plays out. We are influenced by the world around us and vice versa. Accordingly, the body is a space where one encounters the Absolute, and it is the body, as a spiritual place, that undergoes what we have been calling "everything and nothingness." It is within the diversity and complexity of experiences that we encounter God. Embodiment—as a site of spiritual experience and encounter—may be seen as a recurring theme of this book, as seen in its discussions of mystical experiences, Paul's theology of the body, corporality, organicity, notions of affect, racialized bodies, traumatized bodies, the embodied performance of the Scriptures, and so on.

"Everything" may be understood in the broadest sense of the term. It may refer to the culmination of all avenues pursued, plenitude, completion, abundance, totality, the experience of happiness, holism, or the opposite of nothingness. This is not to be confused with capitalist or hegemonic notions of wealth, success, and accumulation. Rather, it may be imagined as the epitome of being an integrated person. This entails the good and bad of life, the vast array of experiences, and the endeavor towards holistic integration, of being shaped by these experiences, as this is grounded in a notion of God and the experience of faith. It may also be seen in the diversity of approaches taken in this book and the wide array of experiences referred herein, from experiences of traumatic loss, tragedy, and poverty to diverse and uncircumscribable experiences of the living God.

"Nothingness" may be understood in a variety of ways; it indeed has a vast reception within the history of ideas, but for our purposes in relation to spirituality it may be used to refer to a variety of notions and experiences, such as the philosophical distinctions of absolute and relative non-being, death, negativity, evil, mystical spirituality, negative theology, as well as metaphors that map the emptiness of "desert" experiences. It may be manifest in the perception of not having something, of poverty, and being oppressed, but it can take on many different forms. Indeed, as the contributors to this book show, human life is constantly bound between the various stages of

---

7. Williams, *Wound of Knowledge*, 2.
8. Rieger, "Introduction," 201.

everything and nothingness, of plenitude and emptiness—and many shades of in-between.

SPIRITUALITY STUDIES IN SOUTH AFRICA—A BRIEF RECEPTION HISTORY

At the outset, we would like to situate this volume within the South African context and offer a very brief history of "spirituality studies" as it is found within this setting. We are aware that the interest in spirituality is indeed a global phenomenon, and that South Africa is of course influenced by worldwide trends and the reactions of modern thought. With this considered, questions concerning what it means to be human and the awareness of our impact on the environment and people around us does occur through a different lens in South Africa, as our history demands it. What is meant by "spirituality" comes even more to the fore as the historical legacy of apartheid, corruption, poverty, and various systemic problems continue to cripple a country in which the population predominantly, and increasingly, identifies as Christian. The current interest in "spirituality" is spurred on by a disillusionment in the formal church as regards its many failures to engage apartheid, and all its legacies, as well as the ongoing experiences of inequality, poverty, and the need for justice. The immense interest in spirituality can be accounted to the fact that traditional religious thought is being questioned, with academic theology being perceived as lacking spiritual nourishment.[9] As Kourie and Kretzschmar remark: "[Spirituality] can no longer be left only to ministers of religion to disseminate the riches of our Christian heritage."[10]

The academic discipline of spirituality is relatively new to the scene, evolving in the 1970s and 1980s as a subdiscipline within theology in Catholic seminaries.[11] In South Africa, spirituality as an academic discipline also trickled into the academic curricula of Roman Catholic and Anglican academic settings. Spirituality as an academic discipline in South Africa traces its origins to the appointment of Felicity Edwards as professor of contemporary spirituality to the Faculty of Divinity, Rhodes University.[12] In 1997, Pieter de Villiers joined her in a position focused on biblical and protestant spirituality. This paved the way as Wil Vosloo (University of Pretoria) and Fika van Rensburg (North-West University) focused on the interaction

---

9. Kourie and Kretzschmar, *Christian Spirituality*, 10.
10. Kourie and Kretzschmar, *Christian Spirituality*, 1–2.
11. Joubert and Lombaard, "Theology and Spirituality," 8.
12. Joubert and Lombaard, "Theology and Spirituality," 20.

between Bible texts, exegesis, and faith, which disseminated into Afrikaans lay and ordained circles, and enabled a greater acceptance of spirituality as an academic discipline. The circles have grown with Christo Lombaard, Pieter de Villiers, Celia Kourie, to name but a few, who have all played an important part in establishing the discipline of spirituality in South Africa. Few institutions have chairs in spirituality still. Unisa currently has Fundiswa Kobo as the chair of spirituality; at the University of Pretoria, Tanya van Wyk is developing a spirituality course. Hugenote Kollege is one of the few Reformed institutions that offers an integrated curriculum with spiritual formation as one of the main subjects. Societies like the Spirituality Association of South Africa (SPIRASA) contribute to the study of spirituality in South Africa. The society was founded by Celia Kourie. In 2000, Celia Kourie, along with Louise Kretzschmar, edited the volume *Christian Spirituality in South Africa*.

It has been twenty-three years since their volume, and much has changed and new and young scholars are starting to make their contributions. The need to rethink the meaning of spirituality in South Africa is recurring and remains relevant—hence, the appearance of the original conference and the present volume.

THE ORIGINAL CONFERENCE

The title for the original conference out which this volume was birthed, namely "South African Spiritualities: Experiencing God in Nothingness and in Everything," originated during a conversation between Annette Potgieter and Christo Lombaard. Potgieter, having been appointed at Hugenote Kollege and lecturing a course on spirituality with "lay ministers" grew interested in what spirituality meant for the everyday person. Wellington is home to the beautiful Andrew Murray Centre for Spirituality; but in the same town, the effects of poverty and COVID-19 are palpable. This garnered the question: What does it mean to practice spirituality? Is spirituality something for a retreat center only for the elite who can afford it? Or does it mean anything to the everyday person? The topic of "spirituality" is still relatively new to the Reformed tradition, although there are various pockets in South Africa that has been *au fait* with spirituality for the past two decades. Lombaard suggested the title of "in nothingness and in everything" in an attempt to foster the conversation. The conference hoped to explore new avenues of thinking about God in difficult circumstances in which ideologies of hope and prosperity are reshaped. The hybrid conference was held at the Andrew Murray Centre for Spirituality and hosted by Hugenote Kollege, with the academic program being incorporated into the chapel rhythm. This made for a unique conference experience.

CHAPTER OUTLINES

The contributions to this study, in various ways, aim to conceptualize experiences of negativity, embodiment, and spirituality through a diverse range of approaches, ranging between historical theology, patristics, critical theory, political theology, qualitative research, phenomenology, biblical scholarship, and trauma theory.

In the opening chapter, Lisel Joubert seeks to clarify the stakes of negative theology; she traces its connections to Christian Neoplatonism, particularly among the likes of Pseudo-Dionysius, but then seeks to articulate a distinct tradition of negative theology among two female mystics, namely Julian of Norwich and Thérèse of Lisieux, and specifically how their embodied mystical experiences transcend any hard distinction between apophatic and cataphatic approaches. She then proceeds to suggest how these two figures may help us to navigate our diverse experiences of nothingness.

In the following chapter, Annette Potgieter draws upon critical space theory and the tools of historical philology to examine the Pauline imagery of the body as it exists between the tension of glory and nothingness, between resurrected life and death. She then goes on to juxtapose the horizon of Paul's eschatological imaginary regarding the body to a discussion of how such imagery may be critically related to some of the existential turmoil of South Africa, particularly as this relates to the persistence of spatial and material apartheid, long after the formal and legal demise of apartheid in 1994.

Staying with the theme of the merging of horizons between ancient and modern, Khegan Delport examines the phenomenon of attention economy via the figure of Evagrius Ponticus. After a critical examination of the way that attention economies are designed to direct and shape our habits of attention, instilling an affective regime beneficial to the acquisitive designs of digital capital, he then goes to commandeer Evagrius's teaching on ascetic practice, "imageless" prayer, and acedia as one possible diagnosis and remedy for the malaise of attention economies.

Calvin Ullrich in his essay turns to the theme of religion in general; specifically, he engages with the controversial thesis of Jan Assmann regarding the drift of monotheistic religion towards a totalization and, sometimes, its violent repression of difference; he suggests, via the work of Emmanuel Falque, that this tendency may be ameliorated through a turn towards a Christian anthropology of the body; here the insights into our common animality and organicity are remembered through incarnational and eucharistic embodiment, beyond the totalizing tendencies of certain religious identifications.

The theme of re-humanization of the self and other also appears in the contribution of Louis van der Riet. In his essay, he brings to the fore the insights of critical race theory within the remits of Christian spirituality. Coming from the perspective of a white minister in the Dutch Reformed Church, with all its historical complicity with white supremacy, nationalism, and apartheid, van der Riet seeks to bring the analysis of "whiteness studies" into conversation with an apophatic anthropology, particularly through the rubric of purgation, in which the undoing of personal and systemic racism, as well as the decentering and dismantling of "whiteness," is seen as part of the spiritual process of relinquishment and sanctification.

In his chapter, Jacques Beukes engages the tools of empirical and qualitative analysis to discern the role of spirituality within environmental activism, especially among young people. His research suggests that among the young people surveyed there was often a lack of spiritual and religious vocabulary for articulating their rationale for engaging in ecological activism. The implications of this study suggest that there is significant work that needs to be done among the theological academy and the church in connecting faith and ecology in a manner that is communicable to the young.

The chapter of Gavin Fernandes begins a series of contributions that focus on biblical texts and their connections to spirituality. He examines the interactions between Pharaoh, Moses, and YHWH in the Exodus narrative, and seeks to unfurl the nuances of the story within the context of Egyptian legal and wisdom texts, particularly in its description of the hardening of Pharaoh's heart. He then attempts to relate this story of the injustice of Pharaoh to recent political events within South Africa, namely the benighted presidential career of Jacob Zuma.

In what has become his typical style, Jaco Gericke brings the tools of philosophical theology and analytical philosophy to elucidate the theology of Qoheleth, with a specific focus here on its theodicy and perspective on poverty. Through his expertise in exegesis and philology, Gericke shows how Qoheleth's theodicy, and God's involvement in poverty and injustice, cannot be subsumed into the framing questions of contemporary philosophical theology (e.g., its assumption of divine goodness). According to Gericke, Qoheleth presents a more ambiguous picture of Elohim and the divinity's involvement in reality of poverty; overall, he makes a plea that comparative philosophy of religion will need to reflect on the background assumptions it brings to the constructions of questions, and this is necessary if we are to evaluate the similarities and differences between philosophical theologies.

In their chapter, Esterhuizen and Groenewald examine the naming of children within the scope of Isa 7–8. Using the lens of trauma theory, they unpack the metaphorical significance of the sign-names given to the children, namely Shear-jashub, Immanuel, and Maher-shalal-hash-baz, as recounted in the prophetic narrative of Isaiah; this naming, in their reconstruction, occurred within the collective and individual suffering experienced in Judah during the reign of King Ahaz, and here especially in connection to the Syro-Ephraimite war. They argue that the very act of naming of children within an environment of depravation and loss gives witness to the experiences of despair and nothingness, within the memory of generational trauma; but in their estimation the act of naming also gives voice to hope in God's accompaniment of Judah, with the promise of restoration and justice for those who continue to trust in YHWH.

In a similar vein, June F. Dickie makes use of trauma, lament, and performance theory to reimagine how biblical texts, such as Ruth and Psalms, can be creatively reimagined within post-apartheid South Africa, especially among marginalized and suffering communities. Using Judith Herman's influential model of the stages of recovery after traumatic loss, she foregrounds orality, ritual, and the connection of biochemical healing to the performance of lament, to argue that the biblical texts can be performatively reappropriated and rephrased in the context of suffering individuals and communities, and that the voicing of trauma within the context of re-enactment may provide an avenue for healing and reintegration in the wake of traumatic experiences.

In the penultimate chapter, Hassan Musa—a Nigerian scholar well-acquainted with the South African context as well—reads the story of Job within his own context of recrimination, violence, and internecine conflict. Drawing upon several Jewish readings of the narrative of Job, he emphasizes the polyphonic texture of the story, its emphasis on the mystery of suffering, and promise of hope within the context of human tragedy.

Christo Lombaard, in the final chapter, tries to show how biblical scholarship, and especially the instruments of historical criticism, are not inimical to spirituality and the processes of meaning-making in the present. Drawing upon the interaction between two weighty personae within the South African discourse of Christian spirituality, namely Celia Kourie and Pieter de Villiers, Lombaard examines a piece of writing by Kourie, as well as the Afrikaans editorialization and translation of the former by the latter, to show how a redaction analysis of the differences between the original and translation are not necessarily destructive, but rather can be imagined as contributing to the production of contemporary meaning. The implication here is that if such a procedure can be gleaned from modern literary examples, then something similar may also be possible with the biblical texts in their ongoing receptions.

Overall, this collection of essays gives indication of contemporary studies of spirituality coming out of the African continent—and the South African setting in particular. We hope that the publication of this volume shows that the field of spirituality studies, despite its somewhat marginal presence within the circuit of higher academia, is still very much a living tradition and discursive field within this context, and that this book serves as something of a gauge of new work being done, particularly by younger graduates and early career academics, showing that questions concerning the experience of divinity within all things—including the differing valences of nothingness—remains on the horizon in the theological landscape of the country.

BIBLIOGRAPHY

Joubert, Lisel, and Christo Lombaard. "Theology and Spirituality." *Journal of Systematic Theology* (2023) 1–41. https://journalofsystematictheology.com.

Kourie, Celia, and Louise Kretzschmar. *Christian Spirituality in South Africa*. Pietermaritzburg: Cluster, 2000.

Rieger, Anna-Katharina. "Introduction." In *Lived Religion in the Ancient Mediterranean World—Approaching Religious Transformations from Archaeology, History and Classics*, edited by V. Gasparini et al, 201–9. Berlin: de Gruyter, 2020.

Schneiders, Sandra M. "The Study of Christian Spirituality: Contours and Dynamics of a Discipline." In *Minding the Spirit: The Study of Christian Spirituality*, edited by Elizabeth A. Dreyer and Mark S. Burrows, 5–24. Baltimore: Johns Hopkins University, 2005.

Williams, Rowan. *The Wound of Knowledge: Christian Spirituality from the New Testament to St. John of Cross*. 2nd ed. London: Darton & Longman, 1990.

Chapter 1

Navigating Nothingness
Spirituality amidst Upheaval

Lisel Joubert

> *Words are the fig leaves we continually grasp in the effort to clothe our nakedness.*—Belden Lane[1]
>
> *We should love what is not, and we should flee what is.*—Mechthild of Magdeburg[2]
>
> *God leads us into a land without a way.*—John of the Cross[3]
>
> *Teach me to go to this country beyond words and beyond names.*
> —Thomas Merton

INTRODUCTION

The COVID-19 pandemic confronted faith communities worldwide with the reality of being, speaking, and believing in a time of trauma, suffering, and powerlessness. Reflecting theologically on the impact of this event on the lives of faith communities asks for an academic format that recognizes our own experience and own observations during this time—despite its

---

1. Lane, *Solace of Fierce Landscapes*, 68.
2. Farley, *Thirst of God*, 63.
3. Lane, *Solace of Fierce Landscapes*, 74.

subjective nature. It is this subjective experience that led to the writing of this chapter.

During the first eighteen months of the pandemic, I was a full-time minister in a congregation consisting mostly of pensioners in a smallish town. Lockdown started with confinement to our own houses and families—a small space with minimum contact. Paradoxically, my overriding experience was that of noise. I have never in my life been bombarded with so many words as in the first month of hard lockdown. I felt I was drowning in words from social media, even though I only use email and WhatsApp; I am not on Facebook, Twitter, or Instagram.

What bothered me even more was the content of this chatter. It seemed everybody felt it was their moral and religious responsibility to give people answers to carry them through the crisis. People were confronted with a veritable banquet of choice, from meditations to sermons (and naturally, the ever-popular end-of-the-world warnings). Where people had the luxury of data and access to social media platforms and the internet, there was no scarcity of devotional material.

But I felt that we were missing out on an opportunity. This feeling led to the formulation of the topic of this chapter: Was abundance really the best choice? A colleague in a nearby town commented wisely that now was the time for people to navigate or practice what we as ministers have been teaching them for years; to let people figure it out for themselves.

I want to propose that the pandemic was, and still is, an opportunity to help people to navigate "nothingness" and loss by giving them less and not more. In this context nothingness is broadly understood to encompass uncertainty, hopelessness, fear, lack of answers, loss of faith. Nothingness is a multi-faceted experience and not purely philosophical nihilism.

What if believers were not bombarded with so-called answers but were left to find God in other places, in nothingness, or not at all?

In this article the language of apophatic mysticism will be used critically as a conversation partner in contemplating the possibility of "navigating nothingness" in a time of upheaval. It will start with a short introduction of the word *apophasis*. The two themes that will be the focus of this work will then be identified, namely "nakedness" and "nothingness." These themes will be discussed in dialogue with an experience of Julian of Norwich and Thérèse of Lisieux. In conclusion some reflective comments and proposals of possibilities for helping believers to navigate nothingness will be presented.

What Does Apophatic Mean?

Apophasis consists of two Greek words, namely *phasis*, the Greek word for speech, and *apo*, which implies a direction, namely "away from." It can be translated with "unsaying" or "saying away." Matter describes it as a tradition of theology "that speaks away rather than affirms."[4] The word *apophasis* has found a home in theological reflection, philosophy,[5] and literature.[6] In theological discourse apophaticism is mostly linked to mysticism, describing a specific experience of God.

Apophaticism as a type of theological discourse refers to the recognition that God is more than our words, speech, and experience of God. Apophatic theology "identifies and stresses the limitations of human knowledge of God."[7] To talk about God is to talk in terms of what he is not. In this sense of "what he is not" apophaticism has also been called negative theology.[8]

This paradox is older than Christianity; the dynamic of being able to talk about the Divine but also recognizing the mystery beyond has always existed.[9] God does overflow "every analogical notion we might use to describe God."[10] This chapter does not aim to delve into the philosophical intricacies of apophaticism but to use it as a lens for the contextual questions arising from existential experiences during this time of dissonance in history:

> Its baffling affirmation of a God who "is not" resists the too-human tendency, never fully checked in the West, to be satisfied with a God who too comfortably "is," and then is too easily dispensed with. Its capacity to hold on before the inexhaustible depths of the reality of God, who is more real than anything we can know or imagine, is not likely to have been exhausted.[11]

Apophaticism in its theological context appropriates specific biblical metaphors and images, for example: desert and mountain, darkness and loss,

---

4. Matter, "*Lectio Divina*," 147–56.
5. Cf. Franke, *Philosophy of the Unsayable*.
6. In the study of rhetoric, *apophasis* is the phenomenon when a writer or speaker brings up a subject by either denying it or denying that it should be brought up.
7. McGrath, *Christian Spirituality*, 118.
8. Lanzetta, *Other Side of Nothingness*, 9. According to Lanzetta "resurgent academic interest in negative theology, especially in fields of mysticism and postmodern theology that has generated a number of comparative studies between Western and Eastern apophatic traditions."
9. Louth, "Apophatic and Cataphatic Theology," 137.
10. Lane, *Solace of Fierce Landscapes*, 67.
11. Louth, "Apophatic and Cataphatic Theology," 146.

cloud, and suffering. Moses is answered by God with a name that enhances the mystery: "I am who I am" (Exod 3:14).

The origins of the apophatic tradition as a theological discourse can be traced to the fourth century, when it emerged within a theological debate. Some theologians claimed that divine nature is entirely knowable.[12] Gregory of Nyssa, a fourth-century Cappadocian, reacted to this certainty of knowing God by referring to Moses's experience of unknowing (*agnosia*) on Mount Sinai and emphasized this inability of the intellect to comprehend the mystery of God.[13] He and his fellow Cappadocians insisted that "reticence benefits the theologian," recognizing that our language is never sufficient, and that God cannot be formulated.[14]

The well-known names in the repertoire of academics writing on apophatic theology are Gregory of Nyssa, Dionysius, John Chrysostom, Meister Eckhart, and the anonymous author of *The Cloud of Unknowing*.

The fourth-century preacher John Chrysostom, for example, exclaims: "His judgements are inscrutable, his ways are unsearchable, what God has prepared for those who love him has not entered into the heart of man, his greatness has no bound, his understanding is infinite."[15]

Gregory of Nyssa uses the word "darkness" as metaphor for this meeting with the divine: "This is the seeing that consists in not seeing, because that which is sought transcends all knowledge, being separated on all sides by incomprehensibility as by a kind of darkness."[16] Dionysius (sixth century) first systematized the theology of *apophasis*.[17] He wanted to move the mind beyond affirmation and denial to a union behind the negation of the negation.

However, from the beginning this speaking about the "not-speaking about God" was full of philosophical concepts, especially from Neoplatonic sources: "The Neoplatonic language of simultaneous divine presence and absence, immanence and transcendence, became the language of Christian apophaticism, giving structure to subsequent centuries of reflection on the divine transcendence."[18]

12. Lane, *Solace of Fierce Landscapes*, 64.
13. Lane, *Solace of Fierce Landscapes*, 64.
14. Lane, *Solace of Fierce Landscapes*, 64.
15. Louth, "Apophatic and Cataphatic Theology," 138.
16. Sheldrake, *New Westminster Dictionary of Spirituality*, 118; McGrath, *Christian Spirituality*, 105, makes it clear that darkness in apophatic thought does not entail sin or doubt but rather "place[s] limits on human knowledge of God."
17. Waaijman, *Spiritualiteit*, 806, describes the work of Dionysius in Dutch as "de overgang van het uiterste naar het alles-voorbij."
18. Sheldrake, *New Westminster Dictionary*, 118; also see detailed discussion on the influence of Greek philosophy in Louth, "Apophatic and Cataphatic Theology."

McIntosh defines this understanding of Neoplatonism as "the procession of all-things from their eternal being in God into created existence, and the return of all into blissful unity with God."[19] For these older writers this cosmic reality was the proper pattern of theology.[20]

In engaging with apophatic concepts, the contrasting cataphatic tradition also comes into play. This tradition (*kata phasis*—toward speech [or according to the image]) makes "generous use of metaphor and analogy in describing the mystery of God. It is concrete and incarnational, speaking of the divine by way of vivid imagery and storytelling."[21] Apophatic and cataphatic are not either/or concepts but different moments in a journey towards, in, and with God.

In the light of the above three critical issues for this chapter are identified: Firstly, the chapter needs to critically engage with the strong Neoplatonic language associated with the apophatic tradition. Should one use this philosophical mindset or rather retrieve the biblical metaphors behind those of desert, darkness, and nothingness? As John de Gruchy critically observes: "Our journey into the mystery of God, is not a flight into a fantasy world, or even into a Neoplatonic moment of illumination, for it begins in Bethlehem, where the mystery is the first disclosed to faith."[22]

The second is the always present paradox of the gospel, namely that the Triune God is beyond our experience, language and understanding but that he became flesh and showed himself to us. We do know and have seen the Jesus who fed the thousands, blessed the children, touched the sick and the blind. Maximus the Confessor recognizes that in this sense we know who God is: "Good theology begins and ends with a recognition that we can never know God completely; but Maximus is careful not to equate this unknowability with utter ignorance, because God *is* knowable in God's qualities or attributes."[23] We journey between knowing, not-knowing, and being known.

Thirdly, much of what has been written on apophatic theology is in the context of mysticism and a desire for God, and in mystical language for union (*unificatio*). This loss of language and understanding is part of the journey that starts with a desire. However, in guiding people into an experience of nothingness, one cannot assume they long for God. One can assume they long for answers, comfort, words, and explanations. The pandemic

---

19. McIntosh, *Mystical Theology*, 122.
20. McIntosh, *Mystical Theology*, 122.
21. Lane, *Solace of Fierce Landscapes*, 64.
22. De Gruchy, *Monastic Moment*, 147.
23. McFarland, "Developing an Apophatic Christocentrism," 200–201.

stripped people of their certainties—which church leaders think they need to replace.

How can this tradition help us to embrace and navigate nothingness? Nothingness denotes nakedness, emptiness, uncertainty, darkness. For the scope of this chapter, the concepts of nakedness and nothingness will be the main focus, which imply the loss of certainty and control.

I decided not to revert to the familiar names (Dionysius, Eckhart, etc.) and their sometimes-clinical descriptions of apophaticism which are not always clearly related to episodes in their own lives but rather to narratives of bodily suffering and struggle. Julian of Norwich and Thérèse of Lisieux were chosen for their grasping at words like nakedness and nothingness amidst their own bodily suffering. The chapter cannot extensively focus on their lives. Therefore, it is admittedly limited in context. The focus is rather on their own experiences of suffering amidst belief and their naming thereof. Both women's interpretations of their experiences can be experienced as strange for a modern reader and maybe even suspect; and therefore, some historical graciousness is needed to digest their profound theological insights in the emptiness.

JULIAN OF NORWICH—NAKEDNESS

To be stripped of words, to "talk away" and let go, implies a loss of covering—a denuding. Metaphorical nakedness can be seen as central to an intensive apophatic experience. To be naked is to be exposed: "to stand 'naked' before God, without the protective interference of language."[24]

The fourteenth-century English anchorite Julian of Norwich uses wordplay in different ways to describe her experience of silence and utter loss of control. Julian asked three things of God: "The first was to have the minde of Christes passion. The second was bodeleye syekenes. And the third was to have of Goddes gifte thre woundes."[25] (The first was vivid perception of Christ's Passion, the second was bodily sickness. And the third was for God to give me three wounds).[26] Her desire thus formulated was the start of a journey into darkness, perplexity, near death, and a struggle with sin and love.

Denys Turner describes Julian's Long Text of *Revelations of Divine Love* as "one of the great works of Medieval theology in any language by an

---

24. Lane, *Solace of Fierce Landscapes*, 65.
25. Watson and Jenkins, *Writings of Julian of Norwich*, Long Text ch 2.
26. Julian of Norwich, *Revelations of Divine Love.*

author of either gender."²⁷ He recognizes that this text does not fit comfortably "within standard taxonomies of theological genre in her own times."²⁸ Julian does not write from a biblical passage like the monastic tradition of her time, or make a statement like the scholastic tradition of her time, but she writes from her own intensive experience. She reflects "through a process of progressive intensification and complex elaboration of particular and personal experience" that lead to her struggle with the cross and the existence of sin but always in dialogue with God.²⁹

Julian describes her book as not complete ("boke is not yet performed") because she intends "theological incompleteness."³⁰ In Julian the paradox of the stripping and the superfluous is evident—both have the same goal, namely, to move beyond and meet the Triune God at the cross. Lane in his discussion of the apophatic images in her work describes it as follows: "It was an experience of knowing herself as "nothing," being wholly stripped of language and identity. Yet this experience-that-was-not-an-experience joined her more closely to Christ than anything she had ever known."³¹ This nothingness was her deepest participation in his suffering on the cross.³²

Turner, who also recognizes the cross as the locus of Julian's thoughts, highlights the other side of her wordplay where she deploys a huge range of affirmative metaphors of God because "her cataphatic confidence is in itself an apophatic strategy, as if by means of, not despite, the proliferation of Trinitarian vocabulary that she achieves the goal of placing God beyond all possible words" in that she maintains an uncanny balance "between the deployment of a maximum range of metaphor about God with a sense that none of it, and not even all of it, does anything more than draw us into unspeakable mystery."³³

Julian uses puns/wordknots to describe this "knowing, noughting, nothing, no thing, this coming to naught."³⁴ Unfortunately, her puns are not always captured in modern English translations. It is in this "coming to naught" that she found her greatest joy.³⁵ She understood her experience as

27. Turner, *Julian of Norwich*, x.
28. Turner, *Julian of Norwich*, x.
29. Turner, *Julian of Norwich*, xi.
30. Turner, *Julian of Norwich*, xii.
31. Lane, *Solace of Fierce Landscapes*, 68.
32. This nakedness and nothingness can also be recognized in the work of John of the Cross with the use of the Spanish word *nada*. Cf. England, "Architectonics of Desire," 79–95.
33. Turner, *Julian of Norwich*, 11.
34. Lane, *Solace of Fierce Landscapes*, 68.
35. Lane, *Solace of Fierce Landscapes*, 68.

"a sharing in the emptiness (the nawtedness) of Jesus," as seen in these words in the last sentence of chapter 18 of the Long Text: "Thus was our Lord Iesus nawted for us, and we stond al in this manner nowtid with hym."[36]

This nakedness reminds of the "kenotic" element that Paul recognizes in the suffering of Jesus, namely the "self-emptying." In her writings Julian empties the big explanations and opts for the small. This nakedness and emptiness can be recognized in her own understanding of word and symbol "The only way she knew how to convey what she had experienced was to offer tiny images that reduced language to a bare minimum" as is seen in her well-known meditation on "a little thing, the quantity of a hazel nut."[37]

In her typical use of puns, she talks about how our "menie meanes" are too mean to grasp the meaning of what he meant.[38] This experience of nakedness before the cross shows the integration of being apophatic and Christocentric: the "more authentically apophatic one is, the more Christocentric one will be."[39]

Julian reverts to wordplay and symbol to describe her experience—"nawtness" and hazelnuts. Lanzetta, in her investigation into apophatic thought as a possible way for interreligious dialogue, focuses on the mercy of God. She sees his mercy in a shared nakedness: "Divinity shares the erasure and nakedness that is the source of divine mercy. God shares the place where *God* disrobes and discards property and name. God shares God's own unbecoming and the rapture of indiscretion on the other side of nothingness."[40] As Turner remarks:

> In our times, wherein we experience so many forms of theological fragmentation consequent upon our school-based divisions of labor, we may have something to learn from a fourteenth-century "unlettered" anchoress who resists those fragmentations because she knows nothing of them, and, had she known of them, would have seen no good reason why they might be justified and right enough she is.[41]

More than six hundred years later a young French woman also talked about God and nothingness in the last months of her life.

---

36. Elizabeth Spearing translates it as follows: "Thus was our Lord Jesus brought low for us, and we are all brought low like him."
37. Lane, *Solace of Fierce Landscapes*, 68.
38. Lane, *Solace of Fierce Landscapes*, 68.
39. McFarland, "Developing an Apophatic Christocentrism," 200.
40. Lanzetta, *Other Side of Nothingness*, 4.
41. Turner, *Julian of Norwich*, 217.

THÉRÈSE OF LISIEUX—NIGHT OF NOTHINGNESS

This nakedness-nothingness-emptiness is not necessarily experienced as an aloneness. It is per se the product of a conceived relation, namely with God. Scholars writing on negative theology also recognize the similarity with some Buddhist ideas.[42] Nakamura for example identifies a relationality in emptiness: "Emptiness is not nothingness or annihilation; it is the abandonment of the contrariety between dualities such as affirmation and negation, being and non-being, eternity and annihilation. In this sense, emptiness is the relationality of all things."[43] There is a universality and specificity in these discussions on nothingness which enables the creation of a dialogue between the young Catholic nun Thérèse of Lisieux with the desolation of postmodern thought as Frohlich does.[44]

Thérèse of Lisieux (1873–97), who was made Doctor of the Church in 2007, longed for suffering; everything she did, from a young age to her death at twenty-four, was done to the fullest. The focus of this chapter is not the life of Thérèse, just as it is not the full life of Julian, but rather their bodily experiences amidst faith which led them beyond certainty and words.

Modern readers find it difficult to understand this type of religiosity. Thérèse ("The Little Flower of Jesus"), a Discalced Carmelite nun, was canonized by Pope Pius XI a mere twenty-eight years after her death. Interpreting her life and works is hindered and complicated by the fact that so many of her words were "censored" by her family and ecclesiastical authorities, as noted by Frohlich,[45] Niven,[46] and O'Reilley.[47] According to O'Reilley, her memoir *The Story of Her Soul* was edited by her sister Pauline, who was mother superior of the Carmelite convent where she lived and died. The editing amounted to seven thousand alterations of the text.[48] Is she just an example of a "safe piety" that thousands can aim to emulate or is there a depth in her work that has not yet been fully plunged?

In the past decade or two there has been a growing critical interest in her thoughts and beliefs—resulting in divergent opinions. Patricia Ranft[49] talks about "Theresian theology." However, because she was "born within a

---

42. Cf. Sebastian, *Cloud of Nothingness*.
43. Nakamura, "Intuitive Awareness," 120.
44. Frohlich, "Desolation and Doctrine in Therese of Lisieux."
45. Frohlich, "Desolation and Doctrine in Therese of Lisieux."
46. Niven, *Thérèse of Lisieux*
47. O'Reilley, "Revisiting Thérèse."
48. O'Reilley, "Revisiting Thérèse," 3.
49. Ranft, "Logotheology of Therese of Lisieux."

deeply pietistic culture, her presentation demands painstaking translation before its theological treasures are apparent."[50] On the other hand O'Reilley, in reading Thérèse's *The Story of a Soul*, experienced it, among other things, as "a story of masochistic pietism sanctioned and encouraged by cultural and conventual authority: much of it with a distinctively female slant. It gave me the willies."[51] She describes Thérèse's journal as sentimental and full of language that fitted her religious context. However, at the end of the same article O'Reilley writes that she felt "as one comes to the last thirty pages, that one has broken through to quite another country. Now we are in a place cold and austere, we are above the tree line. This may be an awful place, but it is *real*."[52]

Why this ambivalence? Thérèse is known for her *little way*, being small and doing small things with big love. She embraced "her invisibility and discovers meaning within it."[53] This almost subservient piety and life of suffering is, however, deconstructed in her own words when she realized she was not bothered by works, heaven, or even faith and hope. In the last eighteen months of her life after she suffered her first hemoptysis during the Easter of 1896 she wrote and talked about her experience of suffering and God. Her bodily suffering stemmed from her tuberculosis but also the treatment of her doctor. A short example gives an idea of the depth of her physical suffering at the hands of those who took responsibility for her physical well-being. Although other treatments were available at the time, her doctor chose the more familiar devices for respiratory disorders, namely suction cups, vesicatories, and fiery needles.[54]

The suction cup or *ventouse* was a glass cup rounded at the bottom, "warmed by a match-lit piece of cotton placed within it, and then applied to the skin for five minutes; the skin was raised, turned violet by the afflux of blood, and incised, scarring the skin."[55] The cup was then emptied. Vesicatories were heated plasters creating blisters with the medical assumption that "vesicators purged the blood removing 'humors' present in the serous or clear fluid that came out with the bleeding"; it literally meant that skin was peeled away. The other option was cauterization, which consisted of subcutaneous cuts of two centimeters. Thérèse received five hundred such

---

50. Ranft, "Logotheology of Therese of Lisieux," 374.
51. O'Reilley, "Revisiting Thérèse," 3.
52. O'Reilley, "Revisiting Thérèse," 19.
53. Ranft, "Logotheology of Therese of Lisieux," 375.
54. Niven, *Thérèse of Lisieux*, 267.
55. Niven, *Thérèse of Lisieux*, 267.

jabs in one session, without anesthetic, which, even during her last days, was not permitted by convent rules.

Manuscript C of *The Story of a Soul* contains her writings up to July 1897. Other information indicates that it a collection of that which she shared with those around her bed during her last days up to her death on September 30, 1897. In the midst of her suffering, she experienced a "night of nothingness." Frohlich describes it as her "radical participation in the 'nothingness' beyond all."[56] Thérèse wrote that she recalls the times when thinking of heaven brought joy but, because of tiredness and fatigue, this memory of a luminous country now only redoubles her torment:

> It seems to me that the darkness, borrowing the voice of sinners, says mockingly to me: "you are dreaming about the light, about a fatherland embalmed in the sweetest perfumes; you are dreaming about the *eternal* possession of the Creator of all these marvels; you believe that one day you will walk out of this fog that surrounds you! Advance, advance; rejoice in death which will give you not what you hope for but a night still more profound, the night of nothingness."[57]

Thérèse uses descriptive words like thick fog, a dark tunnel, "a wall which has been raised up to the sky, covering the starry vault" (*un mur qui s'élève jusqu'aux cieux et couvre le firmament étoilé*). The last describes an experience of being sealed off from the heavenly host, the communion of saints, her deceased family, all.[58] Thérèse wanted to be loved; she clung to love till the end while in this process of letting go of faith, hope, and heaven:

> She died without belief in heaven, the terminus of the Christian faith. She also died without hope of getting there. What she kept to the end was a resilient love for God, even within her knowing that God was the creator of the darkness in which she was situated to the end.[59]

Together with a reference to "night of nothingness," Thérèse also works with the concept of "traces." In the last lines of *The Story of a Soul* she writes: "Since Jesus has reascended into heaven, I can follow Him only in the traces he has left; but how luminous these traces are! How perfumed!"[60]

---

56. Frohlich, "Desolation and Doctrine," 262.
57. Frohlich, "Desolation and Doctrine," 262.
58. Niven, *Thérèse of Lisieux*, 203.
59. Niven, *Thérèse of Lisieux*, x.
60. Thérèse of Lisieux, *Story of a Soul*, 258.

In reflecting on her experience, Frohlich refers to Derrida and his use of apophasis. For Derrida apophasis is not an immediate language-free experience, but an event that may (or may not) leap forth in the midst of intersubjective communication.[61] Frohlich believes that in the last months of Thérèse's life she showed that she is not a negative theologian

> in the rigorous intellectual sense of one who thinks through the affirmations, negations, and negations of negations that are essential to a full-fledged philosophical articulation of who God is and is not. Rather, she lives the aporia of standing in the terrible nowhere between the God she trusts—the loving God "known" in Scripture, liturgy, church, and world—and the abyss, the nothingness, of a God who can never in any way be known, controlled, or grasped. Her resolution—insofar as there can be one—is simply love.[62]

Thérèse herself talks of transferring "nothingness into fire" where mundane acts in the here and now can reveal God.[63] This is an "event of apophasis" amidst daily acts of love. As with Julian of Norwich, her night of nothingness is participation in kenosis of Christ. Participation per se entails communion, not singleness. Like Julian, she participates in the kenosis of Christ; she "had to fall into the abyss of nothingness in order to be fully taken up by the grace of God" beyond all limiting signifiers.[64]

Kathryn Harrison was invited to write on Thérèse in a Penguin Lives series. As a postmodern author she struggled with Thérèse's worldview and language. Harrison in this struggle quotes a citation from Jean Paul Sartre used by a Dominican priest writing on Thérèse: "You see the void above our heads? That is God. You see this hole in the ground? That is God. You see this crack in the door? That's God too. Silence is God. Absence is God. God is human loneliness."[65]

Like O'Reilley, Harrison reflects on Thérèse's writings during the last eighteen months of her life: "At last she has taken her place among us, not so much revealing herself as human as giving birth to her naked self, plummeting to earth, wet and new and terrified. If we allow her to become a saint, if we believe in her, it's because here, finally, she has achieved mortality."[66]

---

61. Frohlich, "Desolation and Doctrine," 273.
62. Frohlich, "Desolation and Doctrine," 273.
63. Frohlich, "Desolation and Doctrine," 274.
64. Frohlich, "Desolation and Doctrine," 274.
65. O'Reilley, "Revisiting Thérèse," 19.
66. Harrison, *Saint Thérèse of Lisieux*, 146.

NAVIGATING NOTHINGNESS

This chapter started with the proposal that in the course of the COVID-19 pandemic and lockdowns religious leaders should not have attempted frantically to cover the nakedness and fill the nothingness. The irony is clear: I will now use words to make proposals to help people navigate nothingness. This is not a theodicy question but has to do with practical proposals for a universal experience grounded in examples from Christian history and tradition. This chapter is written in answer to a mindset that, if there is no explanation, God is not present. Augustine reminds: "If you have understood, then this is not God. If you were able to understand even partially, then you have deceived yourself with your own thoughts."[67]

Just Tell Stories

Through the ages, from biblical times (as is seen in the lament of Habakkuk) till the present day, there are stories and witnesses of believers who are comfortable in loss and do not think that nothingness negates God but rather points to the place God inhabits. As Gregory of Nazianzus wrote, God is unknowable but the presence of God "is beyond doubt."[68] In both the writings of Julian and Thérèse nakedness and nothingness become the inhabitance of God.

In the beautifully written *Gilead* by Marilynne Robinson the main character comes to the insight in the course of his own life journey: "Even that wilderness, the very habitation . . . is the Lord's. I need to bear this in mind."[69] The life narratives of Julian, Thérèse, John of the Cross, and many others did not happen outside relationship or relationality. Their experience of nothingness transpired within a relationship; it was part of. God is also in the nothingness. In the Song of Songs and the work of John of the Cross, darkness relates to love: darkness also has the nocturnal meaning of beloved.[70] Night is a place of rekindled desire, a place of birth and mercy—almost a womb.

Nothingness and emptiness do not negate the presence of God. We can teach people a tradition that recognizes this, a tradition that is sorely needed in a day and age where the presence of God is seen to only be encountered in blessings and prosperity. Telling these life stories of, among others, Julian

---

67. Lane, *Solace of Fierce Landscapes*, 68.
68. McGrath, *Christian Spirituality*, 105.
69. Robinson, *Gilead*, 118–19.
70. McGrath, *Christian Spirituality*, 106.

and Thérèse in the context of the words of Julian "boke is not yet performed," does not present the listener with a moral lesson, a finished product, or an easy application. These narratives ending in an abyss reflect the experiences of people, making them authentic, part of Christian discourse.

These concepts should not be romanticized or clothed in the sometimes toxic language of piety but should be recognized as part of life and love. Nothingness is out there—it does not matter if you desire God or not. A community of faith (and faithless) must tell these stories to counter the grasping for words and certainty which hinders us from the opportunity "to give birth to our naked self," as Harrison sums up Thérèse's struggle. Neither does wandering in the country of no words have a philosophical prerequisite like Neoplatonism. The desert of the Old Testament, the cross of Jesus Christ, and the reality of life are enough.

Learn to Talk All Over Again

People have come to distrust words even though they long for them. Nothingness can be the place to learn to talk all over again: Word for word and very slowly. In the desert tradition the *abbas* and *ammas* taught their disciples "to chew the cud of the word." To be able to sit with a single word for a month: "God is good," good must be tasted, pondered, and negated.

Anthony of the Desert "advised that we should be like camels rather than horses slowly chewing the cud until the food is gradually broken down and absorbed." You are invited to slow down, taste, chew, swallow, and savor.[71] In the desert—a place of nothingness—a word was pondered on for weeks and a whole lifetime, "the word was meant to be wrestled with and slowly grown into."[72] Slow talking also offers time to recognize symbols. In learning to talk again, symbols become words: A cross, a sign of peace, a broken pot, ashes. In learning language anew, we are cleansed of words that are superfluous; our vocabulary is decluttered. As Nisly so poignantly remarks: "Yet in many hymns and praise songs, along with the God-talk common in churches, God's attributes are often delineated with little apparent concern for the ragged edges of human speech and understanding."[73]

We need to find the balance between "saying too much and saying too little."[74] Why, in times of upheaval, do religious leaders opt for saying too much?

71. Wallace, *Preaching to the Hungers of the Heart*, 11.
72. Paintner, *Desert Fathers and Mothers*, 3.
73. Nisly, "Apophatic Theology and Twentieth-Century Novels," 317.
74. McFarland, "Developing an Apophatic Christocentrism," 201.

Accept Silence as a Language

A core reflection in the language of spirituality is that silence is God's first language: "Genuine silence has its own independent existence. It indicates presence, not absence. It is the enduring or surrounding reality that sounds interrupt."[75] Silence, however, is feared by different cultures for different reasons. You may have grown up in a crowded space, always surrounded by people and noise, and even if you live alone, you choose to fill every waking moment with music and voice. Belden Lane refers to the following words of Sam Keen:

> A psychoanalysis of chatter would suggest that our over-verbalization is an effort to avoid something which is fearful—silence. But why should silence be threatening? Because words are a way of structuring, manipulating, and controlling; thus, when they are absent the specter of loss of control arises. If we cannot name it, we cannot control it. Naming gives us power. Hence, silence is impotence, the surrender of control. Control is power, and power is safety.[76]

Words can become a means to negate the presence of nothingness which hinders the discovery of God in the nothingness and in the beauty of everything. McGrath associates silence with wonder: "rather than utter a platitude of truisms, the proper response to being confronted with the full wonder of God is silence."[77] Silence is the place where all theologizing must ultimately end.[78]

To name is to own, to understand, to have power. How does one travel without naming? The paradox is that "words come out of silence."[79] It is from silence that we return to the familiar, the liturgy, the symbol, and the word, but bit by bit—tasting, rediscovering, learning to speak again; naming as if for the first time.

Julian played with words because she understood what they cannot do. Thérèse let go of heaven, faith, and hope; she was stripped to one word, namely "love," which was enough.

---

75. Schiffhorst, "Country beyond Words," 3.
76. Lane, *Solace of Fierce Landscapes*, 68.
77. McGrath, *Christian Spirituality*, 107.
78. McFarland, "Developing an Apophatic Christocentrism," 201.
79. Schiffhorst, "Country beyond Words," 3.

Recognize and Care for the Flesh

Banquets full of words, explanations galore, and constant speaking also prevent us from caring. To wait in vulnerability, emptiness, nothingness makes us aware of our shared humanity and fragility.

Is it possible to focus on bodies, on touch and care rather than speech? Should we be tending bodies rather than waiting for answers? Or are words a flight from our own vulnerability and those of others? Both these women suffered in their bodies; strangely, they thought they had to long for suffering in order to share in the suffering of Christ. But in the end their bodies became the places where their metaphors changed, and their words disappeared.

CONCLUSION

How is nothingness navigated and emptiness lived? There is no certain way, and the multiplicity of words is not the compass. Schiffhorst remarks: "According to the 'negative' mystical way, the closest we can come to experience God in this life is as an apparent absence that is really a presence."[80] Thérèse wrote about "traces." Is it possible that in the franticness of the pandemic and our filling in the gaps we missed the small gestures and traces?

God is still actually waiting for us to finish speaking. She tends not to interrupt.

BIBLIOGRAPHY

de Gruchy, John W. *The Monastic Moment: The War of the Spirit & the Rule of Love*. Eugene, OR: Cascade, 2021.
England, Frank. "An Architectonics of Desire: The Person on the Path to *Nada* in John of the Cross." *Acta Theologica* 33 (2013) 79–95.
Farley, Wendy. *The Thirst of God: Contemplating God's Love with Three Women Mystics*. Louisville, KY: Westminster John Knox, 2015.
Franke, William. *A Philosophy of the Unsayable*. Notre Dame, IN: University of Notre Dame Press, 2014.
Frohlich, Mary. "Desolation and Doctrine in Therese of Lisieux." *Theological Studies* 61 (2000) 261–79.
Harrison, Kathryn. *Saint Thérèse of Lisieux*. Penguin Lives. London: Viking/Penguin, 2003.
Julian of Norwich. *Julian of Norwich: Revelations of Divine Love*. Translated by Elizabeth Spearing. London: Penguin Random House, 1998.

---

80. Schiffhorst, "Country beyond Words," 11.

Lane, Belden C. *The Solace of Fierce Landscapes: Exploring Desert and Mountain Spirituality.* Oxford: Oxford University Press, 1998.

Lanzetta, Beverly. *The Other Side of Nothingness: Towards a Theology of Radical Openness.* Albany: State University of New York Press, 2001.

Louth, Andrew. "Apophatic and Cataphatic Theology." In *The Cambridge Companion to Christian Mysticism*, edited by Amy Hollywood and Patricia Z. Beckman, 137–46. Cambridge: Cambridge University Press, 2012.

Matter, E. Ann. "*Lectio Divina.*" In *The Cambridge Companion to Christian Mysticism*, edited by Amy Hollywood and Patricia Z. Beckman, 147–56. Cambridge: Cambridge University Press, 2012.

McFarland, Ian A. "Developing an Apophatic Christocentrism: Lessons from Maximus the Confessor." *Theology Today* 60 (2003) 200–214.

McGrath, Alister. *Christian Spirituality.* Oxford: Blackwell, 1999.

McIntosh, Mark A. *Mystical Theology.* Oxford: Blackwell, 1998.

Nakamura, Hajime. "Intuitive Awareness: Issues in Early Mysticism." *Japanese Journal of Religious Studies* 12 (1985) 119–140.

Nisly, L. Lamar. "Apophatic Theology and Twentieth-Century Novels." *Religion and the Arts* 22 (2018) 316–33.

Niven, Thomas. R. *Thérèse of Lisieux: God's Gentle Warrior.* Oxford: Oxford University Press, 2006.

O'Reilley, Mary Rose. "Revisiting Thérèse." *The Literary Review* 51 (2008) 3–20.

Paintner, Christine V. *Desert Fathers and Mothers: Early Christian Wisdom Sayings.* Woodstock: Skylight Paths, 2012.

Ranft, Patricia. "The Logotheology of Therese of Lisieux: 'A way that is very straight, very short and totally new.'" *Heythrop Journal* 58 (2017) 374–88.

Robinson, Marilynne. *Gilead.* New York: Farrar, Strauss and Giroux, 2004.

Schiffhorst, Gerald J. "The Country beyond Words: Silence and Christian Mindfulness." *Cithara* 49 (2010) 3–14.

Sebastian, C. D. *The Cloud of Nothingness: The Negative Way in Nagarjuna and John of the Cross.* India: Springer, 2016.

Sheldrake, Phillip, ed. *The New Westminster Dictionary of Spirituality.* Louisville, KY: Westminster John Knox, 2005.

Thérèse of Lisieux. *Story of a Soul: The Autobiography of St. Thérèse of Lisieux.* Translated by John Clarke. 3rd ed. Washington, DC: Institute of Carmelite Studies, 1996.

Turner, Denys. *Julian of Norwich: Theologian.* New Haven: Yale University Press, 2011.

Waaijman, Kees. *Spiritualiteit: Vormen, grondslagen, methoden.* Gent: Kok-Kampen, 2000.

Wallace, James A. *Preaching to the Hungers of the Heart: The Homily on the Feasts and within the Rites.* Collegeville, MN: Liturgical, 2002.

Watson, Nicholas, and Jacqueline Jenkins, eds. *The Writings of Julian of Norwich: A Vision Showed to a Devout Woman and a Revelation of Love.* University Park, PA: Penn State Press, 2006.

Chapter 2

The Spirituality of Space
Locating the Spiritual Body through the Lens of Romans 8:18–30

Annette Potgieter

INTRODUCTION

We become the spaces we have inhabited. It might seem superfluous to note the importance of space in order to understand human activity, especially as humans are bound by space and time.[1] What we do are operations on space, leaving traces that mark its history and its shape.[2] Yet it is worthwhile making some distinctions here: there is a pivotal difference between "place" and "space." A space is an undefined area, but a place is relational and defined by the location attributed to it.[3] There exists an important link between place and identity. Whenever we meet someone new, we are inclined to ask from where do they come from? The place produces information that we associate with the person, and which becomes part and parcel of a person's self-understanding. Accordingly, identity is always placed.[4]

---

1. Stewart, "Space/Spatiality," 114. Ever since the spatial turn in the 1970s, space has featured as a "vital category of discourse" (Berquist, "Critical Spatiality," 14).
2. Berquist, "Critical Spatiality," 15.
3. Sheldrake, *Spirituality and Theology*, 165.
4. When studying communities in historical texts we deal with the perceptions of time and place and can only speak of time and place in terms of the memory of the community, attached to the place where they live; Moxnes, "Landscape and Spatiality," 92.

Paul's use of location is quite striking in Rom 5–8; he continually hints or bluntly states that the body (σῶμα) is the specific place of God's interaction with humans.[5] Paul specifically wants to persuade an already believing Roman audience, with whom he is not acquainted, that Jesus Christ "our" Lord (κυρίου ἡμῶν Ἰησοῦ Χριστοῦ) should be the controlling power of a believers' body. The audience is not just anywhere; they are situated in Rome, the capital of the Roman Empire. The city of Rome was a testament of the glory of the Roman Empire with the architecture, civil ceremonies, and triumphal route boasting their might. Cultural values were evoked by images transforming the Roman interior into a "memory theater" in which the past is constantly re-appropriated and reimagined in a process of maintaining Roman identity and sense of self.[6] Apart from the influence of place, the body is also a site where culture plays out.[7] Paul uses the body of the believer as the place where interaction with God occurs. Paul understands the body is made up of σάρξ (flesh), ψύχη (soul), and πνεῦμα (spirit). When thinking about the resurrected body, Paul again understands this the reconstitution of the whole psychosomatic self—both body and soul.[8] It is the mortal body that needs to continually present itself to God in order to be a place that is truly alive.

In Rom 8:18–30, Paul depicts the believers' mortal body as a place that decays, even as the body also serves as a redemptive space. There is an inherent dichotomy prevalent as a believer is positioned between everything and nothingness. A believer has been put in the position to be righteous before God, but the mortal body continues to be in a state of decay. Death is inevitable, but redemption occurs as the spiritual body continues.

It is these embodied, lived experiences that we study in an attempt to understand how to move closer to God. There are multiple avenues in understanding spirituality; this chapter would like to focus on the idea of spirituality, and here particularity Christian spirituality, from the spatiality of "lived religion" drawn from in Rom 8:18–30.

DEFINING SPIRITUALITY AND SPACE

For someone living in the first century CE the question "What is spirituality?" would be foreign. Life for them integrated what we modern thinkers

---

5. See Potgieter, *Contested Body*.
6. Van den Heever, "Space, Social Space," 209.
7. Pernau, "Space and Emotion," 541.
8. Moss, *Divine Bodies*, 5.

label distinctly as religion, economy, and family.⁹ These things were not separated. Indeed, even today, the term "spirituality" is notoriously difficult to define. On the one hand, there are definitions ranging from understanding spirituality as an escapism and not being relevant to anything contextual.¹⁰ Other definitions state that everyone embodies spirituality whether they are religious or not, so that spirituality refers to the values and commitments people base their lives on.¹¹ Downey identifies two important components for the umbrella term spirituality: (1) an awareness of that there are levels of reality that is not immediately apparent and (2) a quest for personal integration in the wake of the forces of fragmentation and depersonalization.¹² I find the second to be particularly important, as my working assumption is that the explosion of interest in spirituality is undergirded by a modern problem of compartmentalism. We have managed to live with the idea of "I focus on my body when in the gym" and "I focus on my soul when in church or engaged in some religious activity." Accordingly, this oversimplification affects our being in the world, for what happens in our body affects our soul and vice versa. In the postmodern era, we are alerted to the unsustainability of such dualism. We are implicated and complicated beings who are influenced by our surroundings. The Cartesian and modern worldview that has led us to want to categorize and label everything. We want to be in control, and control is often found in naming and defining something. In this regard, Powell remarks that one of the accomplishments of modern biblical study is to recover the Bible's sense of wholeness.¹³ Following from this holistic viewpoint, spirituality may be defined as the lived experience of belief.

Within this matrix, space also plays a vital role. It challenges Cartesian approaches with focused attention on spatial practice, representations of space, historical meditations of space, and the emphasis on the importance of production and reproduction of space.¹⁴ Edward Soja draws on Henri Lefebvre's categories of social space, but refers to them as "Firstspace," "Secondspace," and "Thirdspace."¹⁵ Firstspace indicates the material word. It is the concrete things that can be mapped, and which determines geophysical realities as perceived by society. Secondspace is represented or imagined

---

9. Brent Nongbri, *Before Religion*, argues that there is no similar word for "religion" as we have in the modern sense in the ancient world.
10. Kourie and Kretzschmar, *Christian Spirituality*, 11.
11. Griffin, *Spirituality*, 1.
12. Downey, *Understanding Christian Spirituality*, 14.
13. Powell, *Theology of Christian Spirituality*, 11.
14. Knott, "Spatial Theory," 104.
15. Soja, *Thirdspace*, 74–75.

space. Thirdspace can be thought of as "lived space."[16] By looking at ancient texts from the vantage point of lived space, it becomes possible to ascertain how space is associated with events, architectural design, political boundaries, and personal ambitions.[17] Human existence is bodily. There is no such thing as unspatialized social reality.[18] Henri Lefebvre, one of the founding and key figures in the critical theory of space, drew particularly on the role of Christian bodies in producing spaces.[19] There is no uncertainty about the connection between space and religion as there are many studies of sacred landscapes, pilgrimage routes, places of worship, missionary excursions, and global religious developments.[20]

With these definitions of spirituality and space in mind, I will now move to a recapitulation of Paul's argument in Rom 8:18–30.

PAUL'S ARGUMENT

Romans 8:18–30 should be understood within the scope of Rom 5–8. Paul explains what he means with the justification of sinners following up on Rom 1–4 with the argument framed by Rom 5:1–11 and 8:31–39.[21] Throughout the argument of Rom 5–8, space plays a pivotal role—specifically the believer's body. It becomes clear that the believers are urged to present themselves or orientate themselves to God. An important theme, particularly in Rom 5:1–11, is peace. The notion of enemies being turned into friends (Rom 5:2, 10) results in being rescued from the wrath of God (Rom 5:6–10). Romans 8:31–39 confirms this assurance. The aim of being rescued is the transformation of believers into Christoformity, living peace in the center of the Roman Empire.[22] Paul argues for believers to orientate themselves away from the *Pax Romana* and participate in a peace that is a radical alternative to Rome.

In Rom 5:1–5 Paul focuses on the present as the addressees already stand firm in the favor of God and take pride on the basis of their hope which anticipates the "δόξα of God,"[23] with Rom 5:5 giving a reason why hope will not be in vain as God's love has been poured into our hearts through the

16. Matthews, "Physical Space," 12.
17. Matthews, "Physical Space," 12.
18. Stewart, "Space/Spatiality," 1.
19. Lefebvre, *Production of Space*, 44.
20. Knott, "Spatial Theory," 103–4.
21. See Nils Dahl's seminal paper on Rom 5–8; Dahl, "Two Notes on Romans 5."
22. McKnight, *Reading Romans*, 96.
23. Breytenbach, "Liberation of Bodies," 1.

Holy Spirit that has been given to us. In Rom 8:9–17, this is picked up again and elaborated on. Paul compares the favor of God, in which believers now stand firmly, to the power of God in Rom 5:12–21. The favor of God that leads to justification abounds sin, and in Rom 6:1–7:6 Paul elaborates on the consequences of being baptized into Christ's death. Someone who has been buried with Christ and resurrected with Christ would no longer continue to sin and would not be subjected to the power of sin. It is important to note that δόξα τοῦ θεοῦ (Rom 5:2) becomes δόξα τοῦ πατρός; this is because believers take pride in the basis of hope to experience the δόξα of God, the same δόξα through which Christ resurrected form the dead. Romans 6:4 uses an analogy of the resurrected Christ that believers can live a new life. They will share in the experience of his resurrection (Rom 6:5). In Rom 8:9–11, Paul develops his idea of the interconnectedness of the believers with the Spirit of God who resurrected Christ in more detail.[24]

Romans 7:7—8:17 clarifies the relationship between sin and the Torah. The law is good, but when controlled by sin it leads to death. The battle with sin is particularly prevalent in 7:14—8:4 as Paul restates his main argument, i.e., how are humans freed from captivity by sin? Man is sold to sin like a slave. Romans 7:21, 23 highlights the slave imagery as being taken as a prisoner of war. The image of a prisoner of war is employed, sketching the dire situation of being held captive by sin. The will is taken away when in the captivity of sin. Paul laments in 7:24: Wretched man that I am! Who will rescue me from this body of death? The body is described as a place of death and Paul describe wanting to be saved. The solution comes in Rom 8:1–4. Believers are described in Rom 8:1: there is no condemnation for those who are in Christ, as the law of the spirit which brings life in Jesus Christ, freed from the Torah that was under the power of sin and thus led to death.

Romans 8:18–30 sheds light on the redemption of the body. Important to understanding Rom 8:18–30 is the juxtaposition of σάρξ and πνεῦμα seen in Rom 8:5–9. The intention, mind-set, of the weak human flesh is against God and leads to death. Those who are ἐν σαρκί cannot win God's favor. However, if the spirit of God lives in believers, then they are not "in the flesh." The predicament remains that even if Christ is in them, the body is not dead, but mortal. Romans 8:11 makes clear that mortal bodies will be vivified. Believers have become children of God and will be glorified with Christ, which is clarified in Rom 8:18–30. Sin has become condemned in the Son and believers have been given the Spirit they will become like the risen Son (Rom 8:29).

---

24. Breytenbach, "Liberation of Bodies," 2.

THE LIBERATION OF THE BODY: ROMANS 8:18–30

The argument in Rom 8:18–30 can be understood in three subsections. In Rom 8:18–21, Paul continues the thought of Rom 8:17c, i.e., that believers suffer and will be glorified together with Christ. The sufferings of the present time are not worth in comparison with the coming glory to be revealed in believers (8:18a–b). This period between "already" and "not yet" is not an easy waiting period. The believers experience sufferings (Rom 8:18), momentary affliction (2 Cor 4:17), physical wasting away (2 Cor 4:16), inward groaning (Rom 8:23; 2 Cor 5:2, 4), and a longing for the heavenly dwelling that will replace the "earthly tent of the body" (2 Cor 5:1–2). The present is a moment of great pain.[25] It is clear that the resurrection of Jesus has already happened, but the resurrection of believers is not yet a reality; for the expectation of the creation eagerly awaits the revelation of the sons of God (ἡ γὰρ ἀποκαραδοκία τῆς κτίσεως τὴν ἀποκάλυψιν τῶν υἱῶν τοῦ θεοῦ ἀπεκδέχεται [8:19a–b]); Rom 8:20 explains Rom 8:19 further shedding light on whether the unveiling of the sons of God will receive δόξα. Creation has been subjected to futility (ματαιότης)[26] and is "groaning in labour pains" as it "waits with eager longing for the revealing of the children of God and for freedom from its own "bondage to decay."

The ὅτι clause of Rom 8:21a explains the content of hope (ἐλπίς). The creation will itself also be set free from the slavery of ruin (ὅτι καὶ αὐτὴ ἡ κτίσις ἐλευθερωθήσεται ἀπὸ τῆς δουλείας τῆς φθορᾶς).[27] The employment of the future tense of ἐλευθερόω is significant, especially as the subject is God. The verb ἐλευθερόω ἀπό denotes to cause someone to be freed from domination.[28] The fact that ἐλευθερόω is introduced as contrary to ὑποτάσσω and φθορά as contrast to δόξα. The future liberation is not only liberation from purposelessness and decay, but also freedom with purpose.[29] There is a movement from enslavement to decay to liberation marked by the δόξα of the children of God.

Romans 8:22–27 explicitly describes the redemption of the body with two metaphors, i.e., childbirth and the adoption of children. Paul starts with οἴδαμεν a statement he assumes is common knowledge to him and his audience. In the present, the whole creation groans together and pains together (πᾶσα ἡ κτίσις συστενάζει καὶ συνωδίνει ἄχρι τοῦ νῦν [8:22a–c]). Of course,

25. Weaver, "Redemption of Our Bodies," 10.

26. Pss 38:6; 77:33 LXX.

27. Moo, *Romans*, 516; Michel, *Römer*, 268; Lohse, *Römer*, 247; Schlier, *Römerbrief*, 262.

28. Cf. Bauer (*BDAG*), 317.

29. Breytenbach, "Liberation of Bodies," 4.

the question is, With whom is the whole of creation in pain? It becomes clear it is not just creation, but also believers who have the firstfruits of the Spirit that groan (αὐτοὶ τὴν ἀπαρχὴν τοῦ πνεύματος ἔχοντες [8:23a]). The body is prominent as believers groan within themselves while awaiting the redemption of their body (τὴν ἀπολύτρωσιν τοῦ σώματος ἡμῶν [Rom 8:23]).

Paul mentions hope again, but unlike what is seen in Rom 5:2, 5 is connected with being saved in Rom 8:24. The repetition and chiastic word order in Rom 8:24–25 particularly emphasizes hope. Romans 8:24 elaborates on the state of redemption as the conjunction γάρ marks. Hope describes the situation in which believers live as liberated people.[30] Hope defines believers' aspiration that their mortal bodies will be made alive in such a way that they are no longer affected by sin.[31] The modal dative τῇ ἐλπίδι qualifies the past tense of σῴζω indicating Christ has already saved believers,[32] but the bodily experience of this saving action lies in the future as τῇ ἐλπίδι denotes. Paul differentiates between the present and future in Rom 8:24b–25 with the contrast of ἐλπίς "hope" and βλέπω "to see."[33] The specific character of the Christian ἐλπίς is to expect not only a future good but "what we do not see" (οὐ βλέπομεν ἐλπίζομεν, Rom 8:25; cf. 2 Cor 4:18).[34]

Paul argues nobody hopes on something they see, but hope for something they do not see; the logical deduction which follows is that believers wait patiently for it.[35] Again, Rom 5:3–5 is echoed with the use of ὑπομονή, but in Rom 8:25 ὑπομονή designates "patience."[36] There is no object mentioned to which a person directs their waiting.[37] The preposition διά with ὑπομονή functions as an agent through which a goal is achieved.[38] The verb ἀπεκδέχομαι is powered by patience (δι' ὑπομονῆς ἀπεκδεχόμεθα) in Rom 8:25. The adoption metaphor (cf. ἀπεκδέχομαι Rom 8:19, 23, and 25) sheds

---

30. Lohse, *Römer*, 248. Schlier, *Römerbrief*, 266, notes "we are saved to hope."

31. Breytenbach, "Liberation of Bodies," 208.

32. Lohse, *Römer*, 248; Käsemann, *Römer*, 230; Zeller, *Römer*, 163. Contra Black, *Romans*, 117, who argues it should be viewed as in an instrumental sense rendering "in hope we attained our salvation."

33. Cf. Wolter, *Römer*, 520; Greijdanus, *Rome*, 382. A similar distinction is seen in 2 Cor 5:7, but between ἐλπίς and πίστις.

34. Spicq, *Theological Lexicon of the New Testament*, 488.

35. The creation has been waiting and hoping since Gen 3:17 for restoration in contrast to Jesus followers who first become aware of the hope that waits when they believe Christ and are baptized in Christ as already seen in Rom 5:5, 8. Cf. Wolter, *Römer*, 520.

36. *BDAG*, 1040.

37. Lohse, *Römer*, 248.

38. Porter, *Idioms*, 150.

light on the future body a believer will obtain life. Christ liberates the mortal body making it possible for the believer to obtain life.

In Rom 8:26–27, Paul especially focuses on the role of the Spirit. Paul again assumes that the audience is already knowledgeable, as he states that "we" know that for those who love God (οἴδαμεν δὲ ὅτι τοῖς ἀγαπῶσιν τὸν θεὸν [8:28ab]), all things work together for good (πάντα συνεργεῖ εἰς ἀγαθόν [8:28c]). Romans 8:29 illustrates that believers are predestined to be conformed to the image of his Son. The body is the intended place where the glory of God will be reflected. Believers have metaphorically died to sin within their bodies as their bodies is a space intended to be in the image of Christ (cf. Rom 8:29). This glorification with Christ points to the spiritual body that believers will have, devoid of any suffering. Romans 8:29 depicts believers are predestined to be conformed to the image of the Son. Accordingly, the children and heirs of God suffer with Jesus in their current predicaments, but also will be glorified with him.

THE BODY AS SPECIFIC LOCATION OF GOD'S ENCOUNTER

It becomes clear in Rom 8:18–30, especially, that the body is liberated from sin and corruption when participating in the glory of the children of God. Δόξα is a bodily image in Paul as seen from Rom 6:4. For Paul, life is only worth living when orientated towards God. Jesus Christ dying for "us" is more than just an example of life, but a fundamental bodily experience for believers who are transported through baptism from a body of death to a body of life. The body becomes a place where the hope lies in the awareness that Christ is the victor. The believer needs to participate in the death and resurrection of Jesus (Rom 6:4) to participate in this new reality. The body is a place that although subject to decay is also a redemptive space. Believers' mortal body will decay and die but will be made alive as spiritual bodies.

Paul understands the body of the believer as a creation of God (1 Cor 15:35–49), a "member of Christ" (1 Cor 6:15) and a "temple of the Holy Spirit" (1 Cor 6:19). Resurrection is not, as it was for some of Paul's contemporaries, a matter of freeing one's spirit by divesting oneself of the body.[39] Paul also does not view the body itself as an evil from which one longs to be freed. The body itself is destined for resurrection. Paul assures believers that God "will give life to your mortal bodies" (Rom 8:11). Paul does not elaborate on what the resurrection life will look like (2 Cor 12:1–4); he suggests that more information is not necessary.

39. Weaver, "Redemption of Our Bodies," 9.

However, Paul's use of the glorified body also has an immanent quality. It is not something, someday for the afterlife. Rather, believers are in a process of constantly orientating themselves towards God and taking on a Christoform identity. The reason for the claim that all things work together for the good is provided in Rom 8:29. God already knew beforehand that he decided for believers to have a form identical to the appearance of his Son. To be conformed to the image of his Son (προώρισεν συμμόρφους τῆς εἰκόνος τοῦ υἱοῦ αὐτοῦ [8:29b]) means that the resurrected will be the firstborn within a large family. This also entails a public orientation.[40]

In this regard, Gager describes that Paul uses the idea of future resurrection of Christians in 1 Corinthians as a symbol of transformation and presupposes an undercurrent of protest and alienation. The current body is perishable, dishonorable, weak, and physical whereas the resurrection body of the not-too-distant future will be imperishable glorious, powerful, and spiritual.[41] Viewing the decay of the mortal body and the enlivening of the spiritual body as tension between nothingness and everything might be a modern lens on Paul, but ultimately it offers a view of a "lived theology."

ENVISIONING BODIES

Understanding the body as a site for redemption offers an important lens to consider the importance of spirituality, especially in a country such as South Africa.[42] Isherwood and Stuart argue, as regards the body, that "we have to rethink our concept of redemption."[43] They use it in the context of thinking about the impact of body theology as a *lived theology*.[44] In a South African context, redemption can be interpreted in various ways. The social, economic and political impact of past atrocities remain present realities. The continuing legacies of apartheid should not be denied here. Racism did

40. McKnight, *Rereading Romans*, 28.

41. Gager, "Body-Symbols," 348.

42. As regards "spirituality," there are of course various diverse cultures in South Africa with an array of different understanding of spirituality. In this sense, spirituality can be defined as pertaining to the center of human existence; Kees Waaijman, *Spiritualiteit*, 1, describes spirituality as concerning "de verhouding tot het Absolute." It should be kept in mind that spirituality was originally viewed as something that is "Roman Catholic." The Dutch Reformed Church did not engage with the notion of spirituality, especially during apartheid. The idea is still novel in Dutch Reformed circles today, although there are a few centers of spirituality that have started in the Dutch Reformed Church, e.g., Ooskerk in Pretoria with the *Viam Dei* program and the Andrew Murray Centre for Spirituality in Wellington, to name a few.

43. Isherwood and Stuart, *Body Theology*, 114.

44. Isherwood and Stuart, *Body Theology*, 33.

not arrive in South Africa in 1948 with the rise of the National Party, but the policies of apartheid indeed signalled a dramatic change.[45] History is important: human beings are not born racist but are racialized. We are trained and learn emotional and symbolic values from our surroundings.[46] In the story of South Africa, particularly for the Afrikaner nation, the entanglement of the church in politics caused an alienation with the Scripture,[47] and eventually from all other churches.[48] The Dutch Reformed Church was the church with the most influence, as it was connected to and resembled the Afrikaner nation of the ruling party.[49] When the Dutch Reformed Church used the word "brothers" it was intended for exclusively only their fellow churchgoers.[50] From a Pauline perspective, the church is seen as the body of Christ (e.g., 1 Cor 12:27) and thus it becomes an integral place from which we navigate ourselves.[51] The majority of the South African population identifies as Christian. The Dutch Reformed Church's perception of Paul's use of the "body of Christ" was tainted, and the church was no longer part of

---

45. Racial discrimination was already entrenched in the Union Constitution and determined a lot of the legislation between 1910 and 1948 (de Gruchy and de Gruchy, *Church Struggle*, 51).

46. This is applicable in two ways, firstly concerning how we develop, shape, train, and adorn the body and secondly concerning the emotional and symbolic values we associate with it (Gager, "Body-Symbols," 347).

47. D. F. Malan, a former minister in the Dutch Reformed Church, was instrumental in laying the foundations of legalizing and enforcing apartheid ideas, which Hendrik Verwoerd, often referred to as the "grand architect of apartheid" took further with the term "separate development" (Vosloo, "Christianity and Apartheid," 1–2).

48. In 1936 the Christian Council of South African was constituted in Bloemfontein following the success of the Edinburgh missionary conference in 1910. The ecumenical dream was, however, continually belabored and thwarted by the Afrikaner nationalist ideals (de Gruchy and de Gruchy, *Church Struggle*, 27). The newly formed World Council of Churches (WCC) voiced concern in 1948 with apartheid. Archbishop Joost de Blank demanded the WCC expel the Cape and Transvaal synods: "the future of Christianity in this country demands our complete dissociation from the Dutch Reformed attitude . . . . Either they must be expelled or we shall be compelled to withdraw." The threat of leaving was not received well (de Gruchy and de Gruchy, *Church Struggle*, 61–62). After the Sharpeville massacre in 1960 the WCC facilitated a process at the Cottesloe hostel of the University of Witwatersrand in Johannesburg attended by church representatives, including from the Dutch Reformed churches, releasing the Cottesloe Declaration in which it is affirmed that there is no scriptural base for the prohibition of mixed marriage, and that no one who believes in Jesus Christ may be excluded from any church on the grounds of their race or color (Vosloo, "Christianity and Apartheid," 18).

49. De Gruchy and de Gruchy, *Church Struggle*, 67.

50. De Gruchy and de Gruchy, *Church Struggle*, 67.

51. In this sense, I intend the church in general in South Africa.

the body of Christ in the symbolic sense of the WCC on a global scale.[52] Against such a backdrop, this becomes immensely important in light of how we think of the body as a place of redemption.

Apartheid did not only mean the segregation of bodies according to racial groups, but also the segregation of South African cities. In 1953 the Group Areas Act forced people to live in separate neighborhoods.[53] Whites were placed in green suburbs, Coloreds and Africans in townships with difficult living standards. Some groups were moved from their homes with force to spaces of nothingness, as for example the famous displacement of the District 6 community which forced them to the plains of the Cape Flats. The Cape Flats are known for being sandy and difficult to inhabit.[54] Although apartheid ended in 1994, the pace of change in spatial structures has not been fast enough.[55]

Drawing on the Rom 8:18–30 imagery of the creation groaning, South Africa can be viewed as a space that is groaning. A hopelessness and purposelessness are seen in people who are displaced, as attachments to people and people gives meaningful identities and secure relationships.[56] Dispersed apartheid cities pushed the poor to the periphery and forced them to become commuters to distant jobs.[57] South Africa experiences one of the highest levels of violent crime in the world.[58] Fear of the "other" continues disguised as spatial quarantine.[59] Statistical evidence indicates violent crime is higher in township areas than in the wealthy suburbs.[60] People in the suburbs live with burglar proofing, burglar alarms, electric fencing, steel gates, automatic garage doors, or in gated communities as a defensive mechanism against the violence.[61] Research indicates a nihilistic attitude to violence

---

52. Of course, this is a complex and differentiated history with the role of Christianity and apartheid being deeply ambivalent as on the one hand, churches and missionaries were instrumental in advocating racial separation and others again playing an instrumental role in the struggle against inequality (Vosloo, "Christianity and Apartheid," 1–2).

53. Houssay-Holzschuch and Teppo, "Race," 351.

54. The Cape Flats area is essentially a lowland with the terrain ranging from low-lying sandy plains. Dunes are frequent with the highest dunes approximately sixty-five meters (Adelana et al., "Cape Flats," 462).

55. Houssay-Holzschuch and Teppo, "Race," 352.

56. De Beer and Oranje, "City-Making," 16

57. Lemon, "Separate Space," 2.

58. Bremner, "Demographic Anxieties," 461.

59. Lemanski, "New Apartheid?," 103.

60. Bremner, "Demographic Anxieties," 463.

61. Bremner, "Demographic Anxieties," 464.

and killing among some, in which the death inflicted on a human being is perceived as an embracing of nothing.[62]

We are shaped by our landscape.[63] We learn how to walk, to talk, and to be. We learn who we are by "being in a place." The body is a social product. Apart from our embodied selves, our common experience of place is familiar landscapes.[64] Landscape is molded by human actions or human perceptions.[65] The landscape becomes the reference point for the places where we live,[66] which determines our actions and behavior. Spirituality is concerned with unlearning what the world says, what we have been socialized into, and relearning who God created us to be. In light of history of apartheid in South Africa, it is worth emphasizing this process of unlearning destructive patterns of socialization. Masango mentions that South Africans lost their concept of Ubuntu during apartheid. Ubuntu entails the concept of mutual respect which is guided by the notion of being in the image and likeness of God,[67] as seen in the interpretation of Rom 8:29 which serves as the climax in Paul's argument indicating that believers are to be conformed to the image of the Son. Accordingly, they participate in a larger family along with the Son as they embody the glory of God. Fundamental for creating places of redemption in South Africa is cultivating spiritualities that embrace the regard and respect of fellow humans as created in the likeness in the image of God. This is a core to a redemptive spirituality that needs to be explored and taught.

Along similar lines, this notion of being part of a family and of the body as being a place that reflected the glory of God is crucial in our discussions concerning gender, race, and identity. For a long time, the idea of "body" has been observed as prone to sin and not as important as the mind.[68] In a country where statistics indicate that every twenty-six seconds in South Africa a woman is raped,[69] it is vital to rethink our understanding of bodies and in which manner we respect one another.[70] A spirituality of the body may serve as a starting point in remedying negative and unhealthy

62. Bremner, "Demographic Anxieties," 464.
63. Gager, "Body-Symbols," 347.
64. Sheldrake, *Spirituality and Theology*, 167.
65. Moxnes, "Landscape and Spatiality," 92.
66. Moxnes, "Landscape and Spatiality," 92.
67. Masango, "African Spirituality," 932–33.
68. Isherwood and Stuart, *Body Theology*, 33.
69. Punt, "Paul, Body Theology," 362.

70. The importance of body theology holds the hope of healing patriarchal thinking (Isherwood and Stuart, *Body Theology*, 33).

notions about the body in general and support in embracing the fact that embodiedness is part and parcel of what it means to be human.[71]

De Certeau remarks that space is "practised space."[72] He analyzes the role of space and spatializing by means of storying in constructing the persuasions and inducements that motivate everyday actions.[73] This is helpful in the manner in which we approach the everyday.[74] Spirituality is a confrontation with one's reality. Spirituality is not an escape from reality, but rather an intentional movement to address difficulties and work through it, for example, unlearning racism. A focus on a spirituality of the redemptive body provides an awareness of confronting spaces of privilege, spaces of racism, spaces of violence, and spaces of inequality. It is important to reflect on places as constructed by the humans that inhabit it.[75] Kritzinger refers to this as a "concrete spirituality," i.e., urban people's need for connection with God's presence in their daily struggles to be human in the city. It is being at home in the hard pavement realities of a South African city.[76] Hereby, the link is made between spirituality, body, and place. Overall, we may view this from the lens of Paul's description of the mortal body that is bound to decay, which may be construed as a state of nothingness. The mortal body longs to be freed. The practice of spiritual disciplines aids in the creating an awareness enabling a person to craft a link between spirituality and space. Moreover, it links the mortal body in a state of decay with the future hope of being vivified from decay and death. But to come back to De Certeau's practiced space, spirituality is something that is practiced. It is repeated, recalibrated, and becomes part of the everyday repertoire of being.[77]

A place can never be the same. Space replicates power relations within a society which implies that spaces are both constantly negotiated and changeable.[78] Paul's notion of the eschatological body and the renewal of creation suggests that indeed body and space can undergo experiences of

71. Powell, *Theology of Christian Spirituality*, 11.

72. De Certeau, *Practice of Everyday Life*, 117.

73. De Certeau, *Practice of Everyday Life*, 117–30.

74. Eliade, *Sacred*, 20, 26, refers to the profane as a "formless expanse" consisting of "absolute nonbeing" that devalues every day or mundane spaces.

75. Sheldrake, *Spirituality and Theology*, 195.

76. De Certeau, *Practice of Everyday Life*, 117.

77. Holloway, "Spiritual Practice," 961–74 argues for sacred everyday geographies where spirituality as an embodied practice, outside of traditional spaces associated with the sacred such as a church or a temple, leads to everyday effects becoming a space of a renewed marvelling of the profane. He mentions more research into the notion of the everyday that is worth exploring.

78. Stewart, "Space/Spatiality," 4.

radical transformation. In this regard, it worth mentioning a disclaimer that Paul's use of glorified bodies creates an ideal type of body.[79] In early Christianity, this ideal glorified body was important, as early Christians grappled with the idea of what this body would do and be like in the afterlife. If a person was disabled, would he/she/they be disabled in the afterlife? Candida Moss investigates early Christian depictions of glorified bodies; she illustrates how even though Jesus reverses hierarchies of wealth, social status, gender, and power, the assumption of conventional beauty ideals are in place when thinking about the spiritual body.[80] She states that "when we write about the resurrection, we write about who we are, who we want to be and the modes of our annihilation that most terrify us."[81] The literary depiction of heavenly bodies utilizes language and imagery that was commonly used to describe the bodies of youthful nobles. Ancient philosophers' understanding of beauty is intertwined with the good, but that which is considered good is available to those who can afford it.[82] The aesthetics of the resurrection correspond to the bodies and attire of the rich; in this picture, salvation becomes the process of enrichment that never deconstructs the social hierarchy that it wants to challenge.

We must tread lightly on thinking of the body as individualistic and to be used for personal gain. Paul does not endorse individual activity.[83] For Paul the body is a metaphor that describes the life of Christian communities.[84] The body also functions as a collective and is relational. Applying this to the unequal space in South Africa entails to participate in collective lament and an outcry against ongoing injustices. It is essential to overcome the distance in places with a focus on collective identity. When we think of redemption in South Africa, the body serves as a focal point to keep in mind that places of oppression, corruption, and violence can change. However, the longing to be liberated from these decaying places is not something in which a person is alone, but part of a community where change can continue to occur.

---

79. Moss, *Divine Bodies*, 13.
80. Moss, *Divine Bodies*, 95.
81. Moss, *Divine Bodies*, 3.
82. Moss, *Divine Bodies*, 113.

83. The ancient Mediterranean is a collective culture. This entails that a person's behavior in a collectivistic culture is centered around the pursuits and goals of the group. Identity is conferred from family, ancestral place, rank and role (Malina, "Collectivism," 22).

84. Punt, "Paul, Body Theology," 362.

CONCLUSION

The topic of spirituality is a broad subject with a variety of interpretative nuances to discern, especially in a South African context which is diverse and confronted with an array of challenges. This chapter has aimed in pointing out an intersection between the body as a place and spirituality, using Rom 8:18–30 as a foundation. The body is a place that although subject to decay is also a redemptive space. Space is something that continually changes. Place in particularly is important as it shapes us. We become products of our environment.

A focus on the spirituality of the body as a place of redemption provides an important tool for South African context as the body as a collective serves as starting point for transformation. South Africa continues to be embattled in the inequality and injustices of space caused during apartheid, the physical cities creating the distance between people remain. But in becoming aware of the tension between everything and nothingness, we manage to cultivate and become aware of ways of thinking about redemptive places. The believer's body that will become the place where the coming glory of God will manifest. The body will be freed from its state of decay. It is in the knowledge that the body will be liberated from the decay that one can confront the everyday difficulties and challenges. A focus on the body adds value to understanding redemption is also lived, even in a state of the tension between everything and nothingness.

BIBLIOGRAPHY

Adelana, Segun, et al. "A Conceptual Model for the Development and Management of the Cape Flats Aquifer, South Africa." *Water SA* 36 (2010) 461–74.

Bauer, Walter, et al. *A Greek-English Lexicon of the New Testament and Other Early Christian Literature*. 3rd ed. Chicago: University of Chicago Press, 2000.

Berquist, Jon L. "Critical Spatiality and the Construction of the Ancient World." In *Imagining Biblical Worlds: Studies in Spatial, Social and Historical Constructs in Honor of James W. Flanagan*, edited by D. M. Gunn and P. M. McNutt, 14–29. Sheffield UK: Sheffield Academic, 2002.

Black, Matthew. *Romans*. The New Century Bible Commentary. 2nd ed. Grand Rapids: Eerdmans, 1973.

Bremner, Lindsay. "Bounded Spaces: Demographic Anxieties in Post-Apartheid Johannesburg." *Journal for the Study of Race, Nation and Culture* 10 (2004) 455–68.

Breytenbach, Cilliers. "Creation and the Revelation of God's Children: Liberation of Enslaved Bodies." *In die Skriflig/In Luce Verbi* 47 (2013). http://dx.doi.org/10.4102/ids.v47i2.681.

Dahl, N. A. "Two Notes on Romans 5." *Studia Theologica* 5 (1951) 37–48.

De Beer, S., and M. Oranje. "City-Making from Below: A Call for Communities of Resistance and Reconstruction." *Town and Regional Planning* 74 (2019) 12–22.
De Certeau, Michel. *The Practice of Everyday Life*. Translated by Steven F. Rendall. Berkeley: University of California Press, 2002.
de Gruchy, John, and de Gruchy, S. *The Church Struggle in South Africa*. 3rd ed. Minneapolis: Fortress, 2005.
Downey, Michael. *Understanding Christian Spirituality*. Mahwah, NJ: Paulist, 1997.
Eliade, Mircea. *The Sacred and the Profane: The Nature of Religion*. New York: Harcourt Brace, 1959.
Gager, John G. "Body-Symbols and Social Reality: Resurrection Incarnation and Ascetism in Early Christianity." *Religion* 12 (1982) 345–63.
Greijdanus, S. *De Brief van den Apostel Paulus aan de gemeente te Rome I*. Amsterdam: Van Bottenburg, 1933.
Griffin, D. R. *Spirituality and Society: Postmodern Visions*. New York: State University of New York Press, 1988.
Holloway, Julian. "Make-Believe: Spiritual Practice, Embodiment, and Sacred Space." *Environment and Planning* A 35 (2003) 1,961–74.
Houssay-Holzschuch, Myriam, and Annika Teppo. "A Mall for All? Race and Public Space in Post-Apartheid Cape Town." *Cultural Geographies* (2009) 351–79.
Hultgren, Arland. J. *Paul's Letter to the Romans*. Grand Rapids: Eerdmans, 2011.
Isherwood, Lisa, and Elizabeth Stuart. *Introducing Body Theology*. Sheffield, UK: Sheffield Academic, 1998.
Käsemann, Ernst. *An die Römer—Kommentar zum Paulusbrief*. Berlin: Evangelische Verlagsanhalt, 1978.
Knott, Kim. "Spatial Theory and the Study of Religion." *Religion Compass* 2 (2008) 1,102–16.
Kourie, Celia, and Louise Kretzschmar. *Christian Spirituality in South Africa*. Pietermaritzburg: Cluster, 2000.
Kritzinger, J. N. "Concrete Spirituality." *HTS Theological Studies* 70 (2014) 1–12.
Lefebvre, H. *The Production of Space*. Oxford: Blackwell, 1991.
Lemanski, Charlotte. "A New Apartheid? The Spatial Implications of Fear of Crime in Cape Town, South Africa." *Environment & Urbanization* 16 (2004) 101–12.
Lemon, Anthony. "Separate Space and Shared Space in Post-Apartheid South Africa." *Geography Research Forum* 18 (1998) 1–21.
Lohse, Eduard. *Der Brief an die Römer*. Kritisch-exegetischer Kommentar über das Neue Testament. Göttingen: Vandenhoeck & Ruprecht, 2003.
Malina, Bruce J. "Collectivism in Mediterranean Culture." In *Understanding the Social World of the New Testament*, edited by Dietmar Neufeld and Richard E. DeMaris, 17–28. London: Routledge, 2010.
Matthews, Victor H. "Physical Space, Imagined Space, and 'Lived Space' in Ancient Israel." *Biblical Theology Bulletin: Journal of Bible and Culture* 33 (2003) 12–20.
Masango, Maake J. S. "African Spirituality That Shapes the Concept of Ubuntu." *Verbum et Ecclesia* 27 (2006) 930–43.
McKnight, Scot. *Rereading Romans Backwards—A Gospel of Peace in the Midst of Empire*. Waco, TX: Baylor University Press, 2019.
Michel, Otto. *Der Brief an die Römer*. Kritisch-Exegetischer Kommentar under das Neue Testament Band 4. Göttingen: Vandenhoeck & Ruprecht, 1966.

Moo, Douglas J. *The Epistle to the Romans*. New International Commentary on the New Testament. Grand Rapids: Eerdmans, 1996.

Moss, Candida R. *Divine Bodies: Resurrecting Perfection in the New Testament and Early Christianity*. New Haven, CT: Yale University Press, 2019.

Moxnes, Halvor. "Landscape and Spatiality: Placing Jesus." In *Understanding the Social World of the New Testament*, edited by Dietmar Neufeld and Richard E. DeMaris, 90–106. London: Routledge, 2010.

Nongbri, Brent. *Before Religion—A History of a Modern Concept*. New Haven, CT: Yale University Press, 2013.

Pernau, Margrit. "Space and Emotion: Building to Feel." *History Compass* 12 (2014) 541–49.

Porter, Stanley E. *Idioms of the Greek New Testament*. Sheffield, UK: JSOT, 1992.

Potgieter, Annette. *Contested Body: Metaphors of Dominion in Rom 5–8*. Durbanville: AOSIS, 2020.

Powell, Samuel M. *A Theology of Christian Spirituality*. Nashville: Abingdon, 2005.

Punt, Jeremy. "Paul, Body Theology, and Morality: Parameters for a Discussion." *Neotestamentica* 39.2 (2005) 359–88.

Schlier, Heinrich. *Der Römerbrief*. Herdes Theologischer Kommentar Zum Neuen Testament Band 4. Freiburg: Herder, 1977.

Sheldrake, Phillip. *Spirituality and Theology—Christian Living and the Doctrine of God*. London: Darton Longman & Todd, 1998.

Soja, Edward W. *Thirdspace: Journeys to Los Angeles and Other Real-and-Imagined Places*. Malden, MA: Blackwell, 1996.

Spicq, Ceslas, and Ernest, James D. *Theological Lexicon of the New Testament*. Vol. 1. Peabody, MA: Hendrickson, 1994.

Stewart, Eric C. "New Testament Space/Spatiality." *Biblical Theology Bulletin* 42 (2011) 114–23.

Van den Heever, Gerhard. "Space, Social Space, and the Construction of Early Christian Identity in First Century Asia Minor." *Religion & Theology* 17 (2010) 205–43.

Vosloo, Robert. "Christianity and Apartheid in South Africa." *Journal of Systematic Theology* 2 (2023) 1–41.

Waaijman, Kees. *Spiritualiteit: Vormen, grondslagen, methoden*. Gent: Kok-Kampen, 2000.

Weaver, Dorothy Jean. "The Redemption of Our Bodies—A Pauline Primer on Resurrection." *Vision* (2004) 5–11.

Wolter, Michael. *Der Brief an die Römer. Teilband 1: Röm 1–8*. Evangelisch-Katholischer Kommentar zum Neuen Testament. Göttingen: Neukirchener Theologie Patmos, 2014.

Zeller, Dieter. *Der Brief an die Römer*. Regensburger Neues Testament. Regensburg: Friedrich Pustet Regensburg, 1985.

Chapter 3

The Attention Assemblage and the Machines of Acedia

On Evagrian Practice in the Age of Hyperattention

Khegan M. Delport

THE DEMOCRATIZATION OF SADNESS

The connection between attention and spiritual practice is long-standing; there are numerous routes one could explore in unpacking their social co-investments. The meanings of "attention" are multiple and textured, requiring a hermeneutical and historical sensitivity to the ways that the language of "attention" has been received and deployed throughout history. The theme of "attention" has been addressed by many disciplines, such as neuroscience, philosophy, history, economics, religious studies, theology, and so on. Any comprehensive attempt to do justice to this field would need an adequate grasp of these receptions. In this chapter, I can only hint at some of these avenues; in particular, I would like to say a few things about *attention economy*, and especially its mediation through digital and screen-based technology. My specific purpose is to ask why this cultural process raises challenges for mental and spiritual resilience generally, especially in the wake of the global pandemic. In a time of hyper-visualization, hyper-reality, fake news, and deepfakes, I here make some observations regarding the current reality we face regarding attention economies and why spiritual traditions, like that of Christian mysticism and practice, might provide one avenue for diagnosis and resistance within the inundation of digitalized distractions.

My contribution is rather modest and does not seek to answer how the larger, more embracing "attention ecology"[1] might be altered towards a more humanizing, social consensus. Many strategies could be invoked here (e.g., acceleration, deceleration, etc.); however, any change at a meaningful level would need to include a collective change of behavior on our behalf. Digital platforms tend to entrench and "grammatize"[2] the captured and abstracted data sets of online activity and thus intrench certain habits of digital consumption. Online monopolies do indeed engage in hegemonic tactics of control and surveillance to direct and nudge us towards predictabilities that are beneficial for them. This is now an open secret. But the truth is that for this to change, our collective habits would need to change as well. Social mobilization is required to provoke changes to digital monopolies, and we probably also require a collective imagination reoriented towards alternative models of digital and humane flourishing. However, most of the time, if we are honest, we are willing to enter a Faustian compact because of the ease of living and services thereby provided. So, if we truly want different political and digital options than we currently have, this will imply a transformation of our really existing, analogue modes of being. It would imply a new attention ecology, an ethos of care regarding what we deem as truly valuable, what we would like to change and preserve.

And so, a few qualifications: throughout what follows, it should be clear that I have sympathy with the critics of neoliberal visions of attention economy. In this framing, our visual cultures, leisure time, and even our sense faculties have been commandeered and absorbed into the leviathan of the market. Marxist critics of attention culture, such as Jonathan Beller, have spoken about how within this particular regime and discipline of attention our private lives have been turned into "deterritorialized factories in which [we as] spectators work ... in which we perform value-productive labor."[3] According to *the attention theory of value*, our perceptive interactions are "increasingly bound to production,"[4] our collective attention and sensibility subjected to "economization,"[5] and incorporated into a valorizing of digital capital. Hereby, our engagement with the world is incorporated into an

---

1. Citton, *Ecology of Attention*.
2. The term is taken from Bernard Stiegler.
3. Beller, *Cinematic Mode of Production*, 1.
4. Beller, *Cinematic Mode of Production*, 3
5. Beller, *Cinematic Mode of Production*, 6.

"attentional biopower"⁶ that aims to restrict the sensorium into a predictable "semi-automatization,"⁷ one that can be managed for the maximization of profit. Beller's insights draw upon Jonathan Crary, who argued that this alignment of perception with production is not a new development, but part of *long dureé* of visual modernism that grew out of "*an already reconfigured field* of techniques and discourses about visuality and an observing subject,*"⁸ fomenting a "spectacular culture" in which agents are socially atomized and thus "*inhabit time* as disempowered."⁹

I should also add that my approach should not be equated with "mindfulness" techniques either. "Mindfulness," in its popular promotion, often tends to disembed practices of meditation and contemplation, abstracting them from particular religious traditions, transforming them into a scientistic mode of stress regulation. "Mindfulness" in this variety of practice becomes an empty, floating signifier that can be adopted by just about anyone. The form that "mindfulness" usually takes here is one that fits rather seamlessly into a neoliberal model of market production by transforming meditative practices into an asocial, apolitical, and ahistorical ethos of stress management. Here mindfulness becomes a way of removing distractions so that capitalist labor and production may continue with less friction, or as an outlet for emotional build-up, without inquiring into or critiquing the social context in which such production occurs. By adopting such a posture, it does not investigate the ideological formation of attention economy under neoliberalism. Thus, contemplative practice has become commodified—McMindfulness, Mindfulness©, etc.—and thus turned into one more instantiation of capitalist discipline.[10]

I say this to lay my cards on the table in case I am read as quietist and escapist. However, neither am I claiming for my argument anything too expansive or revolutionary. Rather, in what follows I am suggesting one mode of resistance to this reductive and mechanizing discipline of attention through an *alternative* form of spiritual discipline: a praxis of contemplative prayer as being one avenue for the transformation of our senses and desire. Here, I have chosen the corpus of Evagrius Ponticus (ca. 345–399 CE), a

6. Beller, *Cinematic Mode of Production*, 4.
7. Beller, *Cinematic Mode of Production*, 8.
8. Crary, *Suspensions of Perception*, 6
9. Crary, *Suspensions of Perception*, 3.
10. See Walsh, "Meta-Critique of Mindfulness Critiques." For instance, fans of the Showtime TV series *Billions* will know that Bobby Axelrod, the ruthless and brilliant venture capitalist at the center of the drama, is a practitioner of meditation and mindfulness, and that it is this form of Stoic self-management that precisely enables him to do his job "better" and dispense with rivals from a position of greater poise.

Cappadocian and Egyptian monk, considered to be the one of most influential theorists of the monastic life. The reason why such a tradition might have a particular resonance today is that the tradition of desert monasticism may provide practices and resources for spiritual vigilance and resilience within post-COVID conditions. Columba Stewart, a noted scholar of Evagrius and early monasticism, mentions how his "analysis of the powerful effects of imagery and his concern that we not mistake the virtual for the actual encourage deeper reflection on the effects of imaging technology on religious culture."[11] In particular, the Evagrian diagnostic of *acedia* appears as perceptive analysis, even by today's standards: his description of the workings of the so-called "noonday demon,"[12] in all its antique strangeness, brings to the fore the ways our acquisitive desire for novelty and perpetual productivity transforms our engagement with temporality, space, and the other—whether this be human or divine. The ancient concept of acedia, despite its historical peculiarity and archaeology, has connections to our contemporary experiences of cultural and digital acceleration. Capitalist deterritorialization and desire, with its fantasies of perpetual accumulation, speed, and innovation, and the various means by which it orchestrates our attention, indeed seem to exacerbate a disconnection from the sensuous manifold. In this light, the spiritual teachings of Evagrius, I argue, might provide avenues across the centuries for engaging attentively with screen-based technologies and attentive economies. Such pertinence may be found in his concept of "imageless prayer" as mode of receiving the intellectual light of Trinity within the mind (*nous*), apart from intrusive passions and mental representations.

I am not the first to do this: the Evagrian concept of acedia has been taken up by analysts of media culture, like Richard Seymour: within what he calls "the chronophagic machine" of digital addiction, he speaks of how acedia in desert and medieval spirituality concerns "a lack of care about one's life; a listless, restless spiritual lethargy." It is a condition that leaves "one yearning for distraction and continuing novelty, exploiting one's petty hates and hungers. It dissolves one's capacity for attending, for living as if living mattered, into a series of itches demanding to be scratched. Ultimately, it was dehumanizing, corrosive of meaning: it was spiritual death."[13] Indeed, digital and platform capitalism are machines of acedia, technologies whose imbedded tendencies are towards a "democratization of sadness," to quote

11. Stewart, "Imageless Prayer and the Theological Vision of Evagrius Ponticus," 202.

12. For a description of "the terrors of noontime," see Ankersmit, *History and Tropology*, 230–37.

13. Seymour, *Twittering Machine*, 200.

Geert Lovink.[14] In this digital regime, sadness has been coded into a "techno-sentiment"[15] that keeps us within the cybernetic loop of discontent, so that through the "scrolling, swiping and flipping, we hungry ghosts try to fill the existential emptiness, frantically searching for a determining sign—and failing."[16] Within this context, I believe that we need some kind of connection to spiritual transcendence beyond the algorithmic purgatory of digital capitalism. And so, with all due hermeneutical sensitivity regarding the difference between the time of the desert monks and ours, statements like these suggest something of the present actuality of Evagrius.

THE HYPERATTENTION ECONOMY

Lockdowns and COVID-19 restrictions accelerated the drive of attention and gig economies in general.[17] Isolation, the limitation of non-essential services, and the progression towards a greater reliance on online content increased dependency on screen-based technologies in general—for both work and leisure. One may qualify this in the context of South Africa where poverty, data-costs, a lack of digital literacy, and access to internet limit such developments; but one should also add that it is precisely this paucity which is spurring on companies to expand into Africa. Moreover, access to mobile communications and social media (e.g., Facebook, TikTok, Instagram, etc.), especially among South African millennials, suggests that we too are placed within this burgeoning attention economy.[18]

The language of "attention economy" has been in use at least since the late 1990s. In a seminal text, Michael Goldhaber theorized that the new economy of the internet was not primarily centered on information production, which is infinitely fecund, but rather on the scarcity of attention.[19] In essence, attention economies are predicated on the disparity between the seemingly endless production of content and the inherently circumscribed capacity of human attention. Consequently, more and more information is being added to the database of knowledge, while our innate ability to process this content decreases accordingly. Largely because of digital proliferation, we have seen a generational transition from earlier customs of "deep attention," where longer and focused periods of attention were common,

14. Lovink, *Sad by Design*, 55.
15. Lovink, *Sad by Design*, 50.
16. Lovink, *Sad by Design*, 51.
17. Dé et al, "Impact of Digital Surge during Covid-19 Pandemic."
18. Cf. Duffett and Wakeham, "Social Media Marketing Communications."
19. Goldhaber, "Attention Economy and the Net."

to cultures of "hyperattention" where our attention spans are much shorter and variegated, as argued by Katherine Hayles.[20] Now the classical economic specter of scarcity raises the question: How does one direct human attention? Marketing of course invents techniques whereby attention may be captured and directed repeatedly, and even predictably, towards certain ends within an ever-increasing environment of competition. In distinction from industrial and material economies where reproduction and repeatability are elevated, and producers must financially compete as regards the circulation of products, attention economies are centered upon the ability to stand out from the crowd and the ability to grab and bring your attention into focus. In this regime, attentiveness does not even have to be monetized: sheer celebrity might be considered satisfactory, because this opens wider circles of influence and benefit—including of the fiduciary kind. Clicks, likes, and tweets—as well as *who* is doing the tweeting and liking—are considered a kind of currency on their own. As Georg Franck says: "Nothing seems to attract attention more than the accumulation of attention income, nothing seems to stimulate the media more than this kind of capital, nothing appears to animate advertising space with a stronger power of attraction than the displayed wealth of earned attention."[21] There are some upsides to this: humans naturally seek attention, honor, and recognition. One of the prospects of an attention economy is a trend towards social and relational valuation as a new form of currency, even as one should add the cautionary note that attention economy, like any comparable social arrangement, requires the inculturation of social virtues.[22] Old questions of justice and distribution should indeed be repurposed for the digital age. For the problem remains: Who gets a greater share in this currency? Do some get more than they deserve? And who is valued more within this compact? Moreover, it is quickly apparent that attention-seeking behavior, especially within an online context, can lead to the adoption of extremist or morally degrading tactics that aim to funnel the stream of digital consciousness. Immersed in a deadening surfeit of virtually indistinguishable and derivative content, social influencers may adopt escalating levels of turpitude to garner attraction—like the kind satirized to comical effect in Ruben Östlund's *The Square* (2017) where the marketers for a gallery simulate the sudden displosion of a toddler, all with the aim of inflaming social commentary and viral shares.[23]

20. Hayles, "Hyper and Deep Attention."
21. Franck, "Economy of Attention," 10.
22. See, for example, Milbank and Pabst, *Politics of Virtue*.
23. Social media is replete with examples, but one may mention the conspiracy-laden eructations of Alex Jones, former host and resident troll of the show *Infowars*, who (among other far-right accolades) has touted some rather execrable theories regarding

The other problem with this picture is that *attention assemblages*,[24] systems designed to reproduce attention, are predicated on a variety of social control that needs to be engaged critically: through algorithms and digital protocols, online content providers, like Facebook, seek "to propagate a certain social order of continued participation," according to media theorist Taina Bucher.[25] These systems are often automated and tend to reinforce digital flows, and entrench habits of usage that favor particular kinds of content over against others. Whether we know it or not, our senses, desires, and imaginations are being shaped and sculpted through this process. Moreover, the fact that our perception of reality itself is being altered through these mediums needs to be taken seriously. Franck raises pessimistic prospects regarding "mental capitalism," whereby as the attention economy grows, what is also "expanding is the aspect of reality produced specially to attract attention."[26] Invoking somewhat nightmarish and despairing scenarios comparable to Baudrillardian simulation,[27] Franck argues that the over-production of attention economies creates a world where the distinction between "semblance" and "substance" becomes less and less publicly available. Here, it seems that "immediate reality is not what we perceive as an assembly of touchable, solid things, but that which attention forms out of the stimuli activating our senses. Everything appearing beyond this elementary stratum of perceivability has invariably been selected and actively shaped."[28] The danger here then is that attention economies have the potential to shape us in particular ways, to draw us into their ambit, and delimit our horizons in overly restrictive and potentially harmful ways. In addition to this, in an age of expanding hyperattention, our capacities are

---

the "staging" of the Sandy Hook massacre in 2012, where over twenty children were murdered by a gunman. He is also infamous for using the same online platform for marketing his brand of dietary supplements and dubious pharmacopeia.

24. "Assemblage," while subject to diverse usage in "continental" theory, is a concept largely drawn from Gilles Deleuze and Félix Guattari and is often used to describe the interplay of emergence and structure, the way that open and evolving systems interact to form new logical structures that are not reducible to those systems; see Marcus and Saka, "Assemblage." The *attention assemblage* can therefore be seen as conceptually articulating the interaction between the developing systems of the attention economy with the deployments of algorithmic datasets and digital protocols. This is in line with the way that the language of "assemblage" is often used after Deleuze and Guattari, and Manuel Delanda, to describe the interfacing and combination of human and nonhuman potencies.

25. Bucher, "Technicity of Attention," 17.
26. Franck, "Economy of Attention," 15.
27. Baudrillard, *Simulations*.
28. Franck, "Economy of Attention," 16.

being stretched to the limit. Our attention is being "degraded" and "used-up," implying a depletion of mental and spiritual vitality. The plasticity of the brain and neural pathways within this setup are being molded in ways that impoverish "subjectivity" and our psychic resources. Tiziana Terranova describes the current bind: "on the one hand, in order to participate in the attention economy, [we] must enter a technological assemblage of attention; on the other hand, becoming part of this assemblage implies a dramatic cognitive loss that is translated into a subjectivity more adept at carrying out routine tasks but less capable of reasoning, reflecting and intimacy."[29] The cost of this is our mental health, as recent studies on the relation between social media and mental health have shown during the time of COVID.[30]

Within this context, therefore, I would propose that we need to address practices of attention if we are to instigate cultures of resilience and resistance in an age of hyperattention. Adopting the reflections of Bernard Stiegler,[31] an ecology of attention would firstly need to address the question *what* we attend to, that is, the content of our attention. If something or someone *has* our attention, this means that our energies are being directed towards it in a unique way. But the question is: What is it that comes into focus and grips our attention? Ideally, we need to ask this question repeatedly, instead of just submitting ourselves uncritically to the flows of algorithms, and so on. We need to bring to mind the content of our attention, what continually draws our focus, for it instigates a reflective stance regarding our habits of attention; thus, our being *attentive* to them. This leads to a second point: the asking of these kinds of questions suggests another meaning of "attention": the word *to attend* also carries with it the idea of *taking care* or looking after something, like when I say, "I'm attending to it." It can also carry therapeutic overtones, as when a doctor says, "I'm attending to the patient." One could thus say that our attention should become the object of our *care*, that I should take it up as something I am concerned about. The habits of attention that structure my everyday should be made thematic, since by being made conscious of these patterns I am becoming aware of where my attention is being directed. This is a task, I suggest, which we as individuals should take up. However, as Stiegler also suggests, one could

---

29. Terranova, "Attention, Economy and the Brain," 6. Terranova perceptively goes on to argue that "Theories of the attention economy . . . appear locked within the limits of scarcity, unable to account for the powers of invention of networked subjectivities, falling back into 'herd-like' models of connected sociality, and delegating to speculative mechanisms of financialization the capacity to create value out of partial attention and continuous distraction" (13).

30. Gao et al., "Mental Health Problems and Social Media Exposure."

31. Stiegler, "Relational Ecology and Digital *Pharmakon*."

mention, thirdly, that attention is both a psychic *and* social phenomenon: it is both personal and collective, which means attention implies patterns of being *attended to* by others, in forms interpersonal care and love. I am not simply an individual but have been individuated and formed relationally by others. Moreover, in this social and relational context I am being *called to attention*, as when others make me aware of things that I should be attentive of. The therapy of attention implies a communal task.

The question now remains as to what Christian spirituality might have to contribute to this theme of attention. Broadly speaking, faith traditions can provide adaptive, social mediations for cultivating practices of attention that may become habitual. Simone Kotva has spoken on how attention is an "adaptive power" on the part of human beings that can be "increased and directed through conscious effort."[32] Communities, including religious and spiritual ones, are social networks where certain kinds of attention can be "increased" and "directed," shaped and formed towards desirable spiritual ends. Adopting the terminology of Yves Citton, we may speak of attention as a *vectoral* movement rather than a *scalar* aggregation, that is, as a lived and experienced orientation over-against static, numerical data sets. For Citton, "If attention selects, filters or prioritizes, it does so starting from a principle of orientation. Attention cannot be reduced to a simple given, a static number: it is much less (countable) reality than (unpredictable) 'potential.'" On the other hand, he says, scalarization implies "the operation that translates arrows into numbers," which "denies the fundamental nature of attention, in the same way that putting a bird in a cage denies its nature as a flying creature." It is within this "ubiquitous scalarization," Citton goes on to say, "that we are condemned by the financial logic of capitalism."[33] Reclaiming attention as a vectoral movement implies an "attention 'tends towards' something: it calls for an exit from oneself, a broadening of horizons. It indicates a 'potential' in *excedence* over any predefined and preconfigured identity."[34] It is this idea of attention as *excedence*, as tending towards something, forming a transcendence of the isolated self and algorithmic routine, that I would like to emphasize in my characterization of Evagrian practice.

THE ACTUALITY OF EVAGRIUS

Evagrius was a desert mystic, speculative thinker, and theologian who was deeply influenced by Cappadocian and Alexandrian strands of Christianity.

32. Kotva, "Attention in the Anthropocene," 245.
33. Citton, *Ecology of Attention*, 77.
34 Citton, *Ecology of Attention*, 78.

He is well-known for his reflections on asceticism, especially regarding spiritual struggle within the life of prayer.[35] In particular, he is recognized for his taxonomy and strategies for combatting intrusive and demonically inspired thoughts (λογισμοί), namely, the so-called eight thoughts of gluttony, lust, avarice, anger, sadness, acedia, vainglory, and pride (cf. *On the Eight Thoughts*). In Evagrian anthropology, human beings remain poised between the realms of the angelic and the demonic, and can be pulled in either direction, depending on our spiritual vigilance. Such practice is placed within a larger tripart schema of ascesis (πρακτική), natural contemplation (θεωρία φυσική), and theology (θεολογική), here drawing upon the tradition of Origen and the Stoics (cf. *Praktikos* 1, *Gnostikos* 20; 49). For Evagrius, the ordering of this taxonomy is important: in order to contemplate the *logoi*, the meaning and spiritual principles that activate the world of things, one needs to engage in a practice of discipline that makes one attentive to the way that passions and thoughts seek to distract and lead the monk away from the "imageless" contemplation of the Trinity, as manifested in the light of the intellect.[36] It is only through a moral purification of selfhood that it can attain such contemplation. In his *Scholia on Ecclesiastes*, he speaks of the Preacher, or allegorically of Christ, as "the one who purifies souls by ethical considerations and leads them into natural contemplation" (*Scholia on Ecclesiastes* 1);[37] indeed, "the soul seeks wisdom not by reason, but by purity," so that "after purification, the pure person no longer regards perceptible things as merely busying his mind, but as having been placed in him for spiritual contemplation" (*Scholia on Ecclesiastes* 8; 15). For Evagrius, it is precisely "dispassion" or *apatheia*—that is, the resistance to the passions—that gives forth to love, and it is "love that is the door to natural contemplation" (*Praktikos* 8).[38]

In a gnomic declaration in *Gnostikos* 4, he writes that the "knowledge that reaches us from external [things] tries by means of the *logoi* to indirectly teach material [things]. However the [knowledge] which by God's

---

35. On Evagrius's concept of prayer, see Casiday, *Reconstructing the Theology of Evagrius Ponticus*, 133–66.

36. See Stewart, "Imageless Prayer and the Theological Vision of Evagrius Ponticus." However, to balance things somewhat, cf. Evagrius's comments in the *Paraneticus*: "Consider carefully what I am saying to you, and if some profitable reflection falls on you, let it fill you instead of the Psalms. Do not cast away a gift from God just to uphold your tradition! Prayer without meditation on God and vision of the mind mingled with it is a fatigue to the flesh. Do not rejoice in the quantity of the Psalms you repeat even as a veil is placed on your heart. A single word in proximity to God is better than a thousand at a distance" (Evagrius, "Paraneticus," 83).

37. "Notes on Ecclesiastes," in Casiday, *Evagrius Ponticus*.

38. Evagrius, "Monk: A Treatise on the Practical Life," in *Evagrius of Pontus: The Greek Ascetic Corpus*.

grace is innate [within us] directly presents matters to the mind; and in beholding them, the *nous* welcomes their *logoi*. And opposing the first is <error; against the second is> anger and indignation <and what flows from them>."[39] The suggestion of this passage is that Evagrius imagines two ways that we engage with knowledge: one can reflect upon reality in an "external" way, in a kind of subject-object fashion, which then is liable to the possibility of "error," that is misapprehension, logical defeat, ignorance, and so on. However, the other kind of knowing which is given inwardly by God is opposed by anger—not by "error" or a "mistake" but by an emotional or affective register. In other words, Evagrius thinks that knowledge can be opposed through theoretical failure *and* through an affective engagement that hinders the perception of truth. This is connected again to Evagrian anthropology in which the human person is constituted by three aspects which are susceptible both to the acquisition of virtue and to demonic onslaught. He classifies these as the rational part (το λογιστικών), the concupiscible part (το επιθυμητικών), and the irascible part (το θυμικόν), which become unnatural thorough the generation of evil intentions, passions, and actions (*Kephalaia Gnostika* 3.59).[40] The primordial begetting of evil comes through a distortion of created nature, whose original source is imagined as an archetypal "carelessness" or "privation" whereby some of the created intellects moved away from their original unity, setting in play the motions of spiritual ignorance (*Kephalaia Gnostika* 1.49; 3.28). This vision is supplemented by *On Thoughts* 8 where he makes a distinction between angelic, demonic, and human kinds of thought: whereas angelic thought seeks the "spiritual principles" of things, asking for their reasons and connections, and human thought receives the simple form of things without "any passion of greed," demonic thought seeks "acquisition," to possess and subordinate reality to one's own interests.[41] This again confirms that there are certain affective ways of engaging with the world that hinder a truthful correspondence to reality. To live humanly and naturally, for Evagrius, is to engage

---

39. The critical edition of this text is found in Evagrius, *Gnostique ou a celui qui est devenu digne de la science*. The translation is taken from Luke Dysinger, http://www.ldysinger.com/Evagrius/02_Gno-Keph/00a_start.htm. The words in the brackets have been supplied by Dysinger to explicate the implied meaning of the Greek, while the words between the carats are contained in the critical edition of Antoine and Claire Guillaumont to indicate lacunae in the Greek text. These have been reconstructed through a combination of educated guesswork, since the Greek of the first lacuna forms a *homoioleuton* and coheres with Evagrian terminology used elsewhere, while the second lacuna is restored through a comparison with Syriac and Armenian manuscripts.

40. See *Evagrius's Kephalaia Gnostika: A New Translation of the Unreformed Text from the Syriac*.

41. Evagrius, "On Thoughts," in *Greek Ascetic Corpus*.

with the God, the world, and the neighbor in a fashion that is not swayed by the passion for accumulation, by reducing these engagements to the coordinates of the acquisitive self. For Evagrius, to live in such a fashion is to be guided by the demonic, rather than angelic or human knowledge; and to be guided by the demonic, that is, when the tripartite self is governed by such "thoughts," it hinders the human person from truthfully engaging reality. This is why Rowan Williams has said that Evagrian practice is aimed at the transformation of sense.[42] It is through a combat with the intrusive thoughts and the practice of *apatheia*, instilled through habits of prayer, almsgiving, hospitality, and love, that the self becomes distanced from acquisitive and egotistic behavior, so that thereby the *logoi* of the things and the light of the Trinity may become manifest to the intellect. Evagrian mysticism, rather than closing us off from the world around us, makes an argument for approaching reality and the natural world in a way that exceeds self-serving patterns of accumulation and destructive passion. The aim of the monastic is to harmoniously interrelate the tripartite aspects of the human person towards spiritual contemplation and virtue. As Evagrius says in a characteristic summary: "The rational soul acts according to nature when its concupiscible part longs for virtue, and the irascible part struggles on its behalf, and the rational part perceives the contemplation of beings" (*Praktikos* 86). All of this finds consummation in the theological knowledge of the Holy Trinity: the practice of exterior and internal poverty awakens us to a silence and stillness that lies at the heart of being (ἡσυχία); and it is this awareness that opens us to the knowledge of Trinity and joins our intellect to the gift of "pure prayer" in which the mind is united (*Chapters on Prayer* 3) by grace to "essential knowledge," so that the intellect itself becomes "the seer of the Holy Trinity" (*Kephalaia Gnostika* 3.12; 30).[43] For Evagrius, "essential knowledge" is identical with God alone, because every "rational nature" has something to which it is contrasted and defined over-against—a kind of relative "nonexistence" or negation. Yet nothing can be opposed to God because God is not a created intellect who may experience the immanent conditions of being "opposed" or "over-against" (*Kephalaia Gnostika* 1.89). Likewise, the contemplation of the Holy Trinity cannot be imaged by created intellects. The imageless prayer of the perfect intellect, when sufficiently trained in its practice and kenotic emptying, becomes filled with the divine light: "If someone should want to behold the state of his mind, let him deprive himself of all mental representations, and then he

---

42. Williams, "Embodied Logos: Reason, Knowledge, and Relation," in *Looking East in Winter*, 59–92.

43. See Konstantinovsky, *Evagrius Ponticus*, 77–107.

shall behold himself resembling sapphire or the colour of heaven . . . . The state of the mind is an intelligible height resembling the colour of heaven, to which the light of the Holy Trinity comes in the time of prayer" (*Skemmata* 2; 4).[44] Moreover such action, at the height of contemplation, gives sway to a kind of active passivity in which pure prayer arises without effort, as a "grace from above." Here we discover that our poverty of being, our existence out of nothingness, for "Love possesses nothing of its own apart from God, for God is love itself" (*To Eulogios* 21; 30).[45]

But to achieve *apatheia*, the monastic will have to persevere through spiritual conflict and the continual barrage of passions that seek to agitate the various registers of the tripartite self. These passions lead to mental representations that ultimately distort the monk's perceptions of the world.[46] The most oppressive of these demonically instigated representations is that of *acedia*. In general, the Evagrian analysis of acedia can be summarized as the temptation to abandon the life of prayer,[47] which manifests itself as spiritual despondency and desperation.[48] Evagrius was probably the first to connect the semantic content of ἀκηδείη, with all its resonance of heedlessness and carelessness,[49] to the idea of the so-called "noonday demon," a figure of ancient folklore who brought on "the terrors of noontime" such as sunstroke and other illnesses associated with the conditions of the desert.[50] The noonday demon had previously entered into Christian discourse through Ps 90:6 in the Septuagint (LXX), which is its only occurrence in the Greek Old Testament.[51] Evagrius's description of *acedia*, though present throughout his writings, is contained in a famous passage in *Praktikos* 12 where he describes how the demon of acedia distorts or accentuates the spatio-temporal experience of the monk, creating a sense of unbearable, elongated time which then provokes thoughts of abandoning the monastic life. The demon makes the monk feel that nothing productive is happening in the *stadium* and that the interpersonal conditions of the monastery have

---

44. Evagrius, "Reflections," in *Greek Ascetic Corpus*. On Evagrius's "light-mysticism," see Casiday, *Reconstructing the Theology of Evagrius Ponticus*, 180–84.

45. Evagrius, "To Eulogios," in *Greek Ascetic Corpus*.

46. Gibbons, "Passions, Pleasures, and Perceptions."

47. Aijian, "Fleeing the Stadium."

48. Bunge, *Despondency*; Nault, *Noonday Devil*, 1–36.

49. See the entry for ἀκηδείη in Diggle et al., *Cambridge Greek Lexicon*. Its cognates and semantic domain are also connected to the ties that bind people together (κῆδος) and the failure to grant burial rites (ἀκηδέω)—a sacrilegious act in the ancient world. Also cf. Lampe, *Patristic Greek Lexicon*, 61–62.

50. Worrell, "Demon of Noonday and Some Related Ideas."

51. Riley, "Midday Demon"; Scott-Macnab, "Many Faces of the Noonday Demon."

broken down: that love has departed the desert and that there is somewhere else one will be able to achieve fantasies of success. It is this drive to leave behind the temporal rhythms and monastic space of prayer that is the strategic goal of the noonday demon.

Later, in medieval times and the early modern period, the figure of the noonday demon and acedia was collapsed into the sin of sloth and melancholy. Under the inspiration of Scotus and Ockham, the "natural" orientation of human intention towards the transcendentally good became discounted in some quarters of scholasticism; it was seen to undermine the free arbitration of the subject, which cannot be free if the will is already predetermined—even by the good. This ultimately created dualisms between mysticism and moral practice, between what was reserved for the spiritually elite and what is incumbent on everyone; it created a moralism that was centered on obedience to divine commands and laws, which themselves are metaphysically arbitrary, and not grounded in a prior ordering in nature towards goodness.[52] The earlier Evagrian and Thomistic unity of theological metaphysics and spiritual practice, within the union of *habitus*, was not maintained within this schema. Aquinas had taught that acedia concerned a sadness regarding spiritual goods and the hatred of physical labour, both which he considered to be rejection of the joy of the gospel.[53] After Ockham, sadness becomes melancholia and the disgust with labour becomes equated with sloth or distraction. But the original unity of the Evagrian system has been lost here, along with its fundamentally spiritual and metaphysical vision, which led to a moralizing and de-spiritualizing of the experience of acedia.

But as I said earlier, the contemporary relevance of Evagrius and the spirituality of the desert appears to have once more regained something of its vigor today. The extended periods of lockdown during the heights of the coronavirus pandemic forced many to develop rituals to structure their time. Many of these practices are not productive in the traditional sense and contributed towards what has been called a "therapeutics of attention."[54] These disciplines, such as prayer and seemingly non-productive labour, as was the case analogously for the desert monastics, can form a resistance to the capitalist disciplines of acquisition, productivity, and distraction, as well as those regimes of attention that are bound to them. These rituals may have awakened some of those who engaged in them to the possibility that "distraction partakes of ancient afflictions and that our disciplines of attention are older than machines," thus giving concrete examples of "how to live in another kind of

---

52. Nault, *Noonday Devil*, 96–106.
53. Nault, *Noonday Devil*, 57–95.
54. Dumitrescu and Smith, "Demon of Distraction," 79.

time altogether, learning to tend to the living and the dead."[55] It has pertinent connections to Christian spirituality in the Capitalocene, whereby the natural world has become entwined with the onslaught of capitalist realism and colonial extraction. Within this context, a spirituality inspired by the vision of Evagrius might say something like this: that our acquisitive desire distorts our relation to the contemplation of beings so that our very interaction with nature hereby becomes perverted and "unnatural." For him, acedia creates within us this desire to always be elsewhere so to achieve a more productive life; one desires acceleration and speed to reach the "goal" more quickly. It is a despairing as regards the spiritual life, of waiting on God, and leads the monk (and us) to seek a psychic placebo whereby the tension may be resolved.[56] For the one plagued by acedia is not satisfied with their cell, their place, and their work, and so desires to flee the *stadia*, somewhere else where they imagine they will achieve goals whose consequences are more measurable and calculable (*On the Eight Thoughts* 6.5, 12–13).

In an age of hyperattention, where we are constantly tempted by escapism and the desire to be somewhere else where things are "happening," many are dominated by the fear that by remaining where we are at that, somehow, we are missing out; to this, the witness of Evagrius stands as a mirror for reflecting these fears back on us, forcing us to be attentive to them, to be aware of them, and not to treat them as "natural" reflexes. Our attention spans and practices of attention are spiritually cultivated: they do not exist as a kind of sheer actuality. They are formed and reformed. Our common desire to escape the moment, to leave the place where we find ourselves, needs to be engaged reflectively—and critically if need be. The desert monastics indicate to us that sometimes it is precisely this harsh and caustic landscape, whose silence and brutality refuses to accommodate to our needs, that teaches us the lessons we may need to learn. The estranging and alien beauty of desert evokes wonder but also a sense of our vulnerability and poverty, our relatedness and dependency. In contrast to the fantasies of acedia, Evagrius evokes the virtues of perseverance; of remaining; of continuing in prayer, the common life, and neighborly love. Now of course most of us are not monks nor do we live in literal deserts; such a life requires structures and dedication that most people do not have. However, simple changes of orientation and habit can go a long way in shifting perspectives and behavior. The daily office of prayer or the liturgy of hours, showing care

---

55. Dumitrescu and Smith, "Demon of Distraction," 81. In this regard, Giorgio Agamben's analysis of monasticism in which this form-of-life enters a zone of indistinction with law, beyond the application of extraneous legality, may suggest a way of being in which life may be lived beyond the strictures of capitalist use-value and production; see Agamben, *Highest Poverty*.

56. Vogel, "Speed of Sloth."

regarding our attentive habits, noticing patterns of boredom and distraction, as well as engaging in "non-productive" activity,[57] may be simple practices for resisting acquiescence to machinic flows and nihilistic algorithms.

Drawing focus on my own context of South Africa, we of course remain just as immersed as the rest of the world within the global networks of capitalism. But we have the added legacy of racialized apartheid and white supremacy, whose spatial and economic legacies—in addition to corruption and state capture—continue to produce inhumane levels of inequality, particularly among the black majority. White citizens, by and large, experience lifestyles and living conditions comparable to those of their European and American counterparts. And yet, despite general conditions of prosperity and comfort, the phenomenon of "white flight" and expatriation is significant enough to be a topic of social analysis and commentary. While matters are certainly not simplistic, the connection of these trends to discourses and practices of "white diaspora" and postcolonial "whiteness," both offline and online, have been noted in some of the most influential scholarship on the topic.[58] With this in view, the discourse of acedia adds a spiritual layer to this discussion, especially as regards the feelings of hopelessness and the slowness of tangible social redress that are felt within the country, particularly among the black majority. However, it also may connect to those who desire to flee, for whatever reason, to "safe" and "white" suburbs, or those majority "white" countries of European descent. Bringing this dimension into the discussion may help us to see that "escaping" will not erase the history and legacies that we carry with us, and if we indeed are to practice κῆδος, the art of care for the living and the dead, and the histories in which we are entangled, then this will imply acknowledgment and coming to grips with the nature of those bonds: what do I owe to the other? For among many white South Africans, the machines of acedia and forums of "white talk" continue to promote ahistorical and selective recounting of the ties that bind us within this shared history. Moral panic and pessimism abound within certain enclaves, and these dispersed affects within their analogue and digital versions continue to buttress a narrative of "white" victimization and marginalization. These affects subsidize discontent with the state of the country and legitimize the rationalization for leaving.[59] But for someone like Evagrius, if we are allowed to translate his insights into our own, we need to engage these desires to flee: What is driving us towards such ends? Are we being governed by legitimate

---

57. Odell, *How to Do Nothing*.

58. Cf. Steyn, "'White Talk.'"

59. By saying this, I am not saying that there exist *no* legitimate grounds for such immigration but just pointing out one discursive regime characteristic of "white talk."

fears and needs or are there other, less justifiable, reasons for engaging these fantasies of flight? The spirituality of the desert says that fleeing does not address those fundamental issues with which the monk is concerned, namely God, the self, and the neighbor. The desert, and everything it signifies, is one place where we encounter these realities without distraction and escapism.

CODA

In conclusion, the Evagrian practice of attention transcends the division between the theoretical and the practical. The question of *what* the object of attention is and the question of *how* one cultivates attention appropriate to its object are united in this system. Mysticism and morality are held together. The bringing together of a speculative metaphysics with an embodied way of life has a lot of richness worth exploring. The connection between knowledge and affect is one that also has been engaged deeply in recent times. In this regard, I would like to suggest that the ascetic writings of Evagrius provide techniques of internal vigilance and stillness for addressing the barrage of thoughts and mental representations that distract and deplete spiritual vitality. Evagrian practice, through a stripping away of self-satisfaction, passions, and the constant play of imagery, aims to bring us to a deeper relation with the divine mystery and to live out of a position of detachment. This is particularly relevant in a strongly image-based, digitally mediated culture where the confusion of fantasy and reality is particularly fraught. It also speaks to an attention economy that often aims to reduce our sensorium and desires to one that is beneficial for a neoliberal and digital capitalism, or toxic online cultures that foment affective relations that disconnect us from the world and from one another. For Evagrius, we can only know truly if we are transformed in our body, soul, and intellect through love. Moreover, his contributions help us to understand our experiences today of despair, melancholy, and acedia that are aggravated through the interpellation of attention economies. A spiritual vision inspired by the desert monks suggests that to achieve some kind of affective repair such requires the practice of the spiritual disciplines, contemplation, and imageless prayer, within a community of mutual attention, and moreover that such attending and being attended to might provide one avenue of resistance. And lastly, as Christian doctrine amply teaches, such practice instills a greater receptivity to, and imitation of, that omnipresent love and care that is greater than the world can give; for in orienting our attention to the immaterial and intellectual light of the Holy Trinity, we are directed to that love which surpasses knowledge (Eph 3:19), to the One on whom we cast our cares: the One who *attends* to us (1 Pet 5:7).

BIBLIOGRAPHY

Agamben, Giorgio. *The Highest Poverty: Monastic Rules and Form-of-Life*. Translated by Adam Kotsko. Stanford: Stanford University Press, 2013.

Aijian, Janelle. "Fleeing the Stadium: Recovering the Conceptual Unity of Evagrius' Acedia." *Heythrop Journal* 62 (2021) 7–20.

Ankersmit, Franklin Rudolf. *History and Tropology: The Rise and Fall of Metaphor*. Berkley: University of California Press, 1994.

Baudrillard, Jean. *Simulations*. Translated by Phil Beitchman et al. Cambridge, MA: MIT Press, 1983.

Beller, Jonathan. *The Cinematic Mode of Production: Attention Economy and the Society of the Spectacle*. Lebanon, NH: Dartmouth College Press, 2006.

Bucher, Tania. "A Technicity of Attention: How Software 'Makes Sense.'" *Culture Machine* 13 (2012) 1–23.

Bunge, Gabriel. *Despondency: The Spiritual Teaching of Evagrius Ponticus on Acedia*. Translated by Anthony Gythiel. New York: St. Vladimir's Seminary Press, 2011.

Casiday, Augustine M. *Evagrius Ponticus*. London: Routledge, 2006.

———. *Reconstructing the Theology of Evagrius Ponticus: Beyond Heresy*. Cambridge: Cambridge University Press, 2013.

Citton, Yves. *The Ecology of Attention*. Translated by Barnaby Norman. Cambridge: Polity, 2017.

Crary, Jonathan. *Suspensions of Perception: Attention, Spectacle, and Modern Culture*. Cambridge, MA: MIT Press, 1999.

Dé, Rahul, et al. "Impact of Digital Surge during Covid-19 Pandemic: A Viewpoint on Research and Practice." *International Journal of Information Management* 55 (2020) 1–5.

Diggle, James, et al., eds. *The Cambridge Greek Lexicon. Volume 1*. Cambridge. Cambridge University Press, 2020.

Duffett, Rodney G., and Myles Wakeham. "Social Media Marketing Communications Effect on Attitudes among Millennials in South Africa." *African Journal of Information Systems* 8.3 (2016) 20–44.

Dumitrescu, Irina, and Caleb Smith. "The Demon of Distraction." *Critical Inquiry* 47 (2021) 77–81.

Evagrius Ponticus. *Evagrius of Pontus: The Greek Ascetic Corpus*. Translated by Robert E. Sinkewicz. Oxford: Oxford University Press, 2003.

———. *Evagrius's Kephalaia Gnostika: A New Translation of the Unreformed Text from the Syriac*. Translated by Ilaria L. Ramelli. Atlanta: Society of Biblical Literature, 2015.

———. *Le Gnostique ou a celui qui est devenu digne de la science*. Edited by Antoine Guillaumont and Clare Guillaumont. Paris: Éditions du Cerf, 1989.

———. "Paraneticus." In *The Cambridge Edition of Early Christian Writings, Volume 2: Practice*, edited by Ellen Muehlberger, 80–85. Cambridge: Cambridge University Press, 2017.

Franck, Georg. "The Economy of Attention." *Journal of Sociology* 55 (2019) 8–19.

Gao, J., et al. "Mental Health Problems and Social Media Exposure during COVID-19 Outbreak." *PLOS ONE* 15 (2020) e0231924. https://doi.org/10.1371/journal.pone.0231924.

Gibbons, Kathleen. "Passions, Pleasures, and Perceptions: Rethinking Evagrius Ponticus on Mental Representation." *Zeitschrift für Antikes Christentum/Journal of Ancient Christianity* 19 (2015) 297–330.

Goldhaber, Michael H. "The Attention Economy and the Net." *First Monday* 2 (April 1997). https://journals.uic.edu/ojs/index.php/fm/article/download/519/440.

Hayles, N. Katherine. "Hyper and Deep Attention: The Generational Divide in Cognitive Modes." *Profession* (2007) 187–99.

Konstantinovsky, Julia. *Evagrius Ponticus: The Making of a Gnostic*. London: Routledge, 2009.

Kotva, Simone. "Attention in the Anthropocene: On the Spiritual Exercises of Any Future Science." In *Political Geology: Active Stratigraphies and the Making of Life*, edited by A. Bobbette and A. Donovan, 239–61. Cham: Palgrave Macmillan, 2019.

Lampe, Geoffrey Hugo. *A Patristic Greek Lexicon*. Oxford: Oxford University Press, 1961.

Lovink, Geert. *Sad by Design: On Platform Nihilism*. London: Pluto, 2019.

Marcus, George E., and Erkan Saka. "Assemblage." *Theory, Culture & Society* 23 (2006) 101–9.

Milbank, John, and Adrian Pabst. *The Politics of Virtue: Post-Liberalism and the Human Future*. London: Rowman & Littlefield, 2016.

Nault, Jean-Charles. *The Noonday Devil: Acedia, the Unnamed Evil of Our Times*. Translated by Michael J. Miller. San Francisco: Ignatius, 2015.

Odell, Jenny. *How to Do Nothing: Resisting the Attention Economy*. Brooklyn: Melville House, 2019.

Riley, G. J. "Midday Demon." In *Dictionary of Deities and Demons in the Bible*, edited by Karel van der Toorn et al., 572–73. 2nd ed. Leiden: Brill, 1999.

Scott-Macnab, David. "The Many Faces of the Noonday Demon." *Journal of Early Christian History* 8 (2018) 22–42.

Seymour, Richard. *The Twittering Machine*. London: Indigo, 2019.

Stewart, Columba. "Imageless Prayer and the Theological Vision of Evagrius Ponticus." *Journal of Early Christian Studies* 9 (2001) 173–204.

Steyn, Melissa. "'White Talk': White South Africans and the Management of Diasporic Whiteness." In *Postcolonial Whiteness: A Critical Reader on Race and Empire*, edited by Alfred J. López, 119–35. New York: SUNY Press, 2005.

Stiegler, Bernard. "Relational Ecology and Digital *Pharmakon*." *Culture Machine* 13 (2012) 1–19.

Terranova, Tiziana. "Attention, Economy and the Brain." *Culture Machine* 13 (2012) 1–19.

Vogel, Jeffrey A. "The Speed of Sloth: Reconsidering the Sin of *Acedia*." *Pro Ecclesia* 18 (2009) 50–68.

Walsh, Zack. "A Meta-Critique of Mindfulness Critiques: From McMindfulness to Critical Mindfulness." In *Handbook of Mindfulness*, edited by R. E. Purser et al., 153–66. Switzerland: Springer, 2016.

Williams, Rowan. *Looking East in Winter: Contemporary Thought and the Eastern Christian Tradition*. London: Bloomsbury, 2021.

Worrell, William. "The Demon of Noonday and Some Related Ideas." *Journal of the American Oriental Society* 38 (1918) 160–66.

Chapter 4

Beyond the Totality of Religion
Memories of Violence, Finitude, and the Organic Body

Calvin D. Ullrich

> and when he had given thanks, he broke it and said,
> "This is my body that is for you. Do this in remembrance of me."
> (1 Cor 11:24)
>
> *et gratias agens fregit et dixit hoc est corpus meum pro vobis hoc facite in meam commemorationem*

INTRODUCTION

> "This is my body—do this in remembrance of me."

At the heart of the Christian faith are these twin concerns: the visible and material presence of God (this is my body) and the ritual of memory which keeps this reality alive (do this in remembrance of me). Riffing Immanuel Kant, memory without this body is empty, and this body without the tradition of memory is blind. In what follows, it will be argued (in a sort of roundabout way) not that the acts of memory of this body have become obscured (such would be far too presumptuous a claim), but rather more modestly that an aspect of what is to be remembered has been forgotten, i.e., the organic body—more specifically, the organic body as an unstable substrate for subjectivity. Before turning to the forgetfulness of the body, this organic aspect of our subjectivity, and its important implications for the Christian life of faith, the question of memory and violence will be raised, specifically with reference to the Judeo-Christian memory into which the body has been inscribed. Since it will be impossible to raise the question of the remembrance of the body in any comprehensive manner, the question of the "memory of violence" is highlighted with respect to a thesis concerned with the political-religious structure of Judeo-Christian memory.

In short, this political structure reveals itself as one of othering and exclusivity, often betraying its universalistic claims, resulting in political, colonial, and ethno-nationalist violence. This controversial, hotly debated thesis is that of the German historian Jan Assmann—namely, that the Archimedean point of Judeo-Christian memory involves a "theologization of the political" creating the distinction between friends and enemies. What follows will be a renewed Christian philosophical and theological response. This response argues in the final analysis for a shift in the conversation to the ambivalences of the organic body of Christ and thus of our own. This shift is neither a valorization of suffering which attempts to turn "weakness" or "instability" into a positive condition of subjectivity. Rather what is attempted will be a description of an originary organic suspension in the body itself, or what Aristotle called *sterēsis*, that precedes all distinctions of strength and weakness, or perhaps belief and unbelief. To arrive at this outcome, we pass through what will be called the "memories of finitude" to the "memories of the organic body" to arrive at a common body and thus a common humanity shared by all; a body which is always-already believing just as it is maintained in unbelief and therefore addresses itself beyond the totality of religion and its "memory of violence."

JAN ASSMANN AND MEMORIES OF VIOLENCE

The Judeo-Christian tradition, with its commemorations, rituals, feasts, and festivals, places a deliberate emphasis on the nature of temporality; certainly, with visions of the future (or what we call eschatology) but also with deep-resourced connections to the past. Indeed, with its roots in Judaism, Christianity is rightly called a "memory religion."[1] In the twentieth and twenty-first centuries, memory studies have flourished, perhaps for several reasons, but certainly among them is what Aleida Assmann has called the

---

1. Signer, *Memory and History in Christianity and Judaism*, ix. I am drawing several of these opening points from Robert Vosloo's professorial inaugural lecture at Stellenbosch University, delivered in 2015, with the title "Time in Our Time: On Theology and Future-Orientated Memory."

"modern time regime"—that contemporary experience of temporality which feels ever more scattered and incoherent, emphasizing whatever creative destruction might be necessary to accelerate growth.[2] In this vision there is no more future just a presentism of "the now" and where the word *history* becomes synonymous with an archive for abstracted observation and study. In appealing to memory in this contemporary moment, and in particular, Judeo-Christian memory, therefore, one must become aware of what Paul Ricoeur called "the excesses" of memory.[3]

It is just this awareness of excess which makes it necessary to revisit memories central to the Christian faith. The *hoc est enim corpus meum* is just such a memory, one which as Jean-Luc Nancy has powerfully reminded us, is "*the* repetition par excellence" of an "unconditional certainty of a *THIS IS*," which can "generate the whole *corpus* of a General Encyclopedia of Western Sciences, Arts, and Ideas."[4] Connected to Nancy's analysis of the body and Western reason was of course his project of the deconstruction of Christianity, and in particular a chapter in his *Dis-enclosure* entitled "A Deconstruction of Monotheism."[5] For Nancy, God's expressing of Godself as a paradoxical, ungraspable, distant force, is the present-ing of an absence: that is, the bringing to presence of an absence. Monotheism is thus always in the process of self-deconstruction and describes not just a historical phenomenon but the radical form of modernity's own self-deconstruction. One would have to reserve Nancy's invaluable reflections for a fuller discussion elsewhere, but to stay with this theme of memory and monotheism, we can now invoke the controversial thesis put forward by the renowned German historian and Egyptologist Jan Assmann.

Far be it possible to comment here on the polemics that have arisen among historians, religious, Judaic, cultural studies scholars, theologians, psychoanalysts, and Egyptologists themselves, in response to Assmann's provocations. But at the center of these debates was the critically acclaimed *Moses the Egyptian: The Memory of Egypt in Western Monotheism* (1997), which was followed by several follow-up texts responding to critics.[6] In *Moses the Egyptian*, which develops alongside but also beyond Freud,[7] the so-called "mnemohistory" of Europe's memory of Egypt—that is, not

---

2. See Assmann, "Transformations of the Modern Time Regime."
3. Ricoeur, *Memory, History, Forgetting*, xv. See also Vosloo, "Time in Our Time," 7.
4. Nancy, *Corpus*, 5.
5. Nancy, *Dis-Enclosure*, 29.
6. Assmann, *Moses the Egyptian*; *The Price of Monotheism*,
7. Freud, *Moses and Monotheism*.

necessarily history "as it happened," but how it is remembered[8]—Assmann argued that the psycho-historical defining event of the West is the development of biblical monotheism. Crucial to this development is what he called the "Mosaic distinction," a position which he revised several times,[9] where, in the literary figure of Moses a distinction is made for the first time between true and false religion—that is, between religion understood in the terms of monotheism and polytheism. Through the first commandments of the Decalogue (Exod 20:3–4), monotheism comes to be understood as an intervention that does not dismiss other gods but puts their truth into question. Biblical monotheism, thus, created the requirement for a reflexivity in religious activity (what Assmann later called secondary "religion") that could now no longer be taken for granted. Perhaps more importantly, biblical monotheism also placed a ban on any depictions of the divine, a program of iconoclasm which effectively introduced transcendence and distance into the religious imagination—there was now no longer any bridges between God and human.

Through a combination of these claims of a true God among others and the prohibition of representations *within* the endospheric community of Israel, a particularistic monotheism was produced that required fidelity in terms of the covenant with God as liberator alone and therefore over and above any other fealty, whether temporal or otherwise. While the covenantal theology which comes into emergence emphasized the *voluntary* nature of Israel's participation as well as God's patience and mercy, Assmann still locates within these exclusivist gestures the origins of intolerance, the distinction between friends and foes, and thus too the source of the problem of violence.[10]

Leaving aside questions of anti-Semitism or anti-Christianity (both of which Assmann has been accused), a final development is worth noting,

8. Assmann, *Moses the Egyptian*, 9.

9. *Herrschafft und Heil*; *Exodus: Die Revolution der Alten Welt*. The distinction is later reformulated in terms of fidelity (*Treue*) and infidelity (*Untreue*), which no longer differentiates Israel vis-à-vis other peoples, but now differentiates those within the community who express loyalty/fidelity to the one God and those who do not. See Assmann, "Mose und der Monotheismus der Treue."

10. Assmann, *Invention of Religion*, 86. It is important to note that Assmann does not claim that monotheism is the source of all violence and hatred, as if this didn't exist in the polytheistic contexts; it is rather that the problem of violence and monotheism gets attached to (secondary) religion for the first time as such. It is also, accordingly, for Assmann not a matter of "going back" to a supposedly more peaceful form of polytheism, but "only a way ahead that leads in the direction of a new understanding of monotheism, one that does not apologetically deny its dark sides, but is instead critically reflective." See Assmann, "Ist der neue Mensch ein Eiferer?" For the further distinction between primary and secondary religion see, Assmann, "Monotheismus," 123–24.

however controversial, since it guides an interpretation of Judeo-Christianity as the systematization of a "total religion." As Assmann demonstrates, the later Deutero-Isaian corpus now moves toward an *ontologization* of the distinction between true and false religion, implying that it is not just a matter of friends (those who follow the one True God) and apostates within the community (those who follow pagan gods), but also simultaneously that pagan gods are now in fact non-existent, thus extending the claim of biblical monotheism to a universality.[11] Crucially, for Assmann, the Christian faith combines these two aspects of monotheism, insofar as it makes a particular claim through divine revelation in the person of Jesus Christ precisely as the site where the universality of truth is to be located. Monotheism, in its Christian form, therefore, not only concerns the Jewish people, but it now concerns everyone and everyone totally.[12] On this interpretation, then, Christianity in particular takes on the form of a total religion, especially to the extent that the political and religious are now seen as irreducible. Whereas Egyptian polytheism for example, was able to regulate and legitimize the distinct spheres of law and religion through an immanentism of universal harmony (*Maat*), biblical religion "theologizes" the political, where any visible basis for political order is shifted into the invisible relationship with the divine.[13] Moreover, with the revelation of God in Jesus Christ, Christianity can claim both the universal in the particular, and thus creates the conditions not only for exclusivity (those who remain faithful to God), but also for intolerance and conflict against those who profess competing claims, since these will always in principle be false.[14]

11. Assmann, "Monotheismus der Treue," 252–55.

12. "Die dritte Quelle wenn nicht der Gewalt, so doch der Intoleranz, besteht im christlichen Begriff der Offenbarung mit seiner paradoxalen Verknüpfung von Exklusivität und Universalität. Es gibt viele Religionen, aber mehr als eine absolute, universal Wahrheit kann es nicht geben." See Assmann, "Mose und der Monotheismus der Treue," 33.

13. For a critical reading of Assmann's "theologization of the political" in discussion with Carl Schmitt, see Steinmetz-Jenkins, "Jan Assmann and the Theologization of the Political."

14. It is at this juncture—where the question of the totalization of religion is connected with the problem of violence—that Assmann makes use of, as well as also inverts, the thesis of the famous German jurist, Carl Schmitt. See Assmann, *From Akhenaten to Moses*, esp. chapter 7. With the transferal of political and religious legitimacy to a transcendent, unrepresentable source, the conditions are created for a rising intensity out of which the truth of the situation is revealed. Assmann's preference is not for Schmitt's notion of *Notfall* but *Ernstfall* or earnestness. When the situation of seriousness and earnestness is reached—or in Schmittian terms, the "emergency"—then one is existentially drawn to one's friends, delineating therefore one's enemies. For Assmann, the semantics of God's wrath in response to failures of fidelity to the covenant, as well as

MEMORIES OF FINITUDE

Much ink has been spilled critically evaluating the merits of Assmann's thesis on both theological and philosophical grounds. But for the sake of time, I will pass over this reception. The concern in the following two sections of the chapter is to propose and describe, as a form of my own response to Assmann's provocations of a totalizing religion and its "memory of violence," a philosophically common base that allows the Christian remembering (and not forgetting!)—as brought to bear in the *hoc est corpus meum*[15]—of the first meaning of one's incarnate being: what will be called the bodily-believing of the organic body. In short, a contemporary Christian response to these totalizing tendencies can be anchored in a more primordial bodily-believing that establishes first the primacy of a common humanity before any kerygmatic response (which must of course presuppose it).

In a certain sense, the constructive foil for this argument is to be found in recent theological attempts which aim at combining contemporary continental philosophy with dogmatic theological loci to understand them anew.[16] One such example in the context of our discussion is a proposal developed recently by Rasmus Nagel.[17] Nagel, in direct discussion with Assmann's corpus, advances the Lutheran formula *simul iustus et peccator* (i.e., the simultaneity of justice and sinfulness) alongside the concept of "fidelity," to support the theological-anthropological claim that the persistence of sin requires again and again the unconditional gift of divine grace—thus undermining from the beginning any distinction between friends and enemies of God. In other words, drawing this position together with philosophers like Alain Badiou, Jacques Rancière, and Slavoj Žižek, and therefore unlike Assmann—who accuses Christianity of dividing up peoples into friends and enemies—Christianity for Nagel, in fact, creates a solidarity of unbelief, since Christian identity is always permanently split.

---

the apocalyptic literature which creates the distinction between those who are damned and saved, both serve as suitable examples for originally religious *Ernstfälle* (*From Akhenaten to Moses*, 122). Thus, if for Schmitt, "all significant modern concepts of the state are secularized theological concepts," then for Assmann it is the "theologization of the political" which has come to define modern theories of the state.

15. That is, in terms of the "backlash" of theology on phenomenology as described by Emmanuel Falque. See his *Crossing the Rubicon*.

16. Karl Barth's insight here is apt: "We must try to find some way of making the accustomed unaccustomed again, the well-known unknown and the old new." See Barth, *Church Dogmatics*, 4.1, 224.

17. See Nagel, *Universale Singularität*, especially chapter 2. See also Nagel, "Total Fidelity?"

Nagel's hamartiological realism aims at universalizing humanity's enmity toward God to cut across distinctions between friends and enemies. The strength of this position is the treatment of the category of sin beyond outdated moralizing gestures, and instead to see its symbolic and ontological importance for a theological anthropology within the context of a deeply secularized world. In such a contemporary hamartiology—which should be pursued for today[18]—Nagel agrees that it is the virtue of the Christian believer to first know of their infidelity, but nevertheless understanding this as *not* simply an accidental deficiency of belief, for that would allow believers to distinguish themselves again from non-believers. While *coram Deo*, Christians are deemed righteous in the sight of God, but from the human perspective what is "real" is the fact of sin. Nagel goes a step further, however, with the question: If even believers are always marked by unbelief, then in what concrete sense (and not just in terms of a "hidden belief") is faith among believers to be distinguished? So, the problem is reformulated as follows: *neither everyone believes, nor some, because precisely they know of their unbelief*. The solution for Nagel is to exchange the language of particular-universal for the language of singularity. On this interpretation, and here the influence of Slavoj Žižek and Alain Badiou looms large, the defining feature of Christian identity explicitly comes into view: the latter is not a particular instance of the universal but (as a Christology would have to show) is an identity whose faith corresponds to a constitutive withdrawal of the singularity of Christ. In other words, Christian identity is to be understood as uniquely concerned with the "exclusivity of the excluded" or the "constitutive exception inherent in the universal."[19]

One can be sympathetic to this form of negative dialectics which attempts to identify within Christianity a form of "uncoupling" that can be explicated through a speculative philosophy.[20] Indeed, at least from within a protestant hermeneutic, the fecundity of the category of sin for theological anthropology, which has long been and continues to be criticized,[21] is here not dismissed but reinterpreted. Nevertheless, what can be added to this solution by way of addition, inversion, and radicalization, is the category of *finitude* as a fundamental feature of subjectivity to be lived-through and shared, first and primordially this time, through a *bodily-believing* as

18. Work in hamartiology is very much on the agenda: see, for example, Dalferth, *Sünde: Die Entdeckung der Menschlichkeit*; and Culp, *Vulnerability and Glory: A Theological Account*.

19. Nagel, "Total Fidelity?," 215–16.

20. The language of "uncoupling" belongs to Žižek; see chapter 12 in Žižek, *Puppet and the Dwarf*, 123–30.

21. See, for example, Huizing, *Schluss mit Sünde*.

opposed to unbelief. The methodological proposal followed here is, thus, far more modest and yet hopefully just as far-reaching, and is influenced by the Christian philosopher Emmanuel Falque. Insofar as a Christian response to the accusation of exclusivism makes use of its own dogmatic loci (albeit clarified philosophically) to expound a more *inclusive* religion (as we have seen above) one must nevertheless also avoid the suspicion that it will only ever be on the basis of Christian terms that the non-believer's position could ever be accepted. Instead, the position of the non-believer should be taken seriously in its own right, not for the sake of converting it but to establish a common basis for a shared humanity.[22]

In this respect, it is the clarifying and common term of *finitude* that we are now urged to "remember."[23] Finitude, particularly with reference to Falque, who is strongly informed by Martin Heidegger, is nothing other than the "most ordinary existence of all human beings, including that of the Son of God."[24] By this, Falque does not mean that we are serving theology the latest research in philosophy according to which it should renew itself.[25] It is simply that for him, humanity's *first* shared horizon of experience is that of a blockage, or an "impassable limit of life"—the *Being of Dasein* as "the between" of birth and death which we ourselves *are* and have to live through so as to give it meaning.[26] Crucially, this position of methodological atheism or "axiological neutrality"[27] is the same for the believer, since even a doctrine of Creation—that we are creatures made in God's image—comes to us as we find ourselves *first* "independent of the evidence that will be the revelation of God."[28] This absolute starting point of finitude which excludes an immediate reference to the infinite gives itself, or rather is demanded by Christian theology, in virtue of God's kenosis in him who fully took on human form. Indeed, it is only on the common basis of Christ's assuming a *Dasein* that we ever have access to God's addressing Godself to humanity.[29]

---

22. Falque writes, "The supposed certitude of Christianity as a stance of belief for many Christians corresponds then to the no less striking obviousness of atheism, as an existential stance, for many of our contemporaries. The legitimacy of one (the believer) cannot be said to hold the field at the price of a condemnation of the other (the atheist)." See Falque, *Metamorphosis of Finitude*, 34.

23. Falque enjoins this "memory of finitude" with reference to Feuerbach in his "précis of finitude"; *Metamorphosis of Finitude*.

24. Falque, *Metamorphosis of Finitude*, 13.

25. Falque, *Metamorphosis of Finitude*, 13.

26. Falque, *Metamorphosis of Finitude*, 27.

27. Falque, *Metamorphosis of Finitude*, 27.

28. Falque, *Metamorphosis of Finitude*, 16.

29. Falque, *Metamorphosis of Finitude*, 6; See also Falque, *Crossing the Rubicon*, 99,

One could certainly critically discuss how Falque will go on to retain the specificity of Christian revelation—insofar as he sees the first words of Christianity and of all humanity (finitude) as not *the final* word; indeed, the Word incarnate revealed in the resurrection still shows us there is *more* to humanity than any simple evaluation of oneself within finitude. Nevertheless, it is this *first* word or the "positiveness of finitude," which Falque is interested in, and which allows one then to take seriously the position of the non-believer, and here precisely by affirming the fundamental given of Christianity: that is to say, the doctrine of the incarnation. Thus, on the ground established by this finitude—without the preemption of the infinite over finite[30]—a common basis for humanity comes into view. The task for the Christian thinker, the one who operates from a common understanding of one's finite existence, can then be to *talk to* the non-believer and continue to explore the meaning of this finitude. For Falque, this does not mean doing less theology, but precisely the opposite—to follow his often-repeated formula: "the more we theologize, the better we philosophize."[31] If Christianity is one among many possible options in the twenty-first century, it is incumbent on the Christian to account for the significance and meaningfulness of the finitude which constitutes humanity; and this is not accomplished as an apologetic, but simply as a coherent perspective within a compendium of possibilities that might enrich an understanding of our shared condition whether as believers or not.

MEMORIES OF THE ORGANIC

Returning now to the "inversion" referred to above, and having established the common basis of humanity's finitude, we can now promote in what sense a contemporary hamartiology could be meaningful in response to totalities of violence. Indeed, sin continues to be linked with its outmoded consequences in suffering or biological death and the supposed implications with human imperfections. However, if human finitude (to be distinguished from *the finite*) now refers rather to our simple being-*there*, then death, corruptibility, decay, as well as the organic forces and drives of our bodies, now become features of the *imago Dei* which Christ's incarnation and memory of

---

122. Falque's project, then, should rightly be seen as a reaction to most of the protagonists of the "theological turn" (particularly his doctoral supervisor, Jean-Luc Marion). Indeed, his methodology has far more in common with thinkers like Paul Ricoeur and Jean-Yves Lacoste.

30. Falque, *Metamorphosis of Finitude*, 16–19.
31. Falque, *Crossing the Rubicon*, 147–52.

the body in the eucharistic seeks to demonstrate. The "sinful stance," then, is not the acceptance of our finitude, but rather the turning away or attempting to flee it. In Falque's words: "The distorted image of God in humankind, or the sinful mode of the human being, is thus read less in finitude itself (suffering, aging, death) than in the refusal to accept it as such."[32]

Living through finitude as the first experience of humanity, as well as of the believer, means that we are not content with referring to a universalizable enmity toward God, or the knowledge of our unbelief expressed through the language of singularity (which harbors within it still an ultimately particularizing gesture). Instead, the far more modest claim for our commonality is this finitude as a mode-of-being-there rooted now not in unbelief but in a common faith. This faith, or belief, is understood philosophically through the means of contemporary phenomenology, and by necessity precedes the religious faith of the believer. Let us with brief reference to Edmund Husserl and Martin Heidegger indicate this phenomenological faith, which I will come to describe as a primordial bodily-belief or "memory of the organic."[33]

Confessing belief in God always draws from a more originary belief in others and the world—one could say using the words of Swedish theologian Ola Sigurdson this is one of its "existential preconditions."[34] We may have a choice about belief in this or that, but we have no choice about having a choice, we are always locked into an absolute non-choice of choosing. The question is therefore only about who or how to believe not whether we do believe. Husserl called this originary belief already in *Ideas I*, a "*primal belief or protodoxa*"[35] and devoted much energy to the study of our everyday *doxa* which make up the natural attitude. As he clarifies later in *The Crisis of the European Sciences*, all scientific knowledge or what Plato called *epistēmē* is founded on these originary assumptions, which themselves deserve to be investigated for their own validation within the life-world of practical

---

32. Falque, *Guide to Gethsemane*, 14.

33. The following discussion on primordial belief is also partially drawn from Emmanuel Falque's chapter, "Always Believing," *Crossing the Rubicon*, 77–98.

34. There is much contiguity here with Sigurdson's account of systematic theology's preconditions. See Sigurdson, "Theology in the Middle of Things."

35. Husserl, *Ideas Pertaining to a Pure Phenomenology*; see §104, "Doxic Modalities as Modifications." Falque also points to a fascinating interpretation of Husserl's famous "phenomenological ἐποχή" in *Ideas I*, §32, with reference to Alfred Schütz and Bruce Bègout, where the latter speaks of "the *epoché of the natural attitude*." Or in other words, Husserl's intention to radicalize Cartesian doubt through the *epoché* of our natural belief in the world itself requires a second *epoché* of the *epoché*, where judgment about the judgment of the natural attitude is suspended. See Falque, *Crossing the Rubicon*, 81–82.

engagements.[36] This originary "act" of trust or faith in the world—often viewed with suspicion by religious faith—in fact teaches us of a common abiding or trusting attitude that we all primarily share, and upon which religious faith by necessity takes root and thus should not forget.

In the early Heidegger we also see how this philosophically common faith is demonstrated as well as how its memory is preserved within Christianity. Heidegger's widely commented on 1918 lectures in Freiburg, published as *The Phenomenology of Religious Life*, serves as our source. There, he distinguishes the multiplicities of faith's modalities, again, from a more primordial *doxa* to which they refer. Paradoxically, it is precisely from his investigations of Pauline *theology* that Heidegger arrives at the pivotal *philosophical* insight for an interpretation of faith: namely, as the act of faith takes priority over the content of faith (i.e., to believe *in* or *turning toward* God, is to believe that God exists), a precedence is given to the *mode of being* in religious faith before matters of existence. This ontological discovery of theological faith thus becomes a model for a phenomenological understanding of faith.[37] One could here continue further and indicate how this primordial belief is carried over in different ways in Gadamer, Ricoeur, and Merleau-Ponty, but the point is still the same; whether we are first given over to the world in Husserl, are committed to a horizon of understanding in Heidegger, whether this horizon is irreducibly linked to historicity in Gadamer and Ricoeur, is it impossible to have attained neutrality and to be free of all prejudice. We are *always believing* in the widest possible sense and therefore in a "community of belief," all the while recognizing the amphibology of the term *faith* here in the case of philosophical faith, portrayed above, but also in the act of confession.

We now come finally to the radicalization of this thesis, and which culminates in what is being called "memories of the organic." Without going into too much detail, a path which I have traced elsewhere, it is well known that following the translation of Husserl's *Cartesian Meditations*, much phenomenology, particularly in France, would occupy itself with resisting the supposed primacy of the Transcendental ego at the expense of the body. Several figures including Jean-Paul Sartre, Merleau-Ponty, Luce Irigaray, and others sought to articulate the lived-body (*le corps vivant*) one "is" not that one "has," and which evades the reduction of the body-as-object in the

---

36. Husserl, *Crisis of the European Sciences*; see §34 and §44. This also brings Husserl close to Wittgenstein, who speaks of certainty as grounded in a kind of "animal" belief (Wittgenstein, *On Certainty*, 47, 62).

37. As Falque writes, "We adhere to the world in philosophy as we adhere to God in theology in an originary posture" (*Crossing the Rubicon*, 84).

mechanistic sciences.[38] In recent years, theology too, has integrated these insights to trace a critical somatology within the tradition that re-instates the body as a medium for our experience of the world, with the other, and with God.[39] None of this is particularly new, as even a cursory survey will suggest. What I would like to argue, however, in both theology and philosophy (as phenomenology), an overcorrection has taken place whereby in attempting rightfully to edify the body as it is lived against materialist reductions, the body in its "organicity" or raw materiality, has been left behind or forgotten. A response here should not return to the body as *res extensa*, but rather to a bodily residue that is neither simply constitutive for meaningful experience nor defined in terms of an object in extended space.[40] Indeed this is a body which escapes phenomenality as such but which impresses itself, or rather weighs itself down on me, as foreign to me, yet as of myself.[41] It is our body as a pulsating vital force, unpredictable, and driven by an animality of affects that exceeds intentionality. As to be expected, the memory of this organic body is furnished in the eucharist and calls for investigation as a deepening of the common experience of finitude.[42] If in response to the totalities of violence we began with a common unbelief and a negative dialectics of singularity, which was then inverted to rediscover a common humanity in a primordial belief in the world (and in others) established by the horizon of finitude, then we conclude with a radicalization that summons both philosophy and theology to explore the foundations of our embodied finitude with respect to a primordial and bottomless Chaos of sensations and drives.

CONCLUSION

The implications of this approach reside in an overcoming of a certain irenicism and aestheticization in both philosophy and theology, by which the Real in human subjectivity is acknowledged in all its organic ambiguity. Here the body is neither easily constituted by an intentional consciousness nor is it simply passively open to the world—and in theology our bodily-being is

---

38. See, for example, Merleau-Ponty, *Structure of Behavior*; see John Wild's "Foreword" in Merleau-Ponty, *Phenomenology of Perception*, 88–99, for a description of the famous phantom limb.

39. See Ola Sigurdson's recent tome, *Heavenly Bodies*; Etzelmüller and Weissenrieder, *Verkörperung als Paradigma theologischer Anthropologie*.

40. This is what Falque calls "the spread body." See Falque, *Wedding Feast of the Lamb*, 12–15; Falque, "Toward an Ethics of the Spread Body."

41. Falque, "Extra-Phenomenal."

42. It is possible that this perspective maintains resonances with recent so-called "deep-incarnation" Christologies. See, for example, Gregersen, *Incarnation*.

not easily superimposed by a spiritualization of materiality. Instead, as in Christ's assuming the depths of our animal being, as the "feast of the lamb" indicates, a bodily resistance that incorporates both passive and active forces emerges, and which cannot straightforwardly be covered over. More importantly within the context of this discussion, the political implications of this original organic body which is to be remembered in both philosophy and theology are yet to be properly understood, as bodies undergo movements of tension, force, resistance, disinhibition, and antagonism. As Spinoza recognized already in his *Ethics*: "no one has hitherto laid down the limits of what the body can do."[43] Thus, before all divisions between the faithful and the non-believer, across all the "memories of violence" between friends and enemies that is our shared history, a Christian anthropology for today should reclaim and remember that there is a common humanity (or even animality) which the Son came precisely to inhabit. In this the eating of the bread and the drinking of the wine, we remember Christ's finitude and organicity as of our own, definitely shared by bodies in relation to other bodies—in a veritable community of bodies beyond the totality of religion.

BIBLIOGRAPHY

Assmann, Aleida. "Transformations of the Modern Time Regime." In *Breaking Up Time: Negotiating the Borders between Present, Past, and Future*, edited by C. Lorenz, and B. Bevernage, 39–56. Göttingen: Vandenhoeck & Ruprecht, 2013.

Assmann, Jan. *Exodus: Die Revolution der Alten Welt*. Munich: Beck, 2015.

———. *From Akhenaten to Moses: Ancient Egypt and Religious Change*. Cairo: American University in Cairo Press, 2014.

———. *Herrschafft und Heil: Politische Theologie in Ägypten, Israel und Europa*. Münchin: Carl Hanser, 2000.

———. *Invention of Religion: Faith and Covenant in the Book of Exodus*. Translated by Robert Savage. Princeton: Princeton University Press, 2018.

———. "Ist der neue Mensch ein Eiferer? Über den Preis des Monotheismus." *Neue Zürcher Zeitung* 245 (Oct 2004) 67.

———. "Monotheismus." *Jahrbuch Politische Theologie* 4 (2002) 122–32.

———. "Monotheismus der Treue: Korrekturen am Konzept der 'mosaischen Unterscheidung' im Hinblick auf die Beiträge von Marcia Pallay und Micha Brumlik." In *Die Gewalt des einen Gottes: Die Monotheismus-Debatte zwischen Jan Assmann, Micha Brumlik, Rolf Schieder, Peter Sloterdijk und anderen*, edited by Rolf Schieder, 252–55. Berlin: Berlin University Press, 2014.

———. *Moses the Egyptian: The Memory of Egypt in Western Monotheism*. Cambridge: Harvard University Press, 1997.

---

43. Spinoza, *Ethics*, part III, prop. II.

———. "Mose und der Monotheismus der Treue: Eine Neufassung der 'Mosaischen Unterscheidung.'" In *Monotheismus unter Gewaltverdacht: Zum Gespräch mit Jan Assmann*, edited by Jan-Heiner Tück, 16–33. Freiburg: Herder, 2015.

———. *The Price of Monotheism*. Translated by Robert Savage. Stanford: Stanford University Press, 2010.

Barth, Karl. *Church Dogmatics*. Vol 4.1, *The Doctrine of Reconciliation*. Translated and edited by T. F. Torrance and Geoffrey Bromiley. Edinburgh: T. & T. Clark, 1956.

Culp, Kristine A. *Vulnerability and Glory: A Theological Account*. Louisville: Westminster John Knox, 2010.

Dalferth, Ingolf. *Sünde: Die Entdeckung der Menschlichkeit*. Leipzig: EV Leipzig, 2020.

Etzelmüller, Gregor, and Annette Weissenrieder, eds. *Verkörperung als Paradigma theologischer Anthropologie*. Berlin: de Gruyter, 2016.

Falque, Emmanuel. *Crossing the Rubicon: The Borderlands of Philosophy and Theology*. Translated by Reuben Shank. New York: Fordham University Press, 2016.

———. "The Extra-Phenomenal." Translated by Luke McCracken. *Diakrisis Yearbook of Theology and Philosophy* 1 (2018) 9–28.

———. *The Guide to Gethsemane: Anxiety, Suffering, Death*. Translated by George Hughes. New York: Fordham University Press, 2019.

———. *The Metamorphosis of Finitude: An Essay on Birth and Resurrection*. Translated by George Hughes. New York: Fordham University Press, 2012.

———. "Toward an Ethics of the Spread Body." In *Somatic Desire: Recovering Corporeality in Contemporary Thought*, edited by Sarah Horton et al., 91–116. Lanham, MD: Lexington, 2019.

———. *The Wedding Feast of the Lamb: Eros, the Body, and the Eucharist*. Translated by George Hughes. New York: Fordham University Press, 2016.

Freud, Sigmund. *Moses and Monotheism*. Translated by Katherine Jones. London: Hogarth, 1939.

Gregersen, Niels Henrik, ed. *Incarnation: On the Scope and Depth of Christology*. Minneapolis: Fortress, 2015.

Huizing, Klaas. *Schluss mit Sünde: Warum wir eine neue Reformation brauchen*. Hamburg: Kreuz, 2017.

Husserl, Edmund. *The Crisis of the European Sciences and Transcendental Phenomenology*. Translated by David Carr. Evanston, IL: Northwestern University Press, 1970.

———. *Ideas Pertaining to a Pure Phenomenology and to a Phenomenological Philosophy*. Translated by F. Kersten. The Hague: Martinus Nijhoff, 1982.

Merleau-Ponty, Maurice. *Phenomenology of Perception*. Translated by Colin Smith. London: Routledge, 2002.

———. *The Structure of Behavior*. Translated by Alden L. Fischer. Pittsburgh: Duquesne University Press, 1963.

Nagel, Rasmus. "Total Fidelity? About the Exclusivity of the Excluded." In *In Need of a Master: Politics, Theology, and Radical Democracy*, edited by Dominik Finkelde and Rebekka Klein, 205–18. Berlin: de Gruyter, 2021.

———. *Universale Singularität: Ein Vorschlag zur Denkform christlicher Theologie im Gespräch mit Ernesto Laclau, Alain Badiou und Slavoj Žižek*. Tübingen: Mohr Siebeck, 2021.

Nancy, Jean-Luc. *Corpus*. Translated by Richard A. Rand. New York: Fordham University Press, 2008.

———. *Dis-Enclosure: The Deconstruction of Christianity*. Translated by Bettina Bergo et al. New York: Fordham University Press, 2008.
Ricoeur, Paul. *Memory, History, Forgetting*. Chicago: Chicago University Press, 2000.
Signer, M., ed. *Memory and History in Christianity and Judaism*. Notre Dame, IN: University of Notre Dame Press, 2001.
Sigurdson, Ola. *Heavenly Bodies: Incarnation, the Gaze, and Embodiment in Christian Theology*. Grand Rapids: Eerdmans, 2016.
———. "Theology in the Middle of Things: Existential Preconditions of Systematic Theology." *International Journal of Systematic Theology* (2020) 473–93.
Spinoza, Benedict de. *The Ethics*. Translated by R. H. M. Elwes. Project Gutenberg, 2009. E-book. https://www.gutenberg.org/files/3800/3800-h/3800-h.htm#chap03.
Steinmetz-Jenkins, Daniel. "Jan Assmann and the Theologization of the Political." *Political Theology* 12 (2011) 511–30.
Vosloo, Robert. "Time in Our Time: On Theology and Future-Orientated Memory." Stellenbosch University, SUN MeDIA, 2015.
Wittgenstein, Ludwig. *On Certainty*. Translated by Denis Paul and G. E. Anscombe. Oxford: Basil Blackwell, 1969.
Žižek, Slavoj. *The Puppet and the Dwarf or, Why Is the Christian Legacy Worth Fighting For?* London: Verso, 2001.

Chapter 5

"Wash me, and I shall be whiter than snow"

Exploring the Potential of Purgation for Racialized Spirituality

Louis van der Riet

INTRODUCTION

The theme of this book, "Experiencing God in Everything and Nothingness," gained new meaning for me upon reading the following articulation of nothingness by the late Vuyani Vellem, a leading South African theologian, particularly known for his contributions to black theology of liberation:

> The West has taught us about *creation ex nihilo*, i.e. creation out of nothing. In translating this notion of nothingness and creation, black people were reduced to nothingness, white people as creators! The grasp of what nothingness is what the West finally declares! In the quest for understanding creation, only what the West has created is what the black knows as creation. While blackness is nothing in the eyes of the West, creation out of nothing is equal to the West creating out of the nothingness of blacks... So the West is an architect of black nothingness, a god

that is creating what the black sees and beholds even to imagine the unimaginable about God's creation.[1]

Vellem's words capture the severity of the racialization of theological language, and indeed theological doctrine. This chapter explores this racialization, not merely of theological doctrine, but of Christian spirituality and the spiritual formation required for those racialized as white South Africans to engage with anti-racism work. In an attempt to contribute to a new, shared humanity with the whole body of Christ, the chapter wrestles with the question of how spiritual formation that addresses whiteness can attend to the often abstract and universalist (even imperialist) character of much Western theology—not merely its ability to experience God in "everything," but also to bring reparation to the "nothingness" attributed to blackness. It seeks to contribute to white critical and anti-racist theology by considering how the liberating and reconstructive nature of spirituality can became important, once again, in the South African context.

The first section of this chapter locates and describes how race functions. It considers whiteness as a theological and spiritual problem, and by using personal narrative, locates whiteness within my own spiritual formation. It grapples with how whiteness is a problem to be addressed, not merely *by* or *through* Christian spirituality, but *within* Christian formation.[2] Addressing whiteness as a problem to be "solved" through spiritual formation will require questioning the very Christian imagination informing such an attempt. Therefore, rather than presenting whiteness as a problem to be solved through spiritual formation, I would like to consider the potential of spiritual formation consciously engaging whiteness. This approach attempts to move outside of the problem-solution binary by addressing the topic in the ambit of spiritual formation, where formation denotes a continuing, cyclical process driven less by solution(s) than by an eschatological "ultimate" reality.[3] Moreover, it attempts to avoid both cyni-

---

1. Vellem, "Un-thinking the West," 8.

2. This is a distinction that also pertains to methodology, not merely for this chapter, but for individual attempts of white Christians doing theology and exercising spirituality that seek to address the injustices of whiteness.

3. Dietrich Bonhoeffer writes in *Ethics* on the "ultimate" and the "pen-ultimate" to reflect on human agency and our freedom to act, stating that we are living in the "pen-ultimate" where ethical action is required, with a view to the "ultimate." He writes, "To give the hungry bread is not yet to proclaim to them the grace of God and justification, and to have received bread does not yet mean to stand in faith. But for the one who does something penultimate for the sake of the ultimate, this penultimate thing is related to the ultimate. It is a *pen*-ultimate before the last. The entry of grace is the ultimate" (Bonhoeffer, *Ethics*, 163).

cism and fundamentalism in grappling with the pervasive and complex nature of racialized spirituality.[4]

In light of the description and diagnosis offered, I then suggest *purgation* as a form of Christian spirituality that is well-suited to reimagining the relationship between Christian spirituality and works of justice, reconciliation, and repair for those racialized as white and who seek to minister alongside the embodied theology of black theologians. I stress the value of not sacrificing tradition in developing new contextual language for lived experiences.

I am consciously engaging from where I stand contextually and historically as an ordained minister of the Dutch Reformed Church, where I have been racialized as white.[5] From this position I speak to the witness of my church and its commitment to the gospel imperative of reconciliation; a "broad and deep vision of corporeally, socio-politically, ecologically embodied reconciliation."[6]

WHITENESS AS A THEOLOGICAL AND SPIRITUAL PROBLEM

Whiteness is embedded in a history of structural racism and white supremacy, with an intersection of political, economic, and ideological struggles centered around race. Melissa Steyn, a pioneering researcher on whiteness in the South African context, describes whiteness as follows:

> What, then, is whiteness? I believe it is best understood as an ideologically supported social positionality that has accrued to people of European descent as a consequence of the economic and political advantage gained during and subsequent to European colonial expansion.[7]

As Hunter and van der Westhuizen explain in the introduction to the *Routledge Handbook of Critical Studies in Whiteness*:

---

4. The linguistic landscape of "solutions" for racism and the afterlife of racialized division and injustice in South Africa has grown in recent decades, including reconciliation, restitution, repair, redress, reconstruction, intergroup contact, information acquisition, social cohesion, community building, church unity, reconstruction, multiculturalism, and others. This indicates a multiplicity of assessments of the racialized context of South Africa and reminds one that addressing the racialized dimension of spirituality must remain both realistic and humble in scope.

5. Van der Riet and Van Wyngaard, "Other Side of Whiteness," 1–25.

6. Verwoerd, "Transforming (Christian) Apartheid," 179.

7. Steyn, *Whiteness Just Isn't What It Used to Be*, 121.

> Whiteness works as a formation, a logic, and an assemblage through which global coloniality is enacted relationally in the interconnection between material, symbolic, and affective. From this point of view, there is no such thing as white people, but there are people racialised as white, humans caught up in the racialising logics of global colonial forms of subjectification and who are constantly called to the many material, cultural and affective lures of whiteness.[8]

Attempts to confine whiteness to a neat definition is perhaps of less value than to grasp it broadly as a reference to racialization infused with power, and "a way into understanding the current global intersecting systems of precarization, marginalization, exclusion and abjection."[9]

Both locally and internationally, a theological evaluation of the problem of whiteness has started to become more explicit in recent years.[10] While some significant work has been done in other English-speaking parts of the world, the contemporary public and academic debate on race and whiteness in South Africa has received little participation by white theologians.[11] In his recent doctoral dissertation, "In Search of Repair: Critical White Responses to Whiteness as a Theological Problem—A South African Contribution," Van Wyngaard has put whiteness under the magnifying glass, particularly as a theological problem.[12] Van Wyngaard studies the complexities of theology's discursive power that can construct and disrupt race. Reflecting on the seminal works of Kameron Carter and Willie Jennings on whiteness, Van Wyngaard demonstrates how the "problem" of whiteness in theology is pervasive and indeed inseparable from modern theology:

> To refer to whiteness and modern theology as if these constitute two phenomena which can be neatly separated so that the possibility exists for a theological critique of whiteness would in their analysis be an inadequate description of the problem, and in its inadequacy lack the capacity to present a vision of a future not bound to a racial scale.[13]

---

8. Hunter and van der Westhuizen, *Routledge Handbook of Critical Studies in Whiteness*, 2.

9. Hunter and van der Westhuizen, *Routledge Handbook of Critical Studies in Whiteness*, 4.

10. Some prominent examples from the global North include Jennings, *Christian Imagination*; and Carter, *Race: A Theological Account*.

11. Van Wyngaard, "Responding to the Challenge of Black Theology," 1.

12. Van Wyngaard, "In Search of Repair."

13. Van Wyngaard, "In Search of Repair," 24.

While Van Wyngaard does not use the language of spiritual formation, his concluding chapter does suggest that commitment larger than merely refined doctrine or simplistic ethical imperatives is required:

> Attempting to name the complexity and horrors of whiteness in South Africa and beyond calls for a commitment in the way we live—while we write words to produce arguments, the crisis must find a response in concrete commitments to life.[14]

Van Wyngaard demonstrates that what has contributed theologically to constituting the problem of whiteness is multidimensional and his study serves "to take first steps in illuminating what the theological work of dislodging whiteness from a Christian imagination and forming white Christians into a faith less bound to white racism might look like."[15] His study concludes by looking at three emerging theological themes, that would all require working out in terms of Christian formation: salvation, space/place, and the human.[16]

In this study Van Wyngaard remarks that "'Christians' and the church's questions concerning race and whiteness cannot be addressed by a neat division of doctrine and ethics, and specifically, that racism is not an ethical problem (only)."[17] To expand on this, I argue that these questions concerning race and whiteness need to be addressed as issues of spiritual formation—the practices and ways in which Christians come to internalize the affections, dispositions, and desires of Christ in their own times and places. Furthermore, the observation that whiteness can be understood as an issue beyond mere individual ethical decisions or practices, cautions against its individualization and from seeing its public theological implications. As Hunter and van der Westhuizen note, individualizing whiteness "divorces matters of race from the public domain and politics. Matters of race then become matters of ethics or morals, of personal offence or interpersonal expressions of race hate, or overt expressions of randomly targeted racism."[18]

A spiritual understanding of anti-racism is thus predicated on the understanding that racial formation is more than racist beliefs or even isolated acts or ethical behavior. It is not that white people merely hold prejudiced beliefs with power, it is that whiteness has formed for them racialized liturgies that form, uphold, and repeat the script of whiteness.

14. Van Wyngaard, "In Search of Repair," 262.
15. Van Wyngaard, "In Search of Repair," 250.
16. Van Wyngaard, "In Search of Repair," 247–62.
17. Van Wyngaard, "In Search of Repair," 248.
18. Hunter and van der Westhuizen, *Routledge Handbook of Critical Studies in Whiteness*, 6–7.

In exploring how a focus on spirituality can reach beyond both doctrine and ethics, the observation by Celia Kourie, a South African theologian with long-standing research in Christian spirituality, is of interest:

> A true spirituality transfigures one's understanding of religion: it is no longer seen as primarily doctrinal adherence, institutional affiliation, or even ethical living, but rather a *personal engagement* with God. Christian spirituality effects a new, transformed humanity....[19]

The division of spirituality from Christian theology is also a relatively recent development of the twentieth century,[20] and can be read as a function of whiteness that has dominated the Western academy and has assumed neutrality and the ability to be objective in its production of knowledge about God.

Kobe, a black South African theologian, supports Vellem's thesis that although white theologians "try by all means to move away from white supremacy, faith betrays white theologians because racism is spiritual."[21] This betrayal of racialized spirituality is found in many theological manifestations, in what is frequently described as a move away from apartheid, which is not necessarily the same as a move away from whiteness. This is highlighted in Van Wyngaard's observation that Beyers Naudé, one of the foremost anti-apartheid Afrikaner theologians, initially employed a "normative understanding of a particular form of Western Christendom in order to reject apartheid and Afrikaner ethno-nationalism,"[22] ironically reinforcing its inclination to coloniality and whiteness (in the guise of "Western," "Christian," and "civilized"). Though through engagement with black consciousness in the 1970s, "Naudé shifts his vision on where liberation will come from."[23] This commitment to black leadership and "a growing awareness and recognition that the oppressed must determine the contours of liberation" provides significant insight into the question of where anti-racism work is located for white people, and will be returned to in this chapter.[24]

---

19. Kourie, "What Is Christian Spirituality?" in Kourie and Kretzschmar, *Christian Spirituality in South Africa*, 28–29.

20. McGrath, *Christian Spirituality*, 27.

21. Kobe, "Ubuntu as a Spirituality of Liberation," 3.

22. Van Wyngaard, "Beyers Naudé," 417.

23. Van Wyngaard, Beyers Naudé," 431.

24. While Van Wyngaard is also deeply formed by black theology of liberation, his doctoral dissertation chose to study whiteness from the perspective of white theologians. In his first chapter he acknowledges the importance of social location and states, "This entire thesis is however built on a premise of being critically conscious of how whiteness

While the commitment to racial reconciliation has been a sustained imperative for theologians and ministers focused on dealing with the afterlife of slavery, colonialism, and apartheid in South Africa, what is needed in terms of spiritual formation for this racial reconciliation to take place is neither clear nor obvious. This raises the question of the real cost of Christian discipleship in anti-racism work for white South African Christians. A recent survey among DRC ministers and licensed proponents younger than forty clearly demonstrates that a spirituality that can sustain an anti-racist commitment remains largely unexplored territory.[25] The survey focused on obtaining responses regarding current ecclesial praxis and views on the future calling of the church, particularly by grasping how respondents relate to the church's past, and its historically white identity.

In his analysis of the responses, Van Wyngaard notes that even though racial reconciliation is a core calling and priority for these church leaders, there is a general absence of any strong emphasis on liturgy, prayer, and contemplation in the calling of the church to achieve this vision. Therefore, "the kind of spirituality that would allow this grappling with White complicity and ties to historic injustice" remains unexplored and warrants further exploration.[26] Van Wyngaard states plainly:

> If the task of leading a church so thoroughly intertwined with the history of White supremacy is taken up, it will require not merely a commitment to society, in general, but a spirituality that can sustain an anti-racist commitment over generations. . . . A clear vision on how to guide congregants to draw from their Christian faith in critically disrupting their White racial and racist formation still needs to be outlined.[27]

The insight that the repair of racialized spirituality must assume a move towards the racialized other is found in many post-1994 theologies constructed with an imagination of reconciliation. We see this methodological choice, not least, in the DRC's missional ecclesiology, and in other injunctions to "cross borders."[28] I therefore now consider my own formation, affected by whiteness, by recalling such an experience of the DRC's missional

---

informs theology and developing such consciousness for the sake of a particular responsibility." This is an attempt to consciously give attention to his own history and identity as white in the midst of a racialized society (Van Wyngaard, "In Search of Repair," 5).

25. Van Wyngaard, "Next Generation?"
26. Van Wyngaard, "Next Generation," 153.
27. Van Wyngaard, "Next Generation," 154.
28. Van Wyngaard, "White Christians Crossing Borders."

ecclesiology, noting its limitations and its perpetuation of the "invisibility–ignorance–innocence triad"[29] of whiteness.

"WASH ME, AND I SHALL BE WHITER THAN SNOW"

The reference to Ps 51:7 in the title of this chapter may recall Western memories of how this imagery of the color white has functioned as a symbol of purity, cleanliness, or holiness; of God's forgiveness, justification, and sanctification; of becoming guiltless, blameless, and free. One may also recall the popular hymn "Whiter Than Snow." I have a distinct memory of how this imagery functioned in my formative teenage years as an active member of my congregation's "outreach" projects; missional relief and reconciliation projects in black communities facing the challenges of poverty and unemployment.

My spiritual formation in a Dutch Reformed Church started in 2003 when I entered high school at age thirteen. The membership of my local, suburban DRC congregation, situated in a wealthy neighborhood in the Northern Suburbs of Cape Town, was exclusively white. Over the course of the next five years, I became heavily involved in the many youth outreach programs organized by this well-resourced congregation. Crossing the borders of race, class, and language were reserved for these "outreach" projects, when we travelled to communities far and wide, often to the provinces of Limpopo and the Eastern Cape. While I am not able to recall or assess how successful our efforts at evangelism or community service were, I am able to recall the language, imagery, and actions that I was invited to embody.

As a teenager without any insight or understanding into the history of the DRC's ties to colonialism and apartheid, or the power and privilege afforded to me because of my racialization as white, I became increasingly proud of how I was doing good, reaching out, and spreading the gospel. These neo-colonial experiences cultivated a benevolent though disengaged relationship with racialized inequality, and with little capacity to critically engage the DRC's missional ecclesiology. I did form very meaningful relationships across race, class, and language boundaries, though without interrogating or reflecting on how aspects of my white identity was being shaped by praxis filled with asymmetrical power relations.

A popular activity with children during these outreaches was creating a "wordless Bible"—either a beaded string or keychain holder with five differently colored beads or pieces of paper, each representing an aspect of the

---

29. Hunter and van der Westhuizen, *Routledge Handbook of Critical Studies in Whiteness*, 2.

gospel narrative. The black bead or paper represented sin. The white bead or paper, we proclaimed, was the symbol that Jesus had washed away our sin, had washed us whiter than snow. While this may sound innocent and powerless to enforce whiteness, in the hands of a white student instructing a black child, the violence of this symbolism becomes clearer. Given this context, I understand retrospectively how this symbolism, and this image of Jesus, could not only reenforce the perceived goodness of being white-skinned, but also how it absolved me and others from responsibility for any systemic, historic, institutionalized, and indeed spiritualized, racialized injustice.

I recall this memory, not only to demonstrate how the study of spirituality is self-implicating,[30] but to show the subtlety of racialized spiritual formation; how it can be wrapped in evangelism, protected by gospel narratives, and coated by youthful naivety. The imagination and language of this event evokes a "memory of colonialism" and maintains a "movement of power and privilege" from white to black.[31] It also reflects some of the major tenants observed within Critical Whiteness Studies, "a distinct if loosely constituted area of academic and research inquiry," such as good intentions that collude in racist reproduction via institutionalized whiteness and white ignorance.[32]

The words of Ps 51 could be read as an expression of a desire to be returned to innocence, where individual transgressions need to be forgiven solely by God, mirroring the individualization and spiritualization that challenges white Christians' ability to enter into "the restoration of relational harmony among members of the community or the restitution of social, political or economic structures in the community."[33] This is substantiated by the findings of a four-year-long research project on forgiveness that was conducted with black and white Christians in Cape Town, South Africa, which found that white Christians "largely understood forgiveness in an individual and spiritual manner . . . as being primarily a matter of restoring their spiritual relationship with God. . . . As such, God is the offended party, and forgiveness would have been enacted when God had set them free from the guilt and spiritual culpability of their actions."[34] Considering the social and public effects of racialization, this diagnosis of white Christians' spirituality is particularly telling and leads us to consider the relation between

30. De Villiers, "Spirituality, Theology and the Critical Mind," 112.

31. Rossouw, "Inclusive Communities," 391.

32. Hunter and van der Westhuizen, *Routledge Handbook of Critical Studies in Whiteness*, xx.

33. Forster, "Translation and a Politics of Forgiveness," 83–84.

34. Forster, "Translation and a Politics of Forgiveness," 84. See also Forster, *(im)possibility of Forgiveness*, 184–89.

white and black Christians in locating the spiritual formation required for those racialized as white to engage with anti-racism work.

DISCERNING WHITE RESPOND-ABILITY AND RESPONSIBILITY

In this section I explore what is not merely methodological questions for this chapter, but for doing theology and exercising spirituality as a white Christian and theologian seeking to address the injustices of whiteness. It does this by raising the question of how Christian spirituality and white consciousness can stand in relation to black theology and black consciousness, where anti-racism work is located for white people.

It is worth quoting Vellem's assessment of the problem of racism and whiteness at length:

> There is a need for the liberation of white people from this bondage of racism and superiority complex. The white community is challenged to understand that the Christian God is not only one of liberation and grace, but also one who is extremely angered in the face of injustice. For the liberation of white people to be possible, white consciousness is crucial to deal with. Understanding whiteness and the privilege attached to it in a society set up to benefit white people at the direct expense of black people is an important starting point. Once white people come to such an understanding and listen to the comprehensive argument by BTL [Black Theology of Liberation] prior to negating it, or defending their actions, a healthy conversation is sure to unfold. This has not happened in South Africa. It has not happened even in post-1994 South Africa as it now continues globally.[35]

In looking for a way forward from the theological problems of whiteness, white theologians who bear witness to being conscious of their formation through racialized spirituality, have opted to *respond* to black theology not merely by evaluating it, but with the intent of developing "a theology for a liberating ministry in the white community."[36]

Klippies Kritzinger, a white South African missiologist and a pioneering voice in working on the theological problems of whiteness, has chosen black theology and black theologians as his primary interlocuters in this

---

35. Vellem, "Un-thinking the West," 5.
36. Kritzinger, "Black Theology—Challenge to Mission," 272.

endeavor.[37] This is to give epistemological privilege to victims of oppression in understanding and responding to oppression and developing strategies to overcome it.[38] The work of Klippies Kritzinger helps to place the personal narrative shared in this chapter within a typology and demonstrates its limitations. In 1988, Kritzinger completed his doctoral dissertation on black theology in which he distinguished between three white responses to black theology: rejection, sympathy, and solidarity. He has recently expanded this to a six-fold typology, that he argues can contribute to the task of "re-evangelising" the white community by distinguishing an intentionally liberating white praxis (LWP) from other white praxes.[39] These six responses include rejection (to "strangers"), hostility (to "enemies"), condescension (to "disadvantaged inferiors"), relief (for "suffering fellow human beings"), reconciliation (with "estranged brothers and sisters"), and solidarity (together with, towards "a radically new society").[40] These "outreach" practices of my youth could be described as acts of "relief" that display sympathy rather than solidarity. Engaging with Kritzinger's typology, Vellem echoes his analysis of sympathy as "one of the most vexatious expressions of the supremacy and superiority of white responses"[41] as it stands in an abusive and dangerous relationship to black pain by reenforcing a "white messianic syndrome."[42]

De Gruchy addresses the question of perspective when he writes:

> White South Africans cannot change in isolation from black South Africans. You cannot become a champion of justice if you are not enabled to see injustice through the eyes of those who experience it; you cannot become a worker for liberation if you do not experience something of the pain of oppression. You cannot really hear the gospel in a life-changing way if you only hear it from white voices.[43]

---

37. "[*This White theology*] is not intended as a separate white theology which falls into the trap of apartheid all over again, but a theology which is intimately related to Black Theology, and which unfolds in constant dialogue with it. The missiological nature of this response is also revealed by the fact that it is structured around the different dimensions of the missiological notion of conversion" (Kritzinger, "Black Theology," 273).

38. Kritzinger, "Liberating Whiteness."

39. Kritzinger. "White Responses to Black Theology."

40. Kritzinger, "White Responses," 7. In addition to this typology, Kritzinger has developed a praxis matrix with seven dimensions that shape a particular theology, ministry, or mission. In the center of this model is spirituality.

41. Vellem, "Un-thinking the West," 5.

42. Kobe, "Ubuntu," 3.

43. Mayekiso, *Being Black*, 124.

While one may agree with this observation, it does beg the question of whether true liberation may require something more than this respondability though acts of solidarity and listening. For white South Africans, such exposure and response to black South Africans would need to be held in relation to taking particular responsibility for one's formation as white. The following section explores this taking of responsibility through the spiritual tradition of purgation.

TAKING RESPONSIBILITY THROUGH PURGATION

In *The Ascent of Mount Carmel*, Saint John of the Cross writes:

> To reach satisfaction in all
> desire satisfaction in nothing.
> To come to possess all
> desire the possession of nothing.
> To arrive at being all
> desire to be nothing.
> To come to the knowledge of all
> desire the knowledge of nothing.
>
> To come to enjoy what you have not,
> you must go by a way in which you enjoy not.
> To come to the possession you have not
> you must go by a way in which you possess not.
> To come to what you are not
> you must go by a way in which you are not.[44]

The tradition of apophatic theology presents one way of mapping spiritual formation through the stages of *purgation, illumination,* and *union*. Apophatic theology, with its origins in Origen's mystical theology, and passed on by Evagrius and in the writings of the anonymous sixth-century Syrian monk Dionysius (also referred to as Pseudo-Dionysius due to a change in name to Areopagite), is marked by an experience of knowing God through a process of *unknowing*. This spiritual tradition, with many subsequent exponents in the West, such as Saint John of the Cross, has always had a focus on "the gracious restoration of the divine image in human beings"; "a never-ending process of conversion" that is motivated not merely by a desire for God, but also for the fulfilment of God's purpose for the world.[45] It is the first of these phases or stages, that have become classic in systematic theories

---

44. John of the Cross, *Collected Works*, 150.
45. De Gruchy, *Monastic Moment*, 33.

of Christian spirituality, that I find particularly valuable in reflecting on whiteness, especially as it illuminates the spiritual practice and imagery of being washed "whiter than snow."

Michael Battle, in his latest publication, *Desmond Tutu: A Spiritual Biography of South Africa's Confessor*, gives a detailed account of these concepts by using them to structure his account of Desmond Tutu's spiritual formation. In the first part of the book on purgation, he describes at length how Tutu called for the purgation of racialized identities in South Africa.[46] Reflecting on Tutu's engagement with the purgation of white identity, Battle writes:

> There must be a clear willingness on the part of white South African society to make amends in unequivocal terms. This is called repentance. If such repentance is not forthcoming, white identity might well appear as the incessant oppressor. This means that, as a Christian and as a person who is a member of the church, processes of dehumanization cannot be tolerated.[47]

Within this concept of purgation, one thus sees the Christian practices of contrition, confession, and repentance, dealing not only with sin and guilt, but also with God's justification and sanctification, as in the symbol of the white bead or paper.

In the context of whiteness, this practice may suggest a purgation of white innocence and ignorance,[48] and of the often unconsciousness ability to transform our whiteness, and in doing so, develop practices that interrupt "the social grammar of whiteness and begins the process of cultivating a new self that participates in the reality of God united to the reality of the world in Christ. This gift of the new humanity is a task to be perfected in grace within the body of Christ, worked out in concert with last things, and lived out within the things before the last."[49] This language of purgation is in keeping with Christian spirituality that produced Christian mysticism, and as Battle suggests, can be "extremely helpful in methodologies toward reconciliation."[50] It is this mystical tradition that Tutu has relied on for "destroying idols and hypocritical constructs in which only Europeans are powerful or can live in the double standards of power."[51] Writing about the tragedy of whiteness and its inability to let go its idols, Vellem

---

46. Battle, *Desmond Tutu*.
47. Battle, *Desmond Tutu*, 80.
48. Steyn, *Whiteness Just Isn't What It Used to Be*.
49. Harvey, *Taking Hold of the Real*, 206.
50. Battle, *Desmond Tutu*, 54.
51. Battle, *Desmond Tutu*, 54.

states, "The essence of this tragedy is indeed a matter of faith. It is spiritual. Nothing could be crueller spiritually so, than a way of knowing that suppresses and defends guilt because white people know that they are guilty at least as beneficiaries of the systems that kept black people as underdogs."[52]

Purgation suggests spirituality that resists mastery, one of the clear aspirations of whiteness, as Hunter and van der Westhuizen note: "The key to rehumaning through whiteness is coming to realize that the white subject was never the site of mastery in the first place. By attempting to practise livedness outside of this aspiration to mastery, a different orientation to the white body may be possible."[53] In his book *After Whiteness*,[54] Willie Jennings captures the imagination of formation in Western education. He demonstrates how the process of formation has been centered on the image or persona of the "white self-sufficient male," whose formation is marked by "possession, control, and mastery."[55] Purgation offers a direct challenge to such formation. Writing on Denise Ackermann, "a rare woman of courage," and on the theme of "the risk of spirituality," Douglas Lawrie writes, "Who, indeed, are fully prepared to have their defences demolished, their evasions curtailed, their mechanisms of mastery dismantled?" He continues, "If spirituality is again to become central to theology and Christian life, we must pray for the somewhat discredited virtue of courage."[56] This virtue of courage is indeed a welcome companion to how Lawrie piercingly defines spirituality in light of Ackermann's witness: "Spirituality is the condition of standing with your nerve ends exposed in a place from which there is no line of retreat and in a meeting of which you are not master."[57]

Indeed, a move towards vulnerability and a spirituality of liminality is required by those who seek to confront their whiteness, as Wepener and Nell, two white males teaching theology at (South) African universities describe their own position and observe that "a spirituality of liminality . . . goes hand in hand with ontological and epistemological hospitality."[58] This is the recognition that "subjective vulnerability implies the resistance to the idea of human self-determination. It places whiteness and whitened subjects

---

52. Vellem, "Un-thinking the West," 5, 6.

53. Hunter and van der Westhuizen, *Routledge Handbook of Critical Studies in Whiteness*, 20.

54. Jennings, *After Whiteness: An Education in Belonging*.

55. Jennings, *After Whiteness*, 6.

56. Lawrie, "Risk of Spirituality," 142.

57. Lawrie, "Risk of Spirituality," 135.

58. Wepener and Nell, "White Males Teaching Theology," 4.

in their fullest responsibility with themselves and others." Hunter and van der Westhuizen continue to state:

> This relationality also disrupts the idea of change as coming from within the white body. Social change is not in the gift of "the white master" but achieved through a relationality where subjectivity is enacted by (at the very least) both in relation. It is this relationality which means that it is possible to resist whiteness.

CONCLUSION

It is thus evident that respond-ability and responsibility—exposure and response to black South Africans, and the relinquishing of self-mastery before God and others—is required for the dismantling of whiteness and must form part of Christian spirituality that seeks to engage in anti-racism work. The need for different foci can further be substantiated by noting their respective limitations. A too narrow focus on the realities of whiteness holds the danger of recentering whiteness,[59] while only responding to black theology can translate as sympathy.

Given that this work of formation for white Christians has these different dimensions and focal points, and even points of departure, it raises the question of how different emphases and aspects of this work of formation can best be configured, how they relate to one another. This is to hold in tension the insight that "as a white church the DRC will have difficulties reflecting critically on its own white identity without the help of other voices,"[60] while seriously addressing the reality that there is formation work that only white people can do among themselves.[61] As has been stated in the introduction, I do not suggest purgation here as *the* solution to the problems of whiteness in spiritual formation. Rather, I highlight the value of reimagining the Christian methodology of practicing the presence of God and communion with God—and others—given the realities of white formation, where "white identity rose to the top of a spiritual hierarchy."[62] Perhaps here lies some potential for a deeper, contextual "re-evangelism"[63] and spiritual formation that engages with historical acknowledgment and implication with a posture of vulnerability; that can contribute to the reordering of

---

59. Van Wyngaard, "White Theology in Dialogue with Black Theology," 5.

60. Rossouw, "Inclusive Communities," 384.

61. Van der Riet and Verwoerd, "Diagnosing and Dismantling South African Whiteness."

62. Battle, *Desmond Tutu*, 80.

63. Kritzinger, "Re-evangelising the White Church," 106.

desire; that can move whiteness towards the preparatory work of confession and fruitful nothingness.

BIBLIOGRAPHY

Battle, Michael. *Desmond Tutu: A Spiritual Biography of South Africa's Confessor.* Louisville, KY: Westminster John Knox, 2021.
Bonhoeffer, Dietrich. *Ethics.* Vol. 6 of *Dietrich Bonhoeffer Works Edition*, edited by Clifford J. Green. Minneapolis: Fortress, 2005.
Carter, J. Kameron. *Race: A Theological Account.* Oxford: Oxford University Press, 2008.
de Gruchy, John W. *The Monastic Moment: The War of the Spirit & the Rule of Love.* Eugene, OR: Cascade, 2021.
De Villiers, Pieter G. R. "Spirituality, Theology and the Critical Mind." *Acta Theologica Supplementum* 8 (2006) 99–121.
Forster, Dion. *The (im)possibility of Forgiveness? An Empirical Intercultural Bible Reading of Matthew 18:15–35.* Beyers Naudé Centre Series on Public Theology 11. 1st ed. Stellenbosch, South Africa: SUN, 2017.
———. "Translation and a Politics of Forgiveness in South Africa? What Black Christians Believe, and White Christians Do Not Seem to Understand." *Stellenbosch Theological Journal* 4 (2018) 77–93.
Harvey, Barry. *Taking Hold of the Real: Dietrich Bonhoeffer and the Profound Worldliness of Christianity.* Eugene, OR: Cascade, 2015.
Hunter, Shona and Christi van der Westhuizen, eds. *Routledge Handbook of Critical Studies in Whiteness.* New York: Routledge, 2022.
Jennings, Willie James. *After Whiteness: An Education in Belonging.* Grand Rapids: Eerdmans, 2020.
———. *The Christian Imagination: Theology and the Origins of Race.* New Haven, CT: Yale University Press, 2011.
John of the Cross. *The Collected Works of Saint John of the Cross.* Translated by Kieran Kavanaugh and Otilio Rodriguez. Washington, DC: ICS, 1991.
Kobe, Sandiswa L. "Ubuntu as a Spirituality of Liberation for Black Theology of Liberation." *HTS Theological Studies* 77 (2021) 1–8.
Kourie, Celia, and Kretzschmar, Louise. *Christian Spirituality in South Africa.* Pietermaritzburg: Cluster, 2000.
Kritzinger, J. N. "Black Theology—Challenge to Mission." Unpublished diss., University of South Africa, 1988.
———. "Liberating Whiteness: Engaging the Anti-Racist Dialectic of Steve Biko." In *The Legacy of Stephen Bantu Biko: Theological Challenges*, edited by C. W. du Toit, 89–113. Pretoria: Unisa, 2008.
———. "Re-evangelising the White Church." *Journal of Theology for Southern Africa* 76 (Sep 1991) 106–16.
———. "White Responses to Black Theology: Revisiting a Typology." *HTS Theological Studies* 78 (2022) 1–9.
Lawrie, Douglas. "The Risk of Spirituality." In *Ragbag Theologies: Essays in Honour of Denise M. Ackermann, a Feminist Theologian of Praxis*, edited by Clint Le Bruyns et al., 133–43. Stellenbosch: SUN, 2009.

Mayekiso, Theo. *Being Black—A South African Story That Matters*. Cape Town: Sula, 2020.

McGrath, Alister. *Christian Spirituality*. Oxford: Blackwell, 1999.

Rossouw, Fourie P. "Inclusive Communities: A Missional Approach to Racial Inclusivity within the Dutch Reformed Church." *Stellenbosch Theological Journal* 2 (2016) 381–96.

Steyn, Melissa. *Whiteness Just Isn't What It Used to Be: White Identity in a Changing South Africa*. New York: SUNY Press, 2005.

van der Riet, Louis R., and Cobus G. J. Van Wyngaard. "The Other Side of Whiteness: The Dutch Reformed Church and the Search for a Theology of Racial Reconciliation in the Afterlife of Apartheid." *Stellenbosch Theological Journal* 7 (2021) 1–25.

van der Riet, Louis R., and Wilhelm Verwoerd. "Diagnosing and Dismantling South African Whiteness: "White Work" in the Dutch Reformed Church." *HTS Theological Studies* 78 (2022) 1–9.

Van Wyngaard, Cobus G. J. "Beyers Naudé (1966–1977): Between Western Ideals and Black Leadership." *Stellenbosch Theological Journal* 6 (2020) 415–34.

———. "In Search of Repair: Critical White Responses to Whiteness as a Theological Problem—A South African Contribution." Unpublished diss., Vrije University Amsterdam, 2019.

———. "A Next Generation? Young Dutch Reformed Church Ministers and Their Vision for the Church in South Africa." *Acta Theologica Supp* 30 (2020) 133–57.

———. "Responding to the Challenge of Black Theology: Liberating Ministry to the White Community—1988–1990." *HTS Theological Studies* 72 (2016) 1–9.

———. "White Christians Crossing Borders: Between Perpetuation and Transformation." In *Unsettling whiteness*, edited by L. Michael and S. Schulz, 191–202. Oxford: Inter-Disciplinary, 2014.

———. "White Theology in Dialogue with Black Theology: Exploring the Contribution of Klippies Kritzinger." *HTS Theological Studies* 72 (2016) 1–9.

Vellem, V. S. "Un-thinking the West: The Spirit of Doing Black Theology of Liberation in Decolonial times." *HTS Theological Studies* 73 (2017) 1–9.

Verwoerd, Wilhelm J. "Transforming (Christian) Apartheid." In *Reconciliation, Forgiveness and Violence in Africa: Biblical, Pastoral, and Ethical Perspectives*, edited by Marius J. Nel et al., 171–83. Stellenbosch: African Sun Media, 2020.

Wepener, Cas, and Ian Nell. "White Males Teaching Theology at (South) African Universities? Reflections on Epistemological and Ontological Hospitality." *Academia Letters* (2021) article 3304. doi.org/10.20935/AL3304.

Chapter 6

Youth and Environmental Consciousness
Do Religion, Faith, and Spirituality Matter?[1]

Jacques Beukes

INTRODUCTION

Several youth movements have started to pay attention to the environmental and climate change problem. The capacity of future generations to satisfy their own requirements should not be compromised in order to achieve sustainable development. Sustainable development is defined as development that satisfies the demands of the present generation. Young people are at the center of conversations and actions about (in)justice in the environment, climate change, and environmental awareness. Youth movements like "Extinction Rebellion" and "Fridays for Future" show that young people globally care about the environment and want to do something about climate change. They are one of the most significant and intriguing groups to

---

1. This chapter forms part of the "South African–German Research Hub on Religion and Sustainability" (SAGRaS). SAGRaS is a collaborative initiative of scholars and practitioners at different institutions within the framework of the International Network on Religious Communities and Sustainable Development (IN//RCSD). It is funded by the National Research Foundation (NRF) from 2022 to 2025 (Grant Reference: SAG201111573377). More information on SAGRaS can be found at www.in-rcsd.org/sagras.

learn more about because of their willingness to take action on their own behalf, which makes them one of the most important groups to learn more about while attempting to make people more conscious of environmental concerns. Thus, it is crucial to research how young people participate in these talks, how they raise social awareness of environmental challenges, and how religious beliefs impact this knowledge.

This chapter looks at the link between youth, religion, and caring about the environment. This chapter will look into two different research questions. The first is: How are youths involved in the discourse of environmental issues? Secondly, to what extent does their faith influence their environmental consciousness? This chapter aims to find out if young people's faith and spirituality drive them to be active in environmental and climate change issues.

A (VERY) BRIEF RATIONALE FOR THIS CHAPTER

I have recently listened to a young environmental activist from South Africa during a webinar on the topic of ecological crisis; I could hear the passion in the young activist's voice while he explained the importance of being involved, as well as all the reasons and justifications why awareness, advocacy, dialogue, and most importantly, actions are needed in the fight against environmental injustice. However, the obvious missing argument or reason for being involved was the religious, faith, and spiritual motivation. So, while I was listening to him the following questions came to mind: Does religion matter? Does faith matter? Does spirituality matter? Especially among young people in their motivation to become active in environmental care. This missing piece kept popping into my mind as I was very curious about this missing piece in this young man's argument. At the end of the discussion, I posted the question to him . . . and he responded, *"Yes, religion, faith, spirituality, and church have a role to play."* Although this was the answer, it was sort of an afterthought and also too simplistic, which made me want to investigate the following research questions: How are South African youths involved in the discourse on environmental issues? And to what extent does their faith influence their environmental consciousness or motivate them to become involved?

However, I will first shift my attention to the current phenomenon, namely the environmental crisis.

ENVIRONMENTAL CRISIS

South Africa is influenced by a number of environmental issues including weather-related severe occurrences. Climate change has had a particularly apparent impact on South Africa in recent years.[2] The many natural calamities that happened, such as heatwaves, droughts, floods, wildfires, and storms, demonstrated this.[3] Various elements inside South Africa might create significant variations in climate change. These include rising temperatures, shifting rainfall patterns, and variances in the frequency and severity of catastrophic weather occurrences.[4] Residents of George in the Southern Cape witnessed significant floods only a few days ago. And this is happening, at the time of this writing, as we approach the end of November 2021.

While other sections of our nation face water shortages and changes in color, flavor, and quality, we do not.[5] Soil erosion, land degradation, and a drop in agricultural food production occur in locations where there is less rain. This will have an especially negative impact on children and families. Young children are especially vulnerable, and especially true with threats such as a lack of clean, safe drinking water and enough nourishment—due to the fact that they are physically more vulnerable and have specific nutritional needs.[6] Moreover, the impacts of rising environmental toxicity on children seem to be little recognized. This is so despite the fact that climate change affects the intellectual, mental, social, and physical development of young people. Moreover, increased temperatures have a greater negative impact on youngsters. This is particularly true about heatstroke. The temperature forecast indicates an increase in the frequency of hot days and nights, particularly in the interior of South Africa. The *"urban heat island effect"* might have a significant impact, leading to a rise in metropolitan temperatures. Children who are excessively excluded and underdeveloped will be more severely impacted by climate change.[7]

Climate change has a tremendous impact on education. Drought-related water shortages pose a danger to South African schools. Furthermore, there is a risk of water pollution as a consequence of pathogenic organisms and poisons released by floods. Water safety is of the highest significance in South Africa. This is because 30 percent of educational institutions,

---

2. Beukes, "Seen and Heard," 2.

3. Lethoko, "Children and Youth as Agents," 75; UNICEF, *Exploring the Impact of Climate Change*, 22.

4. UNICEF, *Exploring the Impact of Climate Change*, 7.

5. Nkrumah, "Beyond Tokenism," 4.

6. UNICEF, *Exploring the Impact of Climate Change*, 7.

7. UNICEF, *Exploring the Impact of Climate Change*, 7.

including schools, lack toilets or use pit latrines.[8] Continuing with the unfavorable consequences of climate change, rising temperatures aggravate most diseases that originate in water or food, particularly those containing bacteria. Warmer weather and temperature fluctuations may aggravate asthma in teens. This seems to be more prevalent in teens than in other age groups. Another effect of climate change is a rise in dust and pollen, as well as air pollution. Higher temperatures expose people to more hazardous compounds in the environment. This creates a problem since many South African schools are located near harmful chemicals, such as heavily used highways, mining wastes, and industrial enterprises.[9]

Climate change, in addition to the direct consequences stated above, has indirect effects. A teenager grows biologically and cognitively. This growth happens in the context of their living environment. So, social and economic issues like a lack of food, damage to infrastructure, and migration may all have a big effect on how people of different ages grow and develop. These effects are bad for teens' mental health and could even cause them to kill themselves. These mental health problems often last until a person is an adult. UN data show that one terrible thing happens every week because of climate change.[10] Even if just a tiny fraction of young people are harmed by these tragedies in terms of their mental health, it causes a massive illness burden.

YOUTH INVOLVEMENT AND YOUTH MOVEMENTS ABROAD

The number of people living in South Africa in 2019 was predicted to be 58.8 million in the middle of the year. There were 17 million children under fourteen years old and 20.6 million young people between fifteen and thirty-four years old. This shows that the majority of South Africans (63.9 percent) are children and young people, according to Statistics South Africa (2019). For many years, it was widely accepted in traditional South African culture that *"children should be seen but not heard."*[11] However, today's youth are at the epicenter of discussions about ecological (in)justice, environmental awareness across generations, and climate change discourses and actions.

---

8. Chersich et al., "Climate Change and Adolescents in South Africa," 615.

9. Chersich et al., "Climate Change and Adolescents in South Africa," 616; Nkrumah, "Beyond Tokenism," 4.

10. Chersich et al., "Climate Change and Adolescents in South Africa," 616; Nkrumah, "Beyond Tokenism," 4.

11. Nel, "Children Must Be Seen and Heard," 1.

In today's world, when children and youth are most impacted by climate change, the conventional notion of children being seen but not voiced has been challenged by today's young. This is because they will bear the burdens and issues associated with greenhouse gas emissions (GHGs), pollution, and other environmental risks.[12]

Swedish eighteen-year-old Greta Thunberg popularized the climate school walkout throughout Europe. Thunberg fights environmental injustice and climate change. At the September 2019 UN Climate Change Summit, her "How dare you" speech blasted world leaders for not addressing climate change.[13] This speech sparked debate. This research will not examine Greta Thunberg's speech's replies and provocations, but rather what I want to highlight is how, in only a few months, an adolescent activist has changed worldwide dialogue on the topic of youth and climate change.[14] Greta Thunberg's environmental advocacy and the social movement that sprang from it are also noteworthy.

Greta Thunberg began protesting when she was fifteen years old. She opted not to go to school on Fridays when she was this age. She would rather spend days outside the Swedish parliament.[15] This event was staged to call for increased government action on climate change. Students swiftly followed and did the same, taking to the streets.[16] They launched the "Fridays for Future" school climate strike initiative. Following Greta Thunberg's speech at the United Nations Climate Change Conference in 2018, there has been an increase in youthful resistance throughout the world.[17] Greta Thunberg is credited with organizing over ten million climate strikers.[18] Young people who have joined youth for climate have voiced concern about how climate change may affect their future lives.[19] The youth have also expressed worries about the sluggish pace with which action is being made to combat global warming. In 2019, there were several coordinated multi-city marches involving millions of young people.[20]

---

12. Chersich et al., "Climate Change and Adolescents in South Africa," 615.
13. Beukes, "Seen and Heard," 4.
14. Beukes, "Seen and Heard," 4.
15. Stoecklin, "Transactional Horizons of Greta Thunberg," 1.
16. Stoecklin, "Transactional Horizons of Greta Thunberg," 1.
17. Cf. Stoecklin, "Transactional Horizons of Greta Thunberg."
18. Sabherwal et al., "Greta Thunberg Effect," 322.
19. Lee et al., "Youth Perceptions of Climate Change."
20. Boulianne et al., "School Strike 4 Climate," 208.

YOUTH INVOLVEMENT AND YOUTH MOVEMENTS IN SOUTH AFRICA

In June 2019, the Youth Climate Movement in South Africa got a lot of attention from the media and a lot more people joined.[21] All over South Africa, young people joined the fight for climate justice. South African youth have always been a strong force that could move a movement forward steadily.[22] Ayakha Melithafa, a climate activist from the Western Cape (Eersterivier) in South Africa who is seventeen years old, has also gotten some but not nearly as much attention as Greta Thunberg has in Europe.[23] Melithafa has done a lot to bring attention to the serious climate problems in South Africa. She also made headlines when she joined Greta Thunberg and other teens from around the world to ask the United Nations Committee on the Rights of the Child to hold five of the world's most powerful economic countries accountable for not doing enough to stop the climate disaster.[24] In January 2020, Ayakha Melithafa joined Greta Thunberg on the stage of the World Economic Forum in Davos, Switzerland.[25] Melithafa has also asked that South Africa stop making coal, oil, and gas right away.

On June 14, 2019, young people marched in Pretoria and Cape Town to demand that the government act quickly and urgently to solve the climate crisis.[26] As a follow-up to a march on March 15, 2019, the African Climate Youth Alliance planned this event. Young people in South Africa want the government to admit that there is a climate catastrophe. They also want to stop giving out new permits to mine oil, gas, and coal. They want the whole country to be run on clean energy by 2030. Lastly, the curriculum in schools needs to be changed so that climate change is a required part of it.[27]

WHY ARE THE YOUTH REGARDED AS VALUABLE INTERLOCUTORS?

Idealistic assertions about the necessity of young involvement in an inclusive, democratic society have nearly become cliché in recent years.[28] Politi-

21. Mjiyakho et al., "Young People and the Climate Crisis," n.p.
22. Cf. Booysen, "Introduction."
23. Cf. World Economic Forum, "10 Teenage Change-Makers," 3.
24. Cf. UNICEF, "16 Children."
25. See World Economic Forum, "10 Teenage Change-Makers," 3, for more.
26. Postman and Hendricks, "South African Youth."
27. Postman and Hendricks, "South African Youth."
28. Bessant, "Mixed Messages."

cians, the media, researchers, and activists all say that youth engagement increases civic duty while also involving young people in addressing social issues and delivering services in their communities. However, dominant perceptions about young people in an adult-dominated environment certainly determine their agency, influence, and positions in society, presenting a substantial challenge to democratic values. These ideas drive governmental policies that progressively restrict, regulate, and punish children while limiting government spending to enhance their living conditions.[29] Too frequently, impoverished kids, the youth of color, immigrant youth, and urban adolescents are underserved, with a dearth of programs that accept their unique cultural identities and understand the systemic disadvantages these young people face, as well as their limitless ability for addressing injustice.[30] However, this has started to change as young people understand the agency they have.

Africa has the world's fastest-expanding population. Its current population of 1.2 billion is expected to more than treble to 2.5 billion by 2050.[31] This population is also the world's youngest, contributing to a burgeoning youth population. The continent's youth (those aged fifteen to twenty-four) account for slightly under 231 million people, or 19 percent of the population, according to the United Nations Population Division. If current population growth rates continue, the number of young people might reach 335 million by 2030 and 461 million by 2050. By African Union (AU) standards, these numbers are an underestimation, since the African Youth Charter defines youths as those aged fifteen to thirty-five, placing 420 million individuals—one-third of Africa's population—in the youth category. If Africa and Africans as a people can influence or even reshape the world,[32] how much more can the young, who account for 33 percent of the African population? African children perform an important role that has gone mostly unnoticed.[33]

Despite living on a continent where young people are expected to be "*seen rather than heard*,"[34] young people all throughout Africa are increasingly raising their voices and advocating for climate change action and environmental issues.[35] These young climate activists provide a fresh

29. Sutton, "Social Justice Perspective on Youth," 617.
30. Sutton, "Social Justice Perspective on Youth," 617.
31. Corrigan, "Getting Youth Policy Right in Africa," n.p.
32. Knoetze, "African Youth, African Faith(s)," 1.
33. Beukes, "Youth, Faith and Environmental Consciousness in Africa," 3.
34. Nel, "Children Must Be Seen and Heard," 1.
35. Kosciulek, "Strengthening Youth Participation," 2.

viewpoint to the global discussion. Youths are critical in gaining these insights since they are the group most affected by climate change and hence the most likely to adapt to a climate-changed future.[36] Youth generally launch local climate initiatives, concentrating on topics that are most significant to their situations and experiences. Furthermore, they tend to focus on social justice issues—the surge of youth-led climate change activism in Africa includes social justice issues such as universal access to electricity, water management, bridging the digital divide, employment, and livelihood opportunities, as well as women and girls' empowerment and food security.[37] As a result, youth movements and activism on numerous topics impacting them are on the increase throughout the world, as they want a place at the table. Youth should be involved in primary places, and their voices should guide practice, and services should lead to their empowerment.

The slogan that young people and children should be seen and not heard has become problematic. A paradigm change is required to transition from believing that young people are tomorrow's leaders to believing that they are valued members of the religious community *now* and may make a useful contribution now. I believe that a paradigm shift is required to shift from the concept that young should only be recognized because of their potential usefulness for the future to the understanding that they are valued members of a community today and should make a significant contribution now. However, a paradigm change from *doing for* to *doing with* to *doing themselves* is also required.

Young individuals are often seen as disruptive, unruly, and untrustworthy by their peers. Nonetheless, African youth, according to Kosciulek,[38] are informed, enthusiastic, and engaged. Similarly, Beukes, emphasized why, owing to their unique skills and capacities, young people should be seen as critical role players and participants in the debate over the environmental issue.[39] According to Beukes, the youth see themselves as change agents capable of disturbing the status quo in a variety of ways; they have a history of contributing to change; they are comfortable being disruptive; the youth are technologically oriented, and so on.[40]

Effective participation and inclusion in climate-related policymaking forums and processes, on the other hand, continue to be a significant

---

36. Beukes, "Youth, Faith and Environmental Consciousness in Africa," 4.
37. Kosciulek, "Strengthening Youth Participation," 2.
38. Kosciulek, "Strengthening Youth Participation," 2–3.
39. Beukes, "Seen and Heard."
40. Beukes, "Seen and Heard," 5–6.

hindrance. This is due to a variety of circumstances. First, although public awareness of climate change is increasing, there is still a need for more comprehensive climate change education and capacity development that integrates local knowledge while contextualizing global change and its local implications. Much of the conversation seems to be on a high level, and much more has to be done to link it to the daily reality of innocent young people and their communities. Second, most decision-making locations are unavailable to young people since they are structured to accommodate the demands of older employees.[41]

Efforts to empower young people should not be limited to "once-off" programs or tokenism; rather, young people should be included in the process, not as objects but as main role-players. The notion of integrating the primary stakeholders engaged in the job at hand is acknowledged as the key to success in practically every scenario. For example, we would instantly doubt the efficiency of an organization that serves predominantly people of color if it was controlled completely by white people, or if a women's rights group was entirely directed by males. Similarly, if we are to maintain the integrity of our youth research, young people must be included in its creation. Involving young people in the change process will also guarantee that the choices made make sense for all stakeholders, including the viewpoint of those it is meant to benefit. When young people take their correct seat at any change table, they assert their legitimate status as respected and responsible citizens.

INVOLVED DUE TO FAITH OR RELIGION?

Now that it is clear that the youth are involved and why they are important interlocutors within this environmental and ecological discourse, somehow or another, the question of whether they are involved because of religious beliefs or spiritual motivation will be explored.

I have conducted a literature study on the question of motivational reasons for becoming involved. According to certain research, earlier family experiences, such as time spent outdoors, family appreciation for nature, and larger family norms are major predictors of environmentally friendly behaviors among young people.[42] These family experiences stimulate interest among young people in preserving nature and becoming young

---

41. Beukes, "Youth, Faith and Environmental Consciousness in Africa," 5.

42. Sivek, "Environmental Sensitivity"; Grønhøj and Thøgersen, "Action Speaks Louder Than Words"; Fung and Adams, "What Motivates Student Environmental Activists," 3.

environmental activists. Another motivation for young people to become activists is cultural factors. Cultural variables, such as surrounding oneself with like-minded individuals, also play a crucial influence on environmental activist behavior (for example, being a part of on-campus environmental organizations may help foster these behaviors as well).[43] Other research has shown that topic majors in schools or higher education institutions may have an impact on environmental attitudes and behaviors.[44] As a result, topics in school, college, and university contribute to the motivating reasons for becoming environmental activists.

Furthermore, among the countless causes, possible environmental effects, concern for future generations, and personal fulfilment are among the most prominent.[45] Concern for the environment and a readiness to act to defend it via activism stem from a variety of value orientations, which are broadly classified as egoistic, socio-altruistic, and biophilic.[46] Other research indicates that education, understanding of long-term environmental repercussions, and personal views may all impact interest in and engagement in environmental advocacy.[47] Recently, it has been discovered that activism predicts people's feelings of global citizenship and the belief that they are linked to others who share similar emotions.[48] A study by Phoebe Dolan also showed similar results to what already was mentioned. Nature connection via outdoor activities, family impact and mentoring, witnessing injustice in the community and world, and peer-to-peer learning are the four themes that Dolan discovered. These four became clear categories that sparked the motivation of young people.[49]

In the final empirical study that was conducted,[50] the reason for the youth to become involved in environmental issues can be summarized in the following table:[51]

---

43. Fung and Adams, "What Motivates Student Environmental Activists," 3; Chawla and Cushing, "Education for Strategic Environmental Behavior,"438.

44. Fung and Adams, "What Motivates Student Environmental Activists," 3.

45. Hansla et al., "Relationships Between."

46. Hansla et al., "Relationships Between"; cf. Fung and Adams, "What Motivates Student Environmental Activists," 2.

47. Marquart-Pyatt, "Explaining Environmental Activism across Countries"; cf. Fung and Adams, "What Motivates Student Environmental Activists," 2.

48. Reysen and Hackett, "Activism as a Pathway to Global Citizenship"; cf. Fung and Adams, "What Motivates Student Environmental Activists," 2.

49. Dolan, *Life Events Which Motivate Youth*, 1–32.

50. Fung and Adams, "What Motivates Student Environmental Activists," 2.

51. Fung and Adams, "What Motivates Student Environmental Activists," 2.

EXPERIENCE	Experiences and education from the past (which can be formal education, self-learning, learning from others, or indirect education) can make someone more or less likely to get involved in activism.
AWARENESS	Bringing an issue, idea, concept, problem, etc. to the attention of people by any means (talking to someone, reading, education, etc.).
SELF-IMPROVEMENT	Doing anything to improve one's own life, character, or self-interests.
PASSION	Doing something because you are interested in it or because you have a connection to it.
INCENTIVES	Being motivated to do something by something outside of yourself. Most of the time, this means getting something in return, but this is not a must-have.
PRACTICE/DESIRE	As a way to solve a problem, the desire to *"be the change you want to see."*
COMMUNITY	The desire to do something to help or connect with a community, or to include the community in one's cause.

From the various literature as well as the empirical research mentioned above, it is clear that the religious or spiritual motivation for becoming activists or involved as young people is missing or at least a scarce element in academic contributions. This was also the point made by Smith in her chapter, "Reconnecting with Earth: Ecospirituality as the Missing Dimension in Spirituality and Sustainability Education."[52] However, although this might be the case in academic contributions it is evident in church (denominational and congregational) reports, websites, and toolkits that various programs on youth and environmental consciousness are taking place on the grassroots level.

CONCLUSION

Over the past several decades, there has been an explosion in theological literature, study, institutional commitment, and public action demonstrating the links between religion and the environment.[53] The environmental catastrophe is a spiritual issue, hurting both the intensity and closeness of religious life.[54] Theologians can therefore put many theological and spiritual reasons forward for why religion in the ecological discourse is crucial. Yet,

  52. Smith, "Reconnecting with Earth."
  53. Gottlieb, "Introduction," 1.
  54. Gottlieb, "Introduction," 8.

from the findings of the literature and empirical studies that were conducted among young environmental activists, it is evident that the religious language and religious motivation among the youth for being involved are missing or at least scarce. Therefore, although Gottlieb[55] is of the opinion that if religious leaders begin to preach a green gospel, denouncing human abuse of nature for its impacts on both humans and nonhumans, it is likely to have a greater impact than remarks by a similar number of academics; this still remains for me a great concern for the theology and even religion in general. Does faith matter? Does religion matter? Does spirituality matter . . . for young activists at least in academic spheres and discourses?

BIBLIOGRAPHY

Bessant, Judith B. "Mixed Messages: Youth Participation and Democratic Practice." *Australian Journal of Political Science* 39 (2004) 387–404.

Beukes, Jacques W. "Seen and Heard: The Youth as Game-Changing Roleplayers in Climate Change and Environmental Consciousness—A South African Perspective." *HTS/ Theological Studies* 77 (2021) 1–8.

———. "Youth, Faith and Environmental Consciousness in Africa: A Practical Theology Research Imperative." *Stellenbosch Theological Journal* 7 (2021) 1–19.

Booysen, Susan. "Introduction." In *Fees Must Fall: Student Revolt, Decolonisation and Governance in South Africa*, edited by S. Booysen, 1–20. Johannesburg: Wits University Press, 2016.

Boulianne, Shelley, et al. "School Strike 4 Climate: Social Media and the International Youth Protest on Climate Change." *Media and Communication* 8 (2020) 208–18.

Chawla, Louise, and Debra Flanders Cushing. "Education for Strategic Environmental Behavior." *Environmental Education Research* 13 (2007) 437–52.

Chersich, M. F., et al. "Climate Change and Adolescents in South Africa: The Role of Youth Activism and the Health Sector in Safeguarding Adolescents' Health and Education." *South African Medical Journal* 109 (2019) 615–19.

Corrigan, Terence. "Getting Youth Policy Right in Africa." Africa Portal, Aug 11, 2017. https://www.africaportal.org/features/getting-youth-policy-right-africa/.

Dolan, Phoebe. *Life Events Which Motivate Youth to Become Climate Activists in Sydney and Canberra*. Independent Study Project (ISP) Collection, 2019.

Fung, Cadi Y., and Ellis A. Adams. "What Motivates Student Environmental Activists on College Campuses? An In-Depth Qualitative Study." *Social Sciences* 134 (2017) 1–15.

Gottlieb, Roger S. "Introduction: Religion and Ecology—What Is the Connection and Why Does It Matter?" In *The Oxford Handbook of Religion and Ecology*, edited by Roger Gottlieb, 1–18. Oxford: Oxford University Press, 2006.

Grønhøj, Alice, and John Thøgersen. "Action Speaks Louder Than Words: The Effect of Personal Attitudes and Family Norms on Adolescents' Pro-Environmental Behaviour." *Journal of Economic Psychology* 33 (2012) 292–302.

---

55. Gottlieb, "Introduction," 10.

Hansla, André, et al. "The Relationships between Awareness of Consequences, Environmental Concern, and Value Orientations." *Journal of Environmental Psychology* 28 (2008) 1–9.

Knoetze, Johannes J. "African Youth, African Faith(s), African Environment and Sustainable Development: A Missional Diaconal Calling." *HTS Theological Studies* 77 (2021) 1–8.

Kosciulek, Desirée. "Strengthening Youth Participation in Climate-Related Policymaking: Policy Briefing 225." . South African Institute of International Affairs, December 2020 https://media.africaportal.org/documents/Policy-Briefing-225-kosciulek.pdf.

Lee, Katharine, et al. "Youth Perceptions of Climate Change: A Narrative Synthesis." *WIREs Climate Change* 11.3 (May/Jun 2020) 11:e641. https://doi.org/10.1002/wcc.641.

Lethoko, Mankolo. "Children and Youth as Agents of Climate Change Impact in South Africa." *Commonwealth Youth and Development* 12 (2014) 75–91.

Marquart-Pyatt, Sandra T. "Explaining Environmental Activism across Countries." *Society & Natural Resources* 25 (2012) 683–99.

Mjiyakho, Yakhani Charlotte, et al. "Young People and the Climate Crisis: The Challenge of Building an Intersectional Justice Movement." *Daily Maverick*, Mar 7, 2021. https://www.dailymaverick.co.za/article/2021-03-07-young-people-and-the-climate-crisis-the-challenge-of-building-an-intersectional-justice-movement/.

Nel, Reggie. "Children Must Be Seen and Heard—Doing Postcolonial Theology with Children in a (Southern) African Reformed Church." *HTS Theological Studies* 72 (2016) 1–7.

Nkrumah, Bright. "Beyond Tokenism: The 'Born Frees' and Climate Change in South Africa." *International Journal of Ecology* (2021) 1–10.

Postman, Zoë, and Ashraf Hendricks. "South African Youth Take to the Streets over Climate Change: Hundreds Protest in Johannesburg and Cape Town." *Ground Up*, Jun 14, 2019. https://www.groundup.org.za/article/south-african-youth-take-streets-climate-change/.

Reysen, Stephen, and Justin Hackett. "Activism as a Pathway to Global Citizenship." *Social Science Journal* 54 (2017) 132–38.

Sabherwal, Anandita, et al. "The Greta Thunberg Effect: Familiarity with Greta Thunberg Predicts Intentions to Engage in Climate Activism in the United States." *Journal of Applied Social Psychology* 51 (2021) 321–33.

Sivek, Daniel J. "Environmental Sensitivity among Wisconsin High School Students." *Environmental Education Research* 8 (2002) 155–70.

Smith, Caroline. "Reconnecting with Earth: Ecospirituality as the Missing Dimension in Spirituality and Sustainability Education." In *International Handbook of Education for Spirituality, Care and Wellbeing*, edited by M. de Souza et al, 653–75. International Handbooks of Religion and Education 3. Dordrecht: Springer, 2009.

Stoecklin, Daniel. "The Transactional Horizons of Greta Thunberg." *Societies* 11 (2021) 1–24.

Sutton, Sharon Egretta. "A Social Justice Perspective on Youth and Community Development: Theorizing the Processes and Outcomes of Participation." *Children, Youth and Environments* 17 (2007) 616–45.

UNICEF. "16 Children, Including Greta Thunberg, File Landmark Complaint to the United Nations Committee on the Rights of the Child: Child Petitioners Protest

Lack of Government Action on Climate Crisis." Media release, Sep 23, 2019. https://www.unicef.org/turkey/en/press-releases/16-children-including-greta-thunberg-file-landmark-complaint-united-nations.

———. *Exploring the Impact of Climate Change on Children in South Africa*. Pretoria: UNICEF South Africa, 2011.

World Economic Forum. "10 Teenage Change-Makers at the Annual Meeting 2020." http://www3.weforum.org/docs/WEF_AM20_10_Teenage_Change_Makers_at_AM20_Brochure.pdf.

Chapter 7

Characterizing Pharaoh's Self-Destructive Politics alongside the Plagues and Politics of South Africa

Gavin Fernandes

INTRODUCTION

Those who seek divine spiritual reassurance from the Bible often struggle at what seems to be God manipulating Pharaoh for his own ends. The Plagues Narrative is part of a wider, overarching plot,[1] but concentrates on Pharaoh's recalcitrance in the face of Yahweh's justice. Concerned readers often read the narrative with a hyper-spiritual view of God's power over Pharaoh, as if God was pulling the strings of Pharaoh's heart as though he were a mere puppet. Many of their misconceptions arise because they fail to read the undercurrents of Pharaoh's own self-destructive politics within their original context.

In this chapter, I will be primarily surveying the literary events found in the Plagues Narrative and will draw a number of observations from a narratological perspective, especially looking at the sequence of events that led God to harden Pharaoh's heart. More importantly, I will show how divine

---

1. See, e.g., Utzschneider and Oswald, *Exodus 1–15*, 30.

patience wears thin only after a protracted "posturing" of Pharaonic politics that brings harm to his own people. I will also draw from narrative and political theory to show why God is justified to move to an ever-intensifying response to Pharaoh.

For contemporary spirituality, however, the ancient document must speak to a modern context. I write this chapter with some proficiency in the biblical text of the Hebrew Bible but as a newcomer to South African politics. "What intersection could there be," I asked myself, "between the politics of the leaders, the spirituality of the people, and the text on the page?" I opted to compare the plagues and politics of ancient Egypt alongside Pharaoh's stubbornness and pride to the malefactions of Jacob Zuma, and the effects that these have had on the country. I will explain why I have done so. Suffice it to say that I write this with the riots of July 2021 still fresh in my mind. That time has been billed as the country's "darkest hour." Indeed, it was the worst violence that South Africa had experienced since the end of apartheid. The aftermath of lost lives and material devastation were reminiscent of some scenes from the exodus disasters. I hope to apply my observations from the ancient text to the South African situation in order to offer my readers lessons for a renewed spiritual hope in a just God alongside the devastating effects of what has been regarded as Jacob Zuma's power ploys upon a weary nation.

It should be noted, in this article, because variant versification exists in part of the Exodus Hebrew text in comparison to the English text, both references are supplied. Because this is a scholarly article related to the Hebrew Bible/Old Testament, the first reference is the Hebrew text, the second is the English verse. Readers who are consulting an English Bible should refer to the number in square brackets for the verse number. So, Exod 8:8 [4] would mean 8:8 pertains to the Hebrew text and 8:4 to the English.

PHARAOH'S EGYPT

While Zuma has been proven to be incontrovertibly guilty of self-enrichment at the expense of the people he represented, it comes as a surprise to some that the biblical pharaoh arguably enjoys more sympathy despite the ideology of the Hebrew narrative itself which attempts to portray the Hebrew God as the greater victim and Pharaoh is its capricious and belligerent bully. On the one hand, there are those that would balk at the seeming one-sided nature of God's hardening against a powerless pharaoh,[2] or see the

---

2. E.g., Gunn, "Exodus 1–14," 81; Eslinger, "Freedom or Knowledge," 56–58.

events of the narrative as a "gruesome game"[3] for God, himself "cast as an incalculable despot who penalizes the very error he wishes to bring about."[4] On the other hand, are those of the Judeo-Christian faiths who struggle with what seems to be God manipulating Pharaoh for his own ends.[5] Christian readers frequently come to read the events of the exodus lopsidedly. Many are challenged by the New Testament book of Romans (10:17-18), in which the apostle Paul deliberately highlights the sovereignty of God but also purposefully omits Pharaoh's own responsibility:

> For the Scripture says to Pharaoh, "For this very purpose I have raised you up, that I might show my power in you, and that my name might be proclaimed in all the earth." So, then he has mercy on whomever he wills, and he hardens whomever he wills. (Rom 9:17-18 ESV)

This leads concerned Christian readers to look back at the exodus story and unwittingly adopt what might be termed as a hyper-spiritual view of God's power over Pharaoh, as if God was pulling the strings of Pharaoh's heart, with the Egyptian king being a mere puppet. An earlier, influential article by Beale, for example, continues to be used to justify such a perspective.[6] Beale writes:

> It is never stated in Exod 4-14 that Yahweh hardens Pharaoh in judgment because of any prior reason or condition residing in him. Rather, as stated in the exegetical conclusion, the only purpose or reason given for the hardening is that it would glorify Yahweh. Therefore, the divine hardening of Pharaoh was unconditional. All that can be said is that Yahweh deemed it necessary to include Pharaoh's disobedient refusal in the historical plan, which was to glorify himself.[7]

If we leave the fact that Beale tries hard to make the divine hardening non-contingent on—and independent of—Pharaoh's actions, his perspective still gives the impression that no injustices in Pharaoh, to begin with, led to Yahweh's hardening.

---

3 Houtman, *Exodus*, 103.

4. Krašovec, *Reward, Punishment, and Forgiveness*, 79.

5. McAffee, "Heart of Pharaoh in Exodus 4-15," 331n1; McGinnis, "Hardening of Pharaoh's Heart," 43-64.

6. See, e.g., the currently accessible 2012 article by Justin Taylor, "Hardening of Pharaoh's Heart," hosted by the influential evangelical *Gospel Coalition* blog (TGC).

7. Beale, "Exegetical and Theological Consideration," 129-54.

Jewish readers are equally flummoxed by the narrative. Maimonides believed that no external influence or compulsion is exerted upon a person that constrains him to be either virtuous or vicious.[8] He interprets the hardening of Pharaoh by saying that God prevented the king from allowing the Israelites to leave Egypt on account of his *earlier* free sins of afflicting the Israelites (Exod 1:10).[9] While this places the responsibility squarely within Pharaoh's own behavior, it raises a further problem because Pharaoh ostensibly did not know Yahweh earlier (Exod 5:2) and the Israelites would have been as any other slaves to him.

What I intend to do in the first part of this article is to redress, to some measure, the aforementioned imbalance by incorporating a perspective not only of God's action but also of human behavior; in this specific case, Pharaoh's own politics as destructive to Egypt and its people as a whole, and largely prior to God's hardening. To my mind, it seems that many of the frustrations of Jewish and Christian readers with this narrative's seeming divine determinism arise on account of "missing the wood for the trees," of missing out on its subtle details as to who really is the greater manipulator between Yahweh and Pharaoh. A careful reading of the characterization in the narrative, taken within the political context of the events portrayed, would allay such frustrations.

It is true that a great many explanations already exist which highlight the fact that Pharaoh's own actions must not be discounted. However, these explanations frequently, if not always, fail to analyze especially how Pharaoh's politics bring harm to his own people, leading to God's just reprisals not only as deliverer of the Hebrew people but as judge (of all the earth) of Pharaoh as deceitful king of his people.

Even before God's power is displayed in the Plagues Narrative, in 3:19, Yahweh assesses Pharaoh as a determined individual who would not change "except by a strong arm."[10] Yahweh's assessment of Pharaoh as having a coarse heart is confirmed when the king burdens his Hebrew slaves with greater impositions in response to Moses's and Aaron's opening demand (Exod 5:5–9). Depending on the meaning of the phrase ʿ*am hā ʾāreṣ* "the people of the land," the Egyptian workers may also be directly affected by the new encumbrances.[11] In any case, whether the phrase includes the

---

8. Maimonides, *Eight Chapters of Maimonides on Ethics*, 86.

9. Maimonides, *Mishneh Torah* (*Seffer Madda, Teshuva*, ch. 6.3).

10. Although Propp points out that "the owner of the arm in 3:19 is somewhat uncertain. If it is Yahweh . . . we note that in the ancient Near East, a deity's 'arm' connoted his power to cause wonders, often catastrophic" (Propp, *Exodus 1–18*, 207).

11. There is much debate concerning the phrase ʿ*am hā ʾāreṣ* in 5:5, whether it might refer to the Egyptians or the Hebrews. See Propp, *Exodus 1–18*, 254.

Egyptians or not, Pharaoh's order is not just an act of retaliation against the Hebrews but that of flouting the Egyptian code of *ma'at* (justice). While it is true that the very same concept of *ma'at* was responsible for leading the Egyptian rulers to ruthlessly crush any internal and external rebellion,[12] the narrative suggests that Pharaoh's act of imposition is a step too far. He takes out his rage not on Moses and Aaron but on his own work/slave force, incapacitating them for his own building projects. While Fretheim recognizes that "the story is best heard by viewing it from the various aspects of the oppressive system,"[13] he focuses purely on the oppression against the Israelites. However, this misses a vital element of harshness towards Egypt and its people. At the outset, the narrative introduces to us here the possibility of Pharaoh's self-destructive character, against his country *as a whole*, not just against the Hebrews. His orders affect the Egyptians as much as the foreign workforce. For starters, they hinder progress on Egyptian building projects (perhaps similar to building projects in 1:11, given the extensive brickwork). In addition, the Egyptian *nōgəśê* "taskmasters" of Pharaoh are under pressure, as much as the *šōṭərê* "officers" of the Hebrews are, to produce quotas of bricks despite the lack of raw materials such as straw (Exod 5:14–16). Finally, Pharaoh's unorthodox command goes against Egyptian conventional wisdom which stated, for another scenario, "Do not make the labourer wretched with taxes; enrich him and he will be there for you next year."[14] Extreme frustration is evident in the cries of the foremen to Pharaoh, "Why do you treat your servants like this?" (Exod 5:15) suggesting this was highly unusual for a Pharaoh. Other Egyptian texts, in speaking about excessive impositions on the people as a sign that the ruler's "heart is for himself,"[15] also suggest that Pharaoh's lack of beneficence and disregard for his own kingdom are hinted at here and, I will argue, be confirmed by the narrative as a polemic for God's just opposition.

The signs and wonders of the Hebrew God begin on a low-level footing. The first two signs—the serpents and leprous hand—are devised to end any hostilities before they begin.[16] Pharaoh is but to concede his own impotence to recreate the signs, and all would be over. The narrative, however, runs into an extended battle of wills between Pharaoh on the one hand and his Hebrew counterparts on the other. The first plague, the transformation of

12. Cox, "Expanding the History of the Just War," 372ff. esp. 374.
13. Fretheim, *Interpretation: Exodus*, 84.
14. Parkinson, *Voices from Ancient Egypt*, 71.
15. Black, *World History of Ancient Political Thought*, 23.
16. Although the sign of the leprous hand is not mentioned in Exod 7, I assume that by saying "Moses . . . went to Pharaoh and did just as the LORD commanded" (7:10), the narrator inherently includes the earlier directive to enact the sign of leprosy (4:6–9).

the Nile into blood, is reproduced by the Egyptian magicians, perhaps simulated in some inferior way, and is enough for Pharaoh to retain his pride and stand his ground. It is, however, easy to miss the fact that the narrative also appears to characterize him with an unwholesome self-centeredness beyond his attitude towards the Hebrews and their deity. He also bears an oblivious disregard towards his own people for it is said that "Pharaoh turned and went into his house *and did not take even this to heart*" while his own people "all the Egyptians dug along the Nile for water to drink, for they could not drink the water of the Nile" (7:23–24). Such a characterization is richer and more complex than the simpler us-versus-them scenario that Pharaoh is often characterized with. It develops the earlier, nascent portrayal of a self-destructive leader, who not only resists the Hebrews and their deity, but his own people's plight and later wisdom.

Pharaoh's character is not presented as consistently degrading, however. A few ameliorations offer the reader additional suspense. The first is the most crucial and occurs when the royal magicians are able to reproduce their own version of the second plague (the frog pestilence), whatever that might be, but are unable to exterminate the verminous swell that originates from God. It is at this point, after witnessing four signs (i.e., two plagues) that Pharaoh makes a dramatic U-turn and engages in some crucial political brinkmanship in the narrative. He summons Moses and Aaron, ostensibly in public, in order to strike a deal.

McAffee says, "The fact that Pharaoh exercises this resolve to resist the wishes of a foreign deity may best be interpreted in the religio-political setting of a deified king."[17] One can agree with McAffee's assessment. Yet, this same religio-political setting must be seen to operate in respect to Pharaoh's climbdown also. Despite having previously refuted the Hebrew God with the words "who is Yahweh?" (5:2), the summons of Pharaoh now tacitly acknowledges both his existence and his greatness. After nonchalantly dismissing them earlier, his action legitimizes Moses and Aaron as ambassadors for the Hebrews and their God and should be interpreted as an act of political diplomacy.

The narrative world presupposes the historical existence of a framework of diplomatic protocols. The world of the ancient Near East included a sophisticated system for handling affairs of state and negotiating treaties. It incorporated a framework of international law and protocol that had developed since the third millennium BCE and that had crystallized into what historians today call the First International Age. This is essentially the historical background of the narrative world. Correspondence from that

---

17. McAffee, "Heart of Pharaoh," 335.

period details complex diplomatic and economic exchanges between the "Great Powers" of the time.[18] It is inherent in any framework of laws or rules that they bind those who come within their aegis. In that ancient world, natural calamities, such as the narrative describes, were frequently attributed to divine justice. Steps were subsequently taken to make legal reparation in light of them. For instance, in a text called the *Plague Prayers*, the Hittite king Mursilis identifies the cause of a plague affecting Hatti (1350–1325 BCE) as the breach of a treaty with Egypt by his father, Suppiluliuma I.[19] It is this perspective that leads him to assuage the gods by making reparations to Egypt and returning Egyptian prisoners.

Pharaoh makes his own plague prayer to Yahweh, mediated by Moses, in 8:4 [8:8]. The request, "pray (עתר) to Yahweh," is reminiscent of other prayers in trouble such as Gen 25:21; Job 33:26, etc. Moreover, it is made amply clear from the dialogue that it is Pharaoh himself who initiates diplomatic relations and straightaway names the compensation for services rendered. "If you do this," he effectively says, "I will let your people go." It is important to understand that Pharaoh's act of capitulation is politically risky because he has effectively appealed to the honor of Yahweh, throwing his entire country upon divine mercy and, in return, agreed to cede to the demand of Moses. This arrangement is reminiscent of agreements made in the ancient Near East that involve oversight by a deity. Breaking this kind of diplomatic treaty or oath, for instance, was understood not just as a political betrayal but a violation of the sacred. Sanders provides examples of the Hittites and Assyrians who he says, "saw their own violations of oaths as possible causes of divine anger against themselves *and their country*."[20] The aggrieved country and its pantheon were entitled to utilize any means at their disposal to punish the offending country.[21] Would this, however, apply to Pharaoh's speech in the narrative?

Pharaoh's language in 8:4 [8] appears not to be that of a standard oath, treaty, or covenant but it nonetheless hints at something more than just a gentleman's agreement. A patron-client arrangement could be considered based on mutual exchange of services (removal of plague = removal from slavery) except that scholars restrict such relationships to a longer term, not just to a single transaction.[22] Nevertheless, from the Hebrew word *śîm* in 8:8

---

18. Irvin, "Regional Foundations for Internationalism."
19. Gurney, "Hittite Prayers of Mursili II"; Singer, *Hittite Prayers*, 57–60.
20. Sanders, "God Appeased by Homicide?," 251–54 (emphasis mine).
21. Cox, "Expanding the History of the Just War," 374.
22. See, e.g., Westbrook, "Patronage in the Ancient Near East," 211. However, consider Jonah 1:16 where non-Israelites appear to offer sacrifices and vows to Yahweh for having been given safe passage.

[12], we learn that this agreement has been "set," "arranged" or "fixed." The word itself can be used for a more serious arrangement such as in Job 17:3 where a pledge can be "set." It could, therefore, point to a *pacta sunt servanda* element within the arrangement between Pharaoh and Moses, where agreements are binding. In any event, the principle of *reciprocity*, a cardinal virtue underpinning *ma'at*, would have certainly applied and Pharaoh's failure to reciprocate in kind would be seen in Egypt as unethical and a serious insult to the deity.[23] It is also important to note that Pharaoh's agreement in 8:4 [8] clearly functions as an act of compliant appeasement to God's earlier demand and threat, namely, "But if you refuse . . . I will plague *all your country with frogs*" (7:27 [8:2]). This is the first introduction of a divine demand to comply with accompanying consequences for the entirety of Egypt, following refusal.[24] In Pharaoh's subsequent act of diplomacy to appease Yahweh, should he renege on the set terms, he will have given the deity a legitimate reason to destroy "all his country" with a worse plague. Pharaoh has essentially obligated himself diplomatically to Moses and his deity, and placed his own life and entire country in Moses's (and ultimately Yahweh's) hands. To put this another way, after this second plague, because Pharaoh breaks his agreement according to the diplomatic conventions of the time, God is entitled to afflict Egypt further, and even hold Pharaoh's own life forfeit if he so chooses. He is also able to immediately make good—should he choose to do so—on his very first threat to Pharaoh: that of slaying his firstborn son (4:22–23) if his own "firstborn," the Hebrew people, are not released.

When the frogs are exterminated in accordance with the agreement between Pharaoh and Moses, the narrative shocks the reader that the former "hardened his heart" (8:11 [15]) despite the gravity of the situation. This first appearance of Pharaoh's hardening his heart phrase is now understood better within the orbit of broken disagreement and contrasting integrity. For the latter, Ford sums up nicely:

> YHWH does not wait until Pharaoh has released the people before he removes his plague; rather he responds to a request for relief by bringing relief (8:9 [13]; cf. 2:23–25). Pharaoh, in contrast, responds to a request for relief from suffering by increasing that suffering (5:3, 6–9, 17–18) . . .[25]

God is well within his right to retaliate against both Pharaoh and his country. Yet, the retaliation is surprisingly mild. No blood is forfeit but instead

---

23. See Karenga, *Maat—The Moral Ideal in Ancient Egypt*, 264.
24. Unless the threat of slaying Pharaoh's "firstborn son" in 4:22–23 refers to Egypt.
25. Ford, *God, Pharaoh and Moses*, 139.

a plague of lice (or gnats) is discharged (8:12 [16]). Still, the said plague obviously tests the ability of the court magicians, and they are unable to reproduce the lice, thereby consigning defeat (8:14 [18]). Out of frustration and fear, they acknowledge it is the ʾeṣbaʿ ʾĕlōhîm "the finger of God" that is responsible (8:15 [19]). This phrase occurs elsewhere, within both the Hebrew Bible and the New Testament as the very personal, unmediated action of the deity.[26] Here, it offers us valuable insight into the magicians' recognition of not only the Hebrew God's divine instrumentality but his punitive response. The "finger," as also the "arm," of an ancient Near Eastern deity's connoted his power to cause wonders, often catastrophic—a common perception in the cultures of that time.[27] Further divine reprisals, including a loss of Egyptian human life, would not just be feared but possibly even expected by the Egyptians at this point. In any case, the narrative presents here a first instance where Pharaoh's people openly acknowledge, without fear of their king, the superiority of the Hebrew God over Pharaoh and his judicial hand against him.

Pharaoh should at this point yield to Yahweh post-haste, but the narrative further shocks the reader by introducing a complication to the plot: Pharaoh hardens his heart yet again. Instead of being attentive to his people's responses, it appears he chooses to ignore them (Exod 8:15 [19]).[28] Thus, this pharaoh is portrayed as the polar opposite of the idealistic one. As Antony Black notes, "The highest praise was reserved for those pharaohs who had rescued their country from disaster, disunity, or disorder."[29] It was the pharaoh's proper moral conduct which kept the cosmos running. Not only was the ideal pharaoh meant to be ruthless subjugating foreign enemies, but he was to temper this by being beneficent towards his own subjects. One famous Egyptian text says of Egypt's king, "He is a lord of kindness, great of sweetness. Through love he has conquered. His city loves him more than its own members. It rejoices at him more than at its God. Men and women pass by, exulting at him."[30] Ironically, the biblical pharaoh has

---

26. The phrase appears in relation to the two tablets of the Testimony given to Moses (Exod 31:18; Deut 9:10). In the Christian New Testament, it is also used by Jesus, who used it in relation to the miraculous casting out of demons (Luke 11:19; cf. John 8:6).

27. Propp, *Exodus 1–18*, 207.

28. By "them" here, I understand the narrative to be referring to his own people. There is, however, an ambiguity because the phrase "as the Lord said" might point back to Exod 7:4 denoting that the "them," to whom Pharaoh does not listen, also refers back to Moses and Aaron.

29. Black, *World History of Ancient Political Thought*, 23.

30. Parkinson, *Tale of Sinuhe*, 30–31, lines B65–70.

not only lost the gods' favor and has failed to subjugate the foreign powers, but he is beginning to lose the goodwill of a growing number of his own people because of his behavior.

Pharaoh's obstinacy has now set him and his country on a perilous course. Failing to heed the voice of his people, he foolhardily sets the diplomatic stage for a further challenge by the Hebrew God. Again, despite having every right to retaliate against Pharaoh, God for his part exhibits further restraint and presents a warning of a plague of flies,[31] a surprisingly light reprisal for a how a typical vengeful god might respond. After it happens, Pharaoh attempts to salvage the situation by offering to allow the Hebrews to sacrifice *within the land* (8:21 [25]). This is essentially political backpedaling: "to make a preposterous policy and then be forced—by opposition, by circumstance, by the laws of physics—to retreat"[32] for he has earlier agreed, saying, "I will send the people *away*" (8:4 [8]) which would mean he agreed to Moses's demand of three days into the wilderness (cf. 3:18; 5:3). Moses refuses and Pharaoh agrees to do what he has already promised earlier, saying, "I will send you [all] away" (Exod 8:24 [28]), but then immediately fudges his words by saying, "only you must not go very far away." One presumes this means beyond Egypt's borders but less than a three days' journey outside.

Moses accepts this new (or renewed) agreement but solemnly warns his counterpart, "only let not Pharaoh cheat again by not letting the people go to sacrifice to the LORD" (8:25 [29]). This is further evidence of a binding *pacta sunt servanda*. The word *hā-ṭêl* used here generally means "deceive" but it can have the sense of "cheating" when reneging on an agreement. An example of its use is that of Gen 31:7 where an agreement was made between Jacob and Laban, but the latter cheated the former. It suggests an agreement has been made between Pharaoh and Moses and the former is given another chance to keep it—undeserving of Pharaoh but gracious on the part of Moses and God.

It must also be noted that Moses is no simple messenger in Pharaoh's eyes. Liverani explains the diplomatic mindset of the time, saying, "Genuine diplomatic messages are entrusted to people of rank, high palace officials or relatives of the king. Such people are well acquainted with the problems under discussion and thus capable of adding explanations and even negotiating agreements."[33] Pharaoh would have seen Moses as a full diplomat of the Hebrews; if not at first, at least afterwards when the power of the god

---

31. Many Jewish sources, however, take it as "beasts." See Rendsburg, "Beasts or Bugs," 9–23.

32. Feffer, "Art of the Back Pedal."

33. Liverani, *International Relations in the Ancient Near East*, 72.

they worshiped had become apparent. By now, it should be amply clear that any affront to the terms set by Moses would be an affront to God himself.[34]

With yet another rapprochement, it seems hostilities will soon end. However, the narrative signals to the reader that Pharaoh has sealed his and his people's fate by reneging on *another* promise when it states that he did it *gam bappa ʿam hazzōʾt* "on this occasion also" (8:28 [32]). With a second breach of agreement, Pharaoh should now incur the unmitigated wrath of an ancient Near Eastern deity and monarch scorned. Politics sometimes did permit a "two-strikes-and-you're-out" policy. We find this enshrined in specific cases within legal codes[35] and kings would sometimes give an offender or treaty-breaker another chance.[36] Thereafter, by reciprocity, any reprisal would be swift and its blow of unbounded proportions. The law of reciprocity expressed in the Book of Kheti says, "A blow is repaid for its like, for every action there is a response."[37]

This is why it comes as a surprise that God's reaction is to issue another ultimatum with a further chance. This time, there is an escalation of the threat in the form of a *deber kābēd məʾōd* "a very heavy pestilence" (9:3). The heaviness of the plague is meant to correspond to the heaviness of Pharaoh's heart. To be clear, death itself does not make an appearance until after five plagues or until Pharaoh has rejected seven signs in total. When death does come, it is initially upon the livestock only, to highlight the restraint of God. To further reinforce God's fairness and patience, we are told, "And the LORD set a time . . ." (9:5). In other words, Pharaoh is given opportunity to come up with some kind of mitigating plan for the loss of animal life in the land. In doing something, no matter how little, he would be showing his honorable side and laudably laying down his ego for the good of his country's economy and his people's livelihoods. The narrative maintains a silence, however. It seems as if the king does nothing. He does act but only ex-post facto, *after* Yahweh makes good his warning (9:6), dispatching a delegation the next day to investigate whether the Hebrews' livestock had survived (9:7; cf. 9:4). Despite the confirmation, the reader is surprised to learn he hardens his heart yet again.

After the death of animal life, for the sixth plague, one would expect God to finally strike at human life in Egypt, and sure enough, we do have

---

34. This is also evident in the words "I have made you a God to pharaoh" in Exod 7:1.

35. Consider, for example, Exod 21:29—"If, however, an ox was previously in the habit of goring and its owner has been warned, yet he does not confine it and it kills a man or a woman, the ox shall be stoned and its owner also shall be put to death."

36. E.g., Solomon with Adonijah (1 Kgs 1:52; 2:22–23) and Shimei (1 Kgs 2:36–46).

37. Karenga, *Maat*, 58, 248, 300, 363.

next the beginning of human affliction proper (9:9). People will now be afflicted in a way that previous plagues did not because human life will experience intense pain for the first time although life itself will be spared. A similar escalation is witnessed in Job 2:4–6, when Satan makes a distinction between the sufferings of Job on account of the death of his livestock and children, and his personal affliction from painful skin lesions. Permitting the latter, God adds, "but spare his life."

It is at this time, following this plague, that we are told that God hardens Pharaoh's heart (Exod 9:12). Let us be clear that it is only *after* eight signs (or six plagues), *after* Pharaoh repeatedly hardens his own heart, do we have the verse that the New Testament employs, "But the Lord hardened the heart of Pharaoh" (9:12). Despite the determinism that is often read from Paul's letter, the realized, persistent, selfish actions of Pharaoh render any hard determinism inert. Pharaoh is no puppet and has exercised his own will, according to the narrative, in a selfish manner.

Returning to the narrative, we find that divine patience has worn thin and now both animal and human life is in jeopardy from an unprecedented hailstorm. Themes of escalation and divine forbearance can be found in the warning for the seventh plague of hail, "For this time, I will send all my plagues on you yourself, and on your servants and your people . . ." (9:14). God is himself at pains to say, "For by now I could have put out my hand and struck you and your people with pestilence, and you would have been cut off from the earth" (9:15). Forbearance is reemphasized through the warning which enables any and all to take shelter. Despite the warning, the king again does nothing. At the same time, an irony is presented in that Pharaoh, whose job it is to control chaos, now fosters it, and it is left to "whoever feared the word of the Lord among the servants of Pharaoh" to act upon God's warning (9:20). Once again, we find a number, if not all, of Pharaoh's people defying his own example to act out of step with their leader. Egypt at this time is portrayed to be a divided nation, with some following their leader's policies in doing nothing, others acting against him by heeding the warning. For a second time, Pharaoh's people act more wisely than he does. Although it is not made explicit, the implication of the seventh plague's aftermath is that there has been loss of human life (compare vv. 19, 21, and 25), not just injury. If this is so, this would be the first time that human life has been struck.

The narrative at this point suggests the disregard of Pharaoh not only for the Hebrew God and his directive but for his own people. He has left them to their own devices instead of bringing order in the community. Moreover, his characterization of Pharaoh's insensitivity towards the already precarious situation faced by his own people, implicating them as well as him. It is true that he calls again for Moses and Aaron, saying, "This time I have sinned" (9:27) and that the phrase Pharaoh uses is the typical phrase of a chastised king who subjugates himself to a superior king or a god within the aforementioned diplomatic framework. Ancient Near Eastern kings were mindful not to find themselves on the wrong side of the gods and quickly recanted over their infractions. An Assyrian text, the "Sin of Sargon," highlights how King Sargon ostensibly angered the gods by the breaking of a treaty. We find this phrase used by other kings such as Abimelech (20:9); David (2 Sam 12:13); Hezekiah (2 Kgs 18:14); and Saul (1 Sam 15:24). The irony, however, in Pharaoh's contrition is that he has "sinned" not once but many times. Despite his apparent humility, he is minimizing his own faults because he has broken his agreement many times over. He further minimizes his faults by hiding behind his people, saying, "I and my people are *in the wrong*," literally *hā-rə-šā-'îm* "the evil ones" (9:27). This statement is a blatant fudge since the narrative has already informed us that many of his people were sensible, even obeying the Hebrew God against their king's example. Again, Pharaoh undermines *ma'at* by his speech[38] and is presented as an apotheosis of dishonor, the putrid leader of his people. Lest anyone doubt that the characterization of Pharaoh as callous king is intensified here, the narrative doubles down on the king's dishonor by having his own people call out his obduracy, openly challenging him, "Do you not yet understand that Egypt is ruined?" (10:7). Such is their loss of respect for their pharaoh.

Countering the hard determinism that creeps into religious readings of Pharaoh's hardening, Fretheim makes an important observation at this point, that

> ... an act of hardening does not make one totally or permanently impervious to outside influence; it does not turn the heart off and on like a faucet. This may be illustrated by God's hardening of the heart of Pharaoh's servants (10:1; cf. 9:34). In view of this, their response in 10:7 is striking. Though God's hardening has occurred, they see the negative impact on Egypt, are open to a different future for Israel, and urge Pharaoh to change his ways.[39]

This shows that these servants are not mere "pawns," as Isbell calls them.[40] Indeed, they will later be depicted as being more favorable towards the

---

38. Ma'at, in the context of urging truthfulness, was commanded in the Egyptian religious texts; e.g., "Speak Maat (truth) let it (cling) to your speech." See in Lichtheim, *Late Egyptian Wisdom Literature*, 78.13, 15.

39. Fretheim, *Exodus*, 97.

40. Isbell, "Exodus 1–2 in the Context of Exodus 1–14," 45.

expulsion of the people, for the sake of preserving their own country, than Pharaoh himself (Exod 12:33–36).

In the closing drama surrounding the remaining plagues, Pharaoh continues to harden his heart (10:20), he will once more fudge on the nature of his own "sin" (10:17), and twice more fudge who (and what) among the Hebrews is to be allowed to leave Egypt (8–11; 24–27), pretending he hasn't already agreed the terms and scope of their exodus. Finally, by disallowing Moses to appear before him after the ninth plague (10:28), Pharaoh's self-destructiveness, which began with harsher impositions upon his own slave force, culminates in his destroying his own "early warning system" for what will be the deadliest plague for his own home. Early warnings, thus far, preceded the first (7:15–18), fourth (8:16–19 [20–23]), and seventh plagues (9:13–19). The pattern entails an early warning for the tenth, the next in the sequence. Yet, Pharaoh preemptively prevents its delivery, and the final plague will take his own firstborn. Without reading the narrative in its totality, we feel sorry for him here, perhaps even outraged at what we might perceive to be the Hebrew God's bomber diplomacy. The narrative, however, actually presents a long-in-the-tooth response to Pharaoh's own obduracy and self-destructiveness beginning with the *lex talionis* warning as early as in 4:22–23, "if you refuse to let him [Israel] go, behold, I will slay your firstborn son."[41]

CONCLUSIONS IN READING THE PLAGUES NARRATIVE

Egyptologist Jan Assmann thinks one major plague would have fulfilled the function of compensating the Hebrews for their suffering by punishing their Egyptian tormentors. So, "Why ten of them?"[42] he asks. The reason, of course, is that just as narratives in general have several goals, the Plagues Narrative also has more purposes than just vindicating the Hebrews. Over the course of the plagues, and apart from other functions that could be mentioned, three can be enumerated which are relevant to our focus.

First, the narrative characterizes Pharaoh as a king with total disregard for the loss of life that comes before. In other words, the narrative confirms that when Pharaoh witnessed the loss of life among the people in the seventh plague of hail, he hardens his heart, but only because his own heir was

---

41. However, rather than the conditional construction "if you refuse . . ." this has also been read as an oracle of certainty: "but you refused . . . behold I will kill . . ."; see, e.g., Johnstone, "Reading Exodus in Tetrateuch and Pentateuch," 20.

42. Assmann, "Exodus and Memory," 9.

lost, he relents. God is seen to preserve his people's suffering in contrast to Pharaoh who lets it happen.

Second, because of Pharaoh's self-destructive pride and selfishness, God as the judge of all the earth is justified to strike him as dishonorable shepherd of Pharaoh's own people. This is the point which I believe is discussed the least but should be highlighted more as a crucial aspect in the interpretation of Pharaoh's obduracy in the face of God's hardening.[43] Assmann rightly recognizes that the plagues denude Pharaoh of his divinity and he appears as an ineffectual tyrant of grotesque hubris again and again.[44] However, I would argue that Pharaoh is portrayed as ineffectual and self-destructive, from the time he introduces *isfet* (disorder, injustice) in 5:5–9 and fails to establish *ma'at* thereafter.

Third, the narrative has also brought to the fore that the *ma'at* of Pharaoh is not as good as that of the fairness and justice of the Hebrew God. Although, as Assmann notes, "Pharao *verkörpert die Gerechtigkeit* (Ma'at)"[45]—Pharaoh is meant to be the very *embodiment* of *ma'at*. However, his ploys and posturing, his backpedaling and constant pretense in the narrative reveal his dishonorable politics. The Hebrew God, on the other hand is consistent, clear, conservative, and restrained even for the kind of divine reprisal that is to be expected by the Egyptians. The tenth plague is not the first time that human life is taken but it does come well after the eighth and (from the perspective of Egyptian religio-political culture) is remarkably tardy.

JACOB ZUMA'S SOUTH AFRICA

Before I begin to draw some parallels with Pharaoh's Egypt and Zuma's South Africa, I offer a few disclaimers. First, I recognize that narratives in the media have generally depicted current events as a struggle between two opposing forces: on the one side are a network of dishonorable politicians and other individuals centered on Zuma, all bent on pillaging and self-enrichment; on the other is a band of honorable politicians and citizens intent on rebuilding institutions and the rule of law. This is too simplistic. Even though singling Zuma out as the figurehead of corruption is done

---

43. Although Bills comes close in recognizing that the narrative functions to show that Pharaoh has transgressed against Yahweh's creation order and that "the plagues are an appropriate revocation of Pharaoh's ma'at." See Bills, *Theology of Justice in Exodus*, 120–70.

44. Assmann, "Pharaoh's Divine Role in Maintaining Ma'at (Order)."

45. Assmann, *Exodus: Die Revolution der Alten Welt*, 288 (emphasis mine).

widely in South Africa's media, the country's problems have been shown to run much deeper than him,[46] and have preceded him. Second, I have only lately become aware that the story of the exodus has had something of a controversial history in the consciousness of South Africans. West notes that "since its arrival in Southern Africa, the Bible has been a site of struggle, though often in more complex ways than most post-colonial analysis has acknowledged."[47] Certainly, the exodus narrative of fleeing to the promised land was woven into the self-identity of the Afrikaner in both the Great Trek and the Centenary *Tweede Trek*.[48] It has been used in the construction and justification of apartheid with the advent of the National Party as well as in attempts to dismantle it, for example, by black South Africans who took Mandela to be a new Moses.[49] My own analysis of the narrative and its application to current affairs is entirely devoid of any reliance upon its historical use (or abuse). All was unknown to me until *after* I began working on a comparison between Zuma and the pharaoh of the exodus. Finally, I am fully aware, of course, that Zuma is no longer on the "throne." Technically he is no longer "pharaoh." Yet, he is clearly somebody more significant than a mere has-been politician. He evidently still holds a power base and commands a substantial following. It is for this reason he continues to represent—at this time at least—the ideal candidate for an emblematic, obstinate Pharaoh.

I am certainly not the first to compare social issues in Africa with the biblical stories. A comparative interpretive methodology has characterized African interpretation for decades.[50] Neither—it turns out—am I the first to compare Zuma to the pharaoh of the exodus. This pride of place goes to others in posterity.[51] One of these insightful predecessors is journalist Toby Shapshak, who compares Nelson Mandela to the pharaoh from the Bible that welcomes the Israelites into Egypt; the Israelites represent South Africa's new democracy after apartheid and Zuma is the evil new pharaoh

---

46. As evidenced in von Holdt, *Political Economy of Corruption*.

47. West, *Stolen Bible*, 445.

48. I thank Khegan Delport of Hugenote Kollege for enlightening me as to the use of the exodus narrative in Afrikaner history.

49. Gunda, "Understanding the Role of the Exodus."

50. Five comparative approaches are delineated by West. The second is perhaps the closest to my approach although I am employing literary criticism rather than historical-critical method. My concern is to primarily allow the biblical text to inform contemporary African life rather than the other way round. See West, "Interrogating the Comparative Paradigm," 47–48.

51. E.g., Ekpo, "Pharaoh Who Does Not Know Joseph."

who enslaves the Israelites while sitting pretty in his palace.[52] The biblical pharaoh's exercise of power can be defined as one of tyranny, as opposed to despotism;[53] its characterization in the narrative is essentially a form of government that breaks its own rules because Pharaoh contravenes the code of *ma'at* and several times he ignores the good of his own people for his own self-respect. This is the very starting point that Chipkin and Swilling take to describe the shadowy process of state capture by Zuma in South Africa which, they argue, "became more and more tyrannical as it set itself against the Constitution and the rule of law in an effort to capture the state."[54] Shapshak similarly laments, "The tragedy is that our leaders . . . have forgotten their people. They have forgotten us."[55]

Zuma certainly appears to be guilty of ignoring the good of the very people who he served. In an address at the Rhema Bible Church in 2009, Zuma quotes from one of the favorite books, Exodus chapter 3, "I have indeed seen the misery of my people in Egypt. I have heard them crying out . . . I am concerned about their suffering."[56] Zuma went on to make the pointed assertion that "the Exodus from Egypt has always symbolised the liberatory character of the church." Perhaps. However, just as the biblical pharaoh who, on the face of things, stood for truth and justice is discovered to be a prevaricator, unconcerned with the sufferings of the Egyptians, it seems Zuma has been found out. At this time of writing, Zuma faces several charges of misdemeanor towards the country and people he represented. His administration (from 2009 to 2018) is alleged to have misappropriated a few billion dollars through corruption. In January–March 2022, the Zondo Commission of state capture and fraud published official reports concluding that multiple incidents of state capture took place within South African government departments and state-owned enterprises when Zuma was in power.

Another important comparison with Pharaoh and Zuma concerns the countries they have ruled over. Just as Pharaoh's politics divided the Egyptians, Zuma's jailing has created tensions and widespread unrest within a divided country. I have already alluded to the fact that the riots of 2021 have led many to call this South Africa's "darkest hour"—perhaps not quite like the plague of darkness that pervaded Egypt, but nonetheless leaving a significant shadow upon the perceived radiance of early post-apartheid

52. Shapshak, "How Pharaoh Zuma Destroyed."

53. This distinction stems from Aristotle. Cf. Richter, "Aristotle and the Classical Greek Concept of Despotism," 175–87; Turchetti, "'Despotism' and 'Tyranny' Unmasking a Tenacious Confusion," 159–82.

54. Chipkin and Swilling, "Introduction," in *Shadow State*.

55. Shapshak, "How Pharaoh Zuma Destroyed."

56. West, "Unstructural Analysis of the Bible," 875–76.

South African politics. *The Economist* magazine notes that whatever the precise mix of conspiracy and poverty behind the violence, it was facilitated by failures of security.[57] Apparently, even local police watched as people piled contraband onto pickup trucks. Some may call into question whether Zuma and his allies were directly responsible. Yet, it can be noted that even Zuma's family appears to have cheered the looters on. Allegedly, his daughter, Duduzile Zuma-Sambudla and her twin brother, Duduzane Zuma, said people should steal "carefully" and "responsibly."[58] The government has called it nothing less than "economic sabotage"[59] with Ramaphosa calling it an "insurrection"[60] and "nothing less than a deliberate, co-ordinated and well-planned attack on our democracy."[61] This, it seems to me, parallels the self-destructive Egyptian elitist politics to bring economic ruin to one's own country. People have questioned whether Zuma could really be behind the loss in votes sustained by the ANC. It seems unlikely but then again, as journalist Nomsa Maseko points out, although his "influence in the outcome of this election could well be overstated . . . his supporters had vowed to punish the governing party for jailing him."[62] The party has even lost its majority in KwaZulu-Natal, which is the largest ANC region and also Mr. Zuma's home province, and a recent technical report has concluded that Ramaphosa does not have the same authority in the ANC as did Zuma.[63]

The plagues of Egypt brought an immense weariness to the Egyptians until it came to a standoff between the ruling elite and the masses. I don't want to press the metaphor too far and suggest that the problems of South Africa are a result of God's handiwork, but they are certainly come thick and fast to scourge the country. Apart from the political and social turmoil of 2021, there are other "plagues" besetting the country—the eye-watering unemployment rate (35 percent at the time of writing) and the 22 percent of the population who are said to be hungry,[64] the worsening inequality, and the effects of the pandemic and the lockdowns which are pushing people deeper into poverty.

57. *Economist*, "Shaming of South Africa," 37–39.
58. *Economist*, "Shaming of South Africa."
59. Ramaphosa, "Update on Security Situation."
60. *Economist*, "Shaming of South Africa," 37.
61. *Economist*, "Shaming of South Africa," 37.
62. Maseko, "South Africa Municipal Elections."
63. Chipkin and Vidojević, *Dangerous Elites*.
64. According to the Quarterly Labour Force Survey—Q4:2021, published by South Africa Dept. of Statistics, March 2022. According to *The Economist*, this is the highest jobless rate since comparable data began in 2008; *Economist*, "Shaming of South Africa," 37.

The disillusionment of South Africans with the present political situation is evident in the recent local election results showing that the ANC's hold is weakening. The governing ANC was already losing support in the 2016 election but lately that has dipped below 50 percent of the vote for the first time in South Africa's democratic history.[65] It is clear that people are weary and questioning their leaders. For me, one can now hear echoes of the Egyptians challenging Pharaoh, "do you not yet understand, that Egypt is ruined?"

Despite the biblical pharaoh's tyranny, his own people, divided though they may be, were, in the end, shown to have better sense. Their increasing challenges to him can be read as an attempt to recapture control of power or, at the very least, control of state policies from Pharaoh. In South Africa, the very institutions that Zuma had tried to ransack have now fought back. Albie Sachs, a former anti-apartheid activist and judge on South Africa's constitutional court, specifically names the public protector's office and the constitutional court, the auditor general, the judiciary and the media. "This is a freeing of the state, a capturing of the capturers," he says triumphantly.[66]

The biblical pharaoh's ploys were an act to delay the inevitable judgment. Similarly, Zuma stonewalled the Zondo Commission of Inquiry and now it seems that South Africa's embattled former head of state is simply delaying what the powerful machinery of justice is able to do to him and his kingdom. At this time, he is on medical parole from his fifteen-month prison sentence. The dishonorable Pharaoh Zuma has become the white elephant in the room; he is difficult to get rid of and continues to flex his muscles against the system, allegedly using ill health as an excuse to delay his already drawn-out corruption trial. He and his legal team have also attempted to maneuver around the system by applying to get a prosecutor removed from his corruption case.[67]

Whatever, the future may hold, all the events of the last year bring me to the ultimate question for which many of my readers may be asking: "Where is God in all of this—Can the Plagues Narrative still speak to the South African situation?" Rightly so: this is after all a chapter dealing with South African *spirituality*. The Plagues Narrative can indeed, even now, be applied to the present political situation as it has been done so for other purposes in the past. The story of the exodus, particularly the theme of liberation from slavery, has already played an explicit and implicit role in both sustaining apartheid in South Africa, and in the resistance to and dismantling of it. In

65. *Economist*, "South Africa Is Slowly Souring."
66. Pilling, "'Zexit' Consumes South Africa."
67. *Reuters*, "South African Judge Dismisses Zuma's Attempt."

terms of the latter, Gunda includes the sermons of Desmond Tutu and Allan Boesak.[68] Gunda maintains that "unlike Tutu who was explicit on God being on the side of blacks, Boesak placed God on the side of the righteous people, irrespective of race."[69] One may wish to quibble with Gunda's assertion here but in any case, as Gunda himself notes, the exodus narrative and experience has been widely adopted and adapted by people suffering not just racial discrimination but marginalization and exploitation.[70] Such is clearly the present case of state capture with Zuma and others exploiting the country's institutions and its people. This is not about race anymore, and one can agree with van Aarde, that "in the South African context God is on the side of the righteous, that is those who are motivated by the love of God and neighbor."[71]

If Shapshak's metaphor holds true for the present situation—that the Israelites represent South Africa's new democracy after apartheid—then the exodus narrative now teaches us we can trust God to restore the country's subverted democracy and rescue it from the pervasive, corrupting influences of Zuma. Ultimately, those in South Africa, who are weary of the ongoing political situation and who are searching for divine justice and democracy, can expect the very God who exhibited forbearance in a protracted process with Pharaoh, but who ultimately brought him to justice, to be forbearing with Zuma for a season. Nonetheless, justice must be inexorably wrought, and we would therefore expect that what has been called "a protracted process that now needs to come to an end"[72] will be inevitably completed, leaving Zuma a defeated pharaoh once and for all.

BIBLIOGRAPHY

Assmann, Jan. *Exodus: Die Revolution der Alten Welt*. Munich: Beck, 2015.
———. "Exodus and Memory." In *Israel's Exodus in Transdisciplinary Perspective: Text, Archaeology, Culture and Geoscience*, edited by T. E. Levy et al., 3–15. Heidelberg: Springer, 2015.

68. Gunda, "Understanding the Role of the Exodus," 6.
69. Gunda, "Understanding the Role of the Exodus," 6.
70. Gunda, "Understanding the Role of the Exodus," 5. Cf. Eslinger, who writes many have understood "this story fits times and places far removed from those miserable slaves in ancient Egypt" ("Freedom or Knowledge," 43).
71. Van Aarde, "Black Theology in South Africa," 7.
72. These are the sentiments of the National Prosecuting Authority spokesman, Mthunzi Mhaga. See Magome, "South African Court Rules."

———. "Pharaoh's Divine Role in Maintaining Ma'at (Order)." *TheTorah.com*, 2016. https://www.thetorah.com/article/pharaohs-divine-role-in-maintaining-maat-order.

Beale, Greg. "An Exegetical and Theological Consideration of the Hardening of Pharaoh's Heart in Exodus 4-14 and Romans 9." *Trinity Journal* 5 (1984) 129-54.

Bills, Nathan. *A Theology of Justice in Exodus*. University Park, PA: Eisenbrauns, 2021.

Black, Antony. *A World History of Ancient Political Thought: Its Significance and Consequences*. Rev. and exp. ed. Oxford: Oxford University Press, 2016.

Chipkin, Ivor, and Jelena Vidojević. *Dangerous Elites: Protest, Conflict and the Future of South Africa*. Institute for Security Studies, Mar 14, 2022. https://issafrica.s3.amazonaws.com/site/uploads/sar-49-2.pdf.

Chipkin, Ivor, and Mark Swilling, eds. *Shadow State: The Politics of State Capture*. Johannesburg: Wits University Press, 2018.

Cox, Rory. "Expanding the History of the Just War: The Ethics of War in Ancient Egypt." *International Studies Quarterly* 61 (2017) 371-84.

The Economist. "The Shaming of South Africa." July 24-30, 2021, 37-39.

———. "South Africa Is Slowly Souring on Its Ruling Party." Nov 6, 2021. https://www.economist.com/middle-east-and-africa/2021/11/06/south-africa-is-slowly-souring-on-its-ruling-party.

Ekpo, Friday. "A Pharaoh Who Does Not Know Joseph." *Guardian* April 30, 2015. https://guardian.ng/opinion/a-pharaoh-who-does-not-know-joseph.

Eslinger, Lyle. "Freedom or Knowledge? Perspective and Purpose in the Exodus Narrative (Exodus 1-15)." *Journal for the Study of the Old Testament* 52 (1991) 43-60.

Feffer, John. "The Art of the Back Pedal." Institute for Policy Studies, Oct 23, 2019. https://ips-dc.org/the-art-of-the-back-pedal.

Ford, William A. *God, Pharaoh and Moses: Explaining the Lord's Actions in the Exodus Plagues Narrative*. Eugene, OR: Wipf & Stock, 2007.

Fretheim, Terence E. *Interpretation: Exodus*. Louisville, KY: Westminster John Knox, 2010.

Gunda, Masiiwa Ragies. "Understanding the Role of the Exodus in the Institutionalization and Dismantling of Apartheid: Considering the Paradox of Justice and Injustice in the Exodus." *Religions* 12 (2021) 605. https://doi.org/10.3390/rel12080605.

Gunn, David M. "Exodus 1-14." In *Art and Meaning: Rhetoric in Biblical Narrative*, edited by A. J. Hauser et al., 72-96. JSOTSup 19. Sheffield: JSOT, 1982.

Gurney, Oliver R. "Hittite Prayers of Mursili II." *Annals of Archaeology and Anthropology* 27 (1940) 3-163.

Houtman, Cornelis. *Exodus: Historical Commentary on the Old Testament*. Vol 2. Kampen: Kok, 1996.

Irvin, Aaron. "Regional Foundations for Internationalism in the Ancient Near East: The Case of Canaan." *UC Berkeley: UC World History Workshop* (2007). https://escholarship.org/uc/item/5gh13054.

Isbell, Charles D. "Exodus 1-2 in the Context of Exodus 1-14: Story Lines and Key Words." In *Art and Meaning: Rhetoric in Biblical Narrative*, edited by A. J. Hauser et al., 37-61. JSOTSup 19. Sheffield: JSOT, 1982.

Johnstone, William. "Reading Exodus in Tetrateuch and Pentateuch." In *The Book of Exodus: Composition, Reception, and Interpretation*, edited by T. B. Dozeman et al., 3-26. Supplements to Vetus Testamentum 164. Leiden: Brill, 2014.

Karenga, Maulana. *Maat—The Moral Ideal in Ancient Egypt: A Study in Classical African Ethics*. London: Routledge, 2004.

Krašovec, Jože. *Reward, Punishment, and Forgiveness: The Thinking and Beliefs of Ancient Israel in the Light of Greek and Modern Views*. Leiden: Brill, 1999.

Lichtheim, Miriam. *Late Egyptian Wisdom Literature in the International Context: A Study of Demotic Instructions*. Freiburg: Universitätsverlag, 1983.

Liverani, Mario. *International Relations in the Ancient Near East, 1600–1100 BC*. Basingstoke: Palgrave, 2001.

Magome, Mogomotsi. "South African Court Rules Zuma's Corruption Case to Continue." *AP News*, Oct 26, 2021. https://apnews.com/article/africa-money-laundering-south-africa-jacob-zuma-87b8accb7f37accbe168ff8104c4bbcf.

Maimonides. *The Eight Chapters of Maimonides on Ethics: Shemonah Perakim*. Translated by J. Gorfinkle. New York: AMS, 1966.

———. *Mishneh Torah: The Code of Maimonides*. Edited by Y. Makbili et al. Haifa, Israel: Or Vishua, 2009.

Maseko, Nomsa. "South Africa Municipal Elections: Who Are the Winners and Losers?" *BBC News*, Nov 4, 2021. https://www.bbc.co.uk/news/world-africa-59166081.

McAffee, Matthew. "The Heart of Pharaoh in Exodus 4–15." *Bulletin for Biblical Research* 20 (2010) 331–54.

McGinnis, Claire Mathews. "The Hardening of Pharaoh's Heart in Christian and Jewish Interpretation." *Journal of Theological Interpretation* 6 (2012) 43–64.

Parkinson, R. B. *Voices from Ancient Egypt*. Norman, OK: University of Oklahoma Press, 1991.

———, trans. *The Tale of Sinuhe: And Other Ancient Egyptian Poems 1940–1640 B.C.* Oxford: Clarendon, 1997.

Pilling, David. "'Zexit' Consumes South Africa as Defiant Zuma Clings On." *Financial Times*, Feb 13, 2018. https://www.ft.com/content/b6186552-10bb-11e8-8cb6-b9ccc4c4dbbb.

Propp, William H. C. *Exodus 1–18*. Anchor Bible. New York: Doubleday, 1998.

Ramaphosa, Cyril. "Update on Security Situation in the Country." South African Government, Jul 16, 2021. https://www.gov.za/speeches/president-cyril-ramaphosa-update-security-situation-country-16-jul-2021-0000.

Rendsburg, Gary. "Beasts or Bugs? Solving the Problem of the Fourth Plague." *Bible Review* (2003) 19–23.

Reuters. "South African Judge Dismisses Zuma's Attempt to Remove Prosecutor." Oct 27, 2021. https://www.reuters.com/world/africa/south-african-judge-dismisses-zumas-attempt-remove-prosecutor-2021-10-26.

Richter, Melvin. "Aristotle and the Classical Greek Concept of Despotism." *History of European Ideas* 12 (1990) 175–87.

Sanders, Paul. "God Appeased by Homicide? 2 Samuel 21:1–14 in View of Some Hittite and Assyrian Parallels." In *Violence in the Hebrew Bible*, edited by Jacques van Ruiten and Koert van Bekkum, 229–68. Leiden: Brill, 2020.

Shapshak, Toby. "How Pharaoh Zuma Destroyed Our Promised Land." *Rand Daily Mail*, April 5, 2017. https://www.businesslive.co.za/rdm/lifestyle/2017-04-05-toby-shapshak-how-pharaoh-zuma-destroyed-our-promised-land.

Singer, Itamar. *Hittite Prayers*. Edited by H. A. Hoffner Jr. Atlanta: Society of Biblical Literature, 2002.

Taylor, Justin. "The Hardening of Pharaoh's Heart." *The Gospel Coalition* (blog), Jan 4, 2012. https://www.thegospelcoalition.org/blogs/justin-taylor/the-hardening-of-pharoahs-heart.

Turchetti, Mario. "'Despotism' and 'Tyranny' Unmasking a Tenacious Confusion." *European Journal of Political Theory* 7 (2008) 159–82.

Utzschneider, Helmut, and Wolfgang Oswald. *International Exegetical Commentary on the Old Testament: Exodus 1–15*. Translated by Philip Sumpter. Stuttgart: Kohlhammer, 2014.

van Aarde, Timothy. "Black Theology in South Africa—A Theology of Human Dignity and Black Identity." *HTS Theological Studies* 72 (2016) 1–9.

von Holdt, Karl. *The Political Economy of Corruption: Elite-Formation, Factions and Violence*. Working Paper 10. Witswatersrand: Society, Work and Politics Institute, 2019.

Westbrook, Raymond. "Patronage in the Ancient Near East." *Journal of the Economic and Social History of the Orient* 48 (2005) 210–33.

West, Gerald. "Interrogating the Comparative Paradigm in African Biblical Scholarship." In *African and European Readers of the Bible in Dialogue: In Quest of a Shared Meaning*, edited by H. de Wit and G. O. West, 37–64. Leiden: Brill, 2008.

———. *The Stolen Bible: From Tool of Imperialism to African Icon*. Leiden: Brill, 2016.

———. "Unstructural Analysis of the Bible Reinforcing Unstructural Analysis of African Contexts in (South) Africa?" *Old Testament Essays* 23 (2010) 861–88.

Chapter 8

Spirituality, Poverty, and the Problem of Evil in the Book of Qoheleth
A Comparative Religious-Philosophical Supplement[1]

Jaco Gericke

INTRODUCTION

Perhaps a fitting first sentence in a chapter on poverty and spirituality in Qoheleth should give credit to contributions on these topics already available in related research. This includes a rich (pun not intended) variety of linguistic literary-critical, historical, social-scientific, ideological-critical, theological, comparative-religious, and philosophical readings. The sheer

---

1. This contribution is dedicated to all South African scholars who have made contributions to research on the wisdom literature of the Hebrew Bible, on the topics of poverty and spirituality, and to Dr. Annette Potgieter for everything she has done in making the initial conference and current edited volume possible. For an overview of related local trends, though as viewed a decade ago, see Nel, "Trends in Wisdom Research." For a relatively recent overview of contributions to poverty, see Holter, "'Poor' in Ancient Israel." Some examples of recent notable local contributions on both Qoheleth and poverty although not necessarily both or concurrently have come from the social concerns of people like Gerald West, Madipoane Masenya, Eben Scheffler, Hendrik Bosman, Dirk Human, Alphonso Groenewald, Hulisani Ramantswana, Ndikho Mtshiselwa, Lerato Makoena, Temba Rugwiji, Nathan Esala, Funlola Olojede, and Simon Cezula.

variety of readerly ideologies, contextual pressures, religious interests, and hermeneutical assumptions have contributed to completely divergent claims of what the book of Qoheleth is all about. Consequently, the consensus on themes related to Qoheleth and spirituality is usually more pervasive and serious than on those involving poverty. Considering these two concepts in tandem, neither theme has abstract verbal equivalents in the Hebrew of the book that can be done from a perspective in any given auxiliary discipline's theoretical frameworks, even as much has already been written on the individual themes, sometimes, but not always, as part of discussions—the main focus of which lay elsewhere.[2]

The present study hopes to make an original contribution on poverty and spirituality in Qoheleth by way offering a highly specific and nuanced comparative religious-philosophical supplement. Philosophical perspectives in general, and those related to themes in philosophy of religion in particular, are not in themselves where the novelty of the research focus lies, i.e., the so-called Problem of Evil.[3] Poverty and spirituality are both in more ways than one related to questions concerning suffering in the world and, in research on Qoheleth, to assumptions about divine goodness, conceptions of evil, and whether and in what sense the book offers some form of theodicy. What makes this a new addition to old discussions can be found in the way it seeks to identify correlations and contrasts that lie in wait at the intersection of poverty and spirituality in Qoheleth on the one hand, and the increasingly rich and nuanced typologies constructed for the Problem of Evil in recent analytic philosophy of religion.

---

2. More specific examples of related research will be provided in the discussion of the themes below. On perhaps the highest levels of synthesis, commentaries on Qoheleth in major mainstream series will immediately make the reader aware of the complexities that have to be considered in writing about what prima facie might seem relatively straightforward. Though this applies to the most influential commentaries of the previous centuries, a helpful recent overview of different approaches, and perspectives on the book as a whole, can be found in Weeks, *Critical and Exegetical Commentary on Ecclesiastes*. Earlier noteworthy erudition and attention to detail include those of Schwienhorst-Schönberger, *Kohelet*; Krüger, *Qoheleth*; Fox, *Time to Tear Down and a Time to Build Up: A Rereading of Ecclesiastes*. These give good general background introductions to basic issues in the now and then current debates. As we shall see as the present discussion unfolds, however, once one focuses on a particular subject like poverty and spirituality, in the context of the original contribution intended, the most relevant and in-depth contributions are usually found elsewhere.

3. More references to related research will be included in the main discussion. For an overview of what has been written within this specific set of approaches to Qoheleth, though not yet updated, see Gericke, "Comprehensive Typology of Philosophical Perspectives on Qoheleth."

ADDITIONAL BACKGROUND ON THE "POOR," "SPIRITUALITY," AND "EVIL" IN QOHELETH

In the Hebrew text of Qoheleth there are four explicit occurrences of the word translated as "poor."[4] As has been noted by others before, the Hebrew word used is unique to Qoheleth, i.e., מִסְכֵּן, is of uncertain origin and derivation, and as an adjective refers to a human subject of whom it is predicated.[5] Two of the four occurrences have the determinative and two are indefinite. The four verses and two pericopes in which Qoheleth explicitly refers to the poor shows it to be a relatively marginal yet not completely irrelevant concern within the larger thematic framework. In the first appearance in 4:13 HEB: טוֹב יֶלֶד מִסְכֵּן וְחָכָם מִמֶּלֶךְ the context involves an illustration combining the themes of poverty and wisdom:

> Better is a poor but wise youth than an old but foolish king who will no longer take advice. One can indeed come out of prison to reign, even though born poor in the kingdom. I saw all the living who, moving about under the sun, follow that[a] youth who replaced the king; there was no end to all those people whom he led. Yet those who come later will not rejoice in him. Surely this also is vanity and a chasing after wind (Eccl 4:13–18 NRSV)

The second, third, and fourth references to the poor occur in conjunction in the space of two verses in the context of the narrative again juxtaposing concerns featuring both poverty and wisdom in 9:15a HEB: וּמָצָא בָהּ אִישׁ מִסְכֵּן חָכָם, 9:15b HEB: בָּהּ אִישׁ מִסְכֵּן הַהוּא, and 9:16 HEB: מִגְּבוּרָה וְחָכְמַת הַמִּסְכֵּן בְּזוּיָה וּדְבָרָיו.

> I have also seen this example of wisdom under the sun, and it seemed great to me. There was a little city with few people in it. A great king came against it and besieged it, building great siegeworks against it. Now there was found in it a poor wise man, and he by his wisdom delivered the city. Yet no one remembered that poor man. So I said, "Wisdom is better than might; yet the poor man's wisdom is despised, and his words are not heeded." (Eccl 9:13–16 NRSV)

---

4. For a helpful nuanced discussion of the poor in the context of the entire Old Testament, see the still relevant study by Levin, "Poor in the Old Testament."

5. For an in-depth, influential relevant treatment of Qoheleth's language see Schoors, *Preacher Sought to Find Pleasing Words. A Study of the Language of Qoheleth* and *Preacher Sought to Find Pleasing Words: A Study of the Language of Qoheleth, Part II, Vocabulary.*

Though explicit references to poverty in the form of the adjective "poor" are isolated and marginal in the book, because of the context of wisdom[6] and the socioeconomic source domains of metaphors in the related religious language, it is actually part of an intricate conceptual background in which it is implicitly connected to other words translated as "rich" (noun and verb), toil, profit, portion, business, possessions, money, good and evil.[7]

In other words, the conceptual background of poverty and spirituality is much larger than the immediate semantic field. In fact, poverty and its counterparts are embedded in the larger context of the human condition, of life in the face of death, youth and old age, the fear of and indebtedness to and of the works, gifts, and judgments of God. With such interlinking ideas within the world of the text, it is not surprising that scholarly research on poverty in Qoheleth has not failed to produce findings, comments, and questions that correlate with topics in research on spirituality.

Linking Qoheleth and his references to the poor to "spirituality" is both common and complicated. Of course, this depends on what one means by spirituality in relation to the biblical texts.[8] A classical conceptual analysis listing individually necessary and jointly sufficient conditions for something to fall under the concept of spirituality may not be possible.[9] That been said, in focusing on "philosophical" approaches to spirituality, Qoheleth is often included as a biblical example.[10] Biblical scholars offering anything remotely related to a philosophical perspective on Qoheleth have either taken for granted or employed many elements of such discussions as part of an explicit theoretical framework.

In "critical" scholarship, the spirituality of Qoheleth is often seen in a popular sense as a canonically included justification for seeing doubt[11] and despair[12] as part of faith.[13] Alternatively, those studies that focus on ethical rather than religious-epistemological aspects have often as a theological

---

6. More on this conceptual background in relation to various themes in the book and in ancient Near Eastern comparative counterparts are discussed in the essays published in Schoors, *Qoheleth in the Context of Wisdom*.

7. A helpful overview of the interrelations of recurring phrases can be found in Murphy, *Ecclesiastes*.

8. On this topic, see the helpful local discussion by Lombaard, *Old Testament and Christian Spirituality*.

9. See, e.g., *inter alia*, Coakley, *Powers and Submissions*; Salazar and Nicholls, *Philosophy of Spirituality*; Coakley, "Feminism and Analytic Philosophy of Religion."

10. Rubinstein, *From Ecclesiastes to Simone Weil*.

11. Davidson, *Courage to Doubt*.

12. Walsh, "Despair as a Theological Virtue."

13. Murphy, "Faith of Qoheleth."

corrective emphasized Qoheleth's moderate aestheticism in contrast to the asceticism the book was seen to promote in Late Antiquity.[14] In contrast, more "conservative" contemporary readings with certain dogmas about the nature of the Bible on the one hand and need to paint atheism as nihilism as part of an apologetic and polemical agenda tend to construct Qoheleth's spirituality in one of two ways. Either the texts are interpreted to mean something more amenable to orthodox Jewish or Christian frames of reference or "Solomon" (or Qoheleth) is purportedly painting a picture of the kind of the spirituality of those who try to live life without God. Other current cultural concerns across the theological spectrum include Qoheleth's spirituality as concerned with the question of meaning of life,[15] or what makes life worth living.[16] At times and on formal and thematic grounds Qoheleth has also been assigned a "wisdom spirituality" which is still popular despite the recent questioning of the very idea of a wisdom tradition.[17]

POVERTY AND SPIRITUALITY IN QOHELETH AND THE PROBLEM OF EVIL IN PHILOSOPHY OF RELIGION

The different concepts, concerns and categories associated with the Problem of Evil in philosophy of religion has been helpfully mapped in the overview by Tooley to which the structure of the present discussion will be partly indebted.[18] On this view, the epistemic question posed by evil for Qoheleth at the intersection poverty and spirituality, is not whether the world in the text as he describes parts thereof contains undesirable states of affairs that provide the basis for an argument that makes it unreasonable to believe in the existence of God. Qoheleth is not as such a discussion of poverty and spirituality with special attention to the Problem of Evil from any ancient or contemporary religious-philosophical perspective. Consequently, correlations and contrasts have to be approached from a holistic, historically conscious point of view. As both Hebrew Bible scholars and philosophers of religion themselves recognize, a difference in the initial conditions means a

---

14. A helpful overview remains Christianson, *Ecclesiastes through the Centuries*.

15. A helpful introduction to this concern in relation to Qoheleth can be found in Keefer, "Meaning of Life in the Book of Ecclesiastes."

16. For example, see Kaiser, *Anweisungen zum gelingenden, gesegneten und ewigen Leben*.

17. See the variety of views related but not identical to the present discussion in Sneed, *Was There a Wisdom Tradition*.

18. Tooley, "Problem of Evil."

complete reconfiguration of what is problematic about evil for poverty and spirituality, as well as for who, how, why, when, and where.

In terms of the concept of evil in Qoheleth and philosophy of religion a few remarks may be added to the preliminary considerations of what has already been researched in related literature.[19] The word רַע translated as "evil" (or in related terms depending on what is being predicated or nominalized) occurs thirty-one times in the book. It is one of Qoheleth's recurring explicit terms and related to both poverty and spirituality as well as to a host of other interconnected terms (e.g., riches, toil, profit, business, possessions). Evil has both moral and axiological undertone and occurs in contexts featuring conditions indirectly linked poverty-related conditions complicating wisdom spirituality.

For example, there is a reference to life as the "evil" business God has given humans that can be found already in Qoheleth's initial summary of his assessment thesis (cf. 1:13). Qoheleth deems it evil when someone is hardworking and wise yet must leave riches behind to those who are neither (2:21). He also insists it is better not to have been born and to have seen the unrequited evil done to the oppressed (4:3). It is evil to toil for a living and not having anyone else to live for (4:8). Evil can be further qualified by its effects as grievous when not being poor involves being hurt because of one's possessions (5:16). Even when not living in poverty, one might lose everything again despite doing everything right, dying as poor as when one was born after a lifetime of futile labor. No longer being poor but working towards preventing poverty with someone else consuming the profits (6:1). Because one does not know what evil may occur in the future, it's better to have multi-located assets (11:2). Other references to evil not mentioning poverty-related matters but are general enough to link to ways in which wisdom spirituality and not being poor makes no difference to the suffering involved (5:1; 9:11–12; 10:1, 5; 11:2; 12:1).

As with poverty, there is more to evil in Qoheleth than the explicit references. Consequently, when commentators discuss evil in Qoheleth it is not only with reference to problems of suffering or theodicy but also in connection to a web of related motifs in the book, e.g., time, death, freedom and determinism, wisdom and folly, pleasure and pain, youth and old age, health, and sickness, etc. When theodicy is the topic of choice, related

---

19. Besides discussing the Problem of Evil, philosophers of religion also seek to clarify the concept of evil, often with helpful historical overviews offered in conjunction with arguments. See, e.g., Angier, *History of Evil in Antiquity: 2000 BCE—450 CE*; Calder, "Concept of Evil"; Gellman, *History of Evil from the Mid-Twentieth Century to Today: 1950–2018*; Meister and Moser, *Cambridge Companion to the Problem of Evil*; Meister and Taliaferro, *History of Evil* (6 vols).

research tends to use the associated terminology from theological backgrounds without considering the theoretical frameworks developed in contemporaneous philosophy of religion. That is, between evil as problem of versus as argument, between different versions of both the aforementioned, between different kinds of evil, and between these and defenses, theodicy, and other categories.[20]

Correlated and contrasted to current typologies in the Problem of Evil, one further preliminary framing question may be asked, as is customary: What fundamental ontological assumptions about what the divine was underlie Qoheleth's religious language related to poverty, spirituality, and evil?[21] Here one of the first comparative-philosophical challenges that arises is linked to the inexact metaphysics of the book whose main concerns lay elsewhere. It seems impossible to place Qoheleth's assumptions about divinity and ontology into the known categories despite the ways in which the world of the text features the divine as creator intimately bound up with initial conditions and associated causal relata.

This brings us to a next distinction between Qoheleth's Problem of Evil related to poverty and spirituality and

> any version of the argument from evil claims that there is some fact concerning the evil in the world such that the existence of God—understood as at least a very powerful, very knowledgeable, and morally very good person, is either logically precluded, or rendered unlikely, by that fact. But versions of the argument often differ quite significantly with respect to what the relevant fact is.[22]

In Qoheleth's religious language, divine power, knowledge, and goodness are constructed from a highly specific religious-historical and socio-cultural context as a source domain for the supervening metaphors as metaphysics. If one had to choose where in relation to the divine attributes the problem is located for Qoheleth in the contexts of poverty and spirituality, one might be with reference to how he constructs the nature of divine goodness. Not because Qoheleth thinks the divine is not also good or against most forms of evil; instead, it is primarily because divine goodness was conceptualized through culturally contingent senses of the meanings of these words in the source domains. The socio-political metaphors

---

20. See, e.g., *inter alia*, Crenshaw, *Defending God*; Gese, "Crisis of Wisdom in Koheleth," 141–53; Sanders, "Wisdom, Theodicy, Death," 263; Carny, "Theodicy in the Book of Qoheleth," 71–81; Schoors, "Theodicy in Qoheleth," 375–409.

21. Gericke, "'Qoheleth's Concept of Deity."

22. Tooley, "Problem of Evil."

supervening on wisdom spirituality mean that while there is no denial of divine knowledge or power, this kind of divine knowledge and power—like the portrayal of divine goodness—is very role specific and never simply a free for all.

Axiological assumptions[23] in Qoheleth's wisdom spirituality values the concept of a hidden and sovereign deity in ways that supervene on perceived relations with the world, including the world of the poor. In this way, one cannot separate discussions of the poor and spirituality in Qoheleth from his assumptions about the nature of religious language, his religious epistemology, his concept of God, the existence of God, the relationship between religion and morality, culture, history, politics and science of the day, religious diversity, pluralism and disagreement and his view of personhood and the afterlife.

As far as Qoheleth's assumptions about the moral properties of divinity linked to poverty and spirituality is concerned, it is readily apparent that in the text God is assumed to instantiate a form of goodness that does not preclude never intentionally bringing harm to humans for no justified reasons.[24] Or for that matter ignoring the cries of the oppressed. Unlike the case for most readers of Qoheleth today, the divine did not need to instantiate the property of being good in a maximally great sense, and not evil in any sense, as necessary conditions to be deemed worthy of worship. In Qoheleth divine power and commands are a sufficient condition for all cultic activities. Spirituality is assumed to be possible even when the fear of God is meant quite literally and where the wisdom that informs it does not prevent poverty and its value relativized thereby.

Regarding different evils in philosophy of religion's discussion of the Problem of Evil, metaphysical, natural, and moral evils are all acknowledged in wisdom spirituality. These can be distinguished but not separated in the context of poverty.[25] That is, things like time, death, futility, contingency, or the physical anguish experienced in poverty, or the human contribution to the creation of the poor in society are often intertwined. They are all included in evil in Qoheleth's sense of "bad business" and "grievous evil." As for different forms of the Problem of Evil, there are certainly elements of what has later come to be distinguished as the logical, evidential, and additional sub-types. Though none of these are formulated as arguments in the world of the text, some of them are implicit and the associated propositional

23. See Gericke, "Axiological Assumptions in Qohelet."
24. See Crenshaw, *Whirlpool of Torment*. I understand not everyone shares the views as discussed by Crenshaw, but they seem both concise and philosophically relevant to me.
25. Stump, *Wandering in Darkness*.

content can be roughly identified and reconstructed from the relevant related assumptions.

A comparative-philosophical reconstruction of the propositional contents of the logical form of the problem as it arises in some contexts in Qoheleth with reference to the poor in the context of wisdom spirituality of Qoheleth might looks as follows:

1. Elohim exists.
2. Elohim has the power to give riches and change the fate of a poor person.
3. God knows about the sufferings of the poor, including poor wise people.
4. God cares whether people fear him and gives good things to humans.
5. Evil exists in the form of the oppression of the poor.

This reconstruction does not purport to be a sound, valid, and descriptively adequate reduction of the complexity of the deity's perceived relationship to the poor in the reasoning behind the (ir)religious language of Qoheleth's wisdom spirituality. It only features some implicit premises that are indeed present.[26] It also reflects something of the way in which the deity is conceptualized in some contexts, is related to evil therein, and in ways that are a problem for Qoheleth's own paraconsistent informal logic in his expressions related to it. Partly because of the contradictions in the book, partly because Qoheleth's views on evil do not map directly onto any presupposition, problem, or perspective in contemporary typologies of the Problem of Evil in philosophy of religion, and partly because of this reader's own imperfections, one can simply admit that there are both correlations and contrasts between other texts as regards the logical problem of the pros and cons of such a reconstruction. In a way it shows qualified correlations and contrasts between what is nascent in some of Qoheleth's concepts and concerns and the adopted, adapted, and applied logical Problem of Evil in philosophy of religion.[27]

From the reconstruction of something approximating the logical dimensions of associated assumptions in the religious language in Qoheleth

---

26. For more on implicit relations with different Greek philosophical and ancient Near Eastern skeptical theological traditions representing higher-order thinking in Qoheleth, see Crenshaw, "Sipping from the Cup of Wisdom," 41–62.

27. To be sure, there are exceptions, and many scholars working in more comparative varieties of philosophy of religion as opposed to the primarily Christian tradition are exceptions to some of the general statements about research in the field throughout the present chapter. A good example of this is Griffiths-Dickson, *Philosophy of Religion*, which discusses all the major loci albeit adapted to perspectives that do not presuppose conceptions of the divine in classical (mono)theism.

and related to the Problem of Evil is a deductive hypothetical argument. As such it attempts to show that according to Qoheleth, certain facts about the world with reference to the poor are implied to be logically incompatible with certain traditional ideas of God held in common in wisdom spirituality. Alternatively, something more like the so-called "evidential (or inductive/probabilistic) versions of the argument could be put together by considering the specific instances of references to the suffering of the poor and everything related to the broader semantic field against the background of his wisdom spirituality. The latter (evidentialist) version, with its correlations and contrasts, would have to be inferred from the more reserved remarks on the part of Qoheleth that imply that the events related to poverty have made it unlikely for him to believe that certain traditional versions of the God conceptualized in other wisdom texts have any instances in the world of the text.

Of course, Qoheleth does not say as much, and his Problem of Evil is not an argument from evil against divine existence. But that does not mean what is for him some sort of Problem of Evil has led to a conception of the divine which, given what it is implies, that gods with very different attributions or relations to the word do not exist. To formulate an evidential argument from evil implicit in Qoheleth with special attention to poverty and wisdom spirituality, one may therefore look to the broader ancient Near Eastern and Greek philosophical conceptual background for quantitatively and qualitatively significant ways in which scenarios featuring evil is observed "under the sun." As has been argued elsewhere,[28] the polemical and rhetorical significance and conceptual-historical background of this phrase, appearing almost thirty times throughout the book, has very likely been misinterpreted in different ways and for different reasons. A brief summary of the relevant points will be provided with special attention to their relevance for discussing Qoheleth, poverty, and spirituality in relation to the Problem of Evil.

Qoheleth's repeated references to the evils "under the sun" is usually either over- or under-interpreted. Over-interpretation is present in readings which claim Qoheleth associates this domain with a "life without God." Under-interpretation occurs where the phrase is simply seen as Qoheleth's way of referring to this world "under heaven."[29] The former seems to have apologetic motivations in light of the book's heterodox ideas and does not seem correct in view of Qoheleth's constant references to and concerns with the divine in this realm. The latter reading does not seek to promote the

---

28. Gericke, "Injustice under the Sun?"
29. Jones, "Values and Limits of Qoheleth's Sub-Celestial Economy."

text as cohering with dogmas about the Bible, but in turn it seems unable to account for why there is the need to use the phrase so frequently, as though there is anywhere else his observations could be assumed to have taken place.

In the estimate of the present author and in connection with the themes of poverty and spirituality in the book, Qoheleth's use of "under the sun" thirty times has a polemical undertone directly related to a problem with evil. But there is more to it once the broader ancient Near Eastern cultural conceptual background is considered. For Qoheleth, to "see" so many scenarios evidencing injustice under the sun when solar deities were responsible for maintaining the moral order seems quite deconstructive (cf. Shamash in the Epic of Gilgamesh). As does the idea that knowledge of what is good in life is so intertwined with הבל "under the sun" in relation to depersonalized solar mythology in ancient Greek philosophy (cf. the image of the sun in the Allegory of the Cave as symbol of Enlightenment). In this way Qoheleth's wisdom spirituality and his observation regarding the poor under the sun may be seen as a polemic against ideas prevailing in Egyptian, Babylonian, and Greek solar theologies at the time of narration (Hellenistic period). This along with Qoheleth's deity working "under the sun" selectively usurping many functions of solar deities (judgment, retribution, giving knowledge/health), albeit in a qualified manner could be seen as both a theodicy and an argument from evil (injustice) of sorts, and as two sides of the same coin.[30]

As far as Qoheleth's relation to the concept of theodicy in discussions of the Problem of Evil in philosophy of religion are concerned, it is clear that certain theodicies are not options in the world of Qoheleth's text. Because the existence of evil is never seen as an argument for broad atheism, Qoheleth does not require the kind of theodicy that attempts to show how the divine could exist despite the problems of injustice his wisdom spirituality highlights in relation to the poor. Neither would Qoheleth think a theodicy whereby post-mortem existence can be appealed to as justification of the divine makes any sense. In Qoheleth the afterlife in Sheol is without any connection to either a heaven/hell or anything related that could be appealed to against the evil in the world.[31] No promise of immortality is required to motivate spirituality. Neither is divine retribution, in this life or the next. Because in Qoheleth's anthropology, the human self as dust animated by divine breath (which in the text overlaps with the air element) is no different from animals, poverty in the context of his wisdom spirituality also does not fit any soul making theodicy. Last but not least, the intricate

---

30. Gericke, "Injustice under the Sun?"
31. Cf. Imray, "Qohelet's Philosophies of Death."

relations between free will and determinism in the book[32] and elements of deontological ethics, without a soteriological frame of reference, also make the free-will theodicy non-applicable to Qoheleth.

Every statement in comparisons like these deserves to be qualified. For Qoheleth as for some philosophers of religion, some evils associated with poverty and spirituality are logically necessary for there to be certain good things in the world. But why they are necessary relates to the divine and human conditions in ways very different from what one finds in current religious philosophical counterpart debates. While in some texts the deity is concerned with the good of humans and with humans that are good and with giving them riches in others there is no such concern or connection, and in fact it would be more descriptively apt to say that in Qoheleth God has neither the desire, ability, nor motivation to eliminate poverty.

Of course, there are exceptions when his words hint at a critical assessment or connection of the divine with evil in a manner that hints at his thinking it less than ideal, and in that sense he can conceive of a greater possible world that the one of his text. But for the most part, these words are words of a-posteriori inferences, with the divine as explanatory factor and made in a spirit of resignation. Instead of imagining a different conception of the divine, or coming up with some error theory, Qoheleth settles for an extreme form of metaphysical pessimism (which is not the same as pessimism about everything in life in general). The deity, like the humans, is implied to be hopelessly locked up its own innate behavior and not only foils the efforts of the wise and the rich but is passive when moral evils make the life of the poor worse. From the perspective of Qoheleth's wisdom spirituality, there is very little if anything to be done about it in most cases: things are what they are, they are more often than not very bad, and no amount of human planning and effort can do anything to make the world other than it is or its problems cohere.

Exactly to what extent poverty is caused by or related to human free will or divine determinism or both is impossible to identify with certainty or precision. Qoheleth's peculiar brand of wisdom spirituality sees the poor as sometimes the cause of their own condition, sometimes the victims of socio-political upheaval (whether instigated in acts of moral evil or not) and on other occasions as the pawns of inscrutable divine operations.[33] What is more certain is that, as already hinted at, the causal link between wisdom spirituality and those of fools and riches/poverty is severed on many levels

---

32. For an in-depth discussion of related concerns, see Rudman, *Determinism in the Book of Ecclesiastes*.

33. Cf. Forti, "'Yet, No One Remembered that Poor Man,'" 149–64.

in many contexts (but not always). This does not mean the different ways in which human and divine moral evils participate in the causal relata of poverty are reconciled in Qoheleth's brand of wisdom spirituality, or for that matter, that he is comfortable with contradictions or with upholding dialectical tensions.

A further aid to understand the relative valuation of poverty for Qoheleth is in the way divine goodness and even riches are themselves part of the Problem of Evil. Not only with reference to ways in which the deity gives and takes but already in the experiment conducted in the royal fiction at the beginning of the book. Qoheleth's wisdom spirituality enabled him to become the opposite of the poor, yet in the end this too was הבל. The latter fact and is part of what he considers grievous evils and does not exclude the role of the deity, associated actions of which are themselves הבל (1:13; 2:24–26; 6:1–2).[34]

Because suffering is never eradicated, and only changes form in rich as opposed to poor conditions (cf. Schopenhauer), Qoheleth's wisdom spirituality and its qualified *carpe diem* motifs are both presented as recommendations and as part of what is הבל. Because the deity is depicted as both good and evil across different forms of evil, Qoheleth's embryonic and idiosyncratic versions of the Problem of Evil does not exclude there being a problem of goodness because of the הבל supervening thereon. That being said, how goodness is a problem with reference to poverty in particular and to wisdom spirituality in general is not the same as in the Problem of Evil.

CONCLUSION

In our discussion of poverty and spirituality in Qoheleth, which was done with a nod to scholarly discussions of evil, suffering, and theodicy in the book, an original contribution of was made through supplementing it with an additional clarification concerning the religious-philosophical conceptual background involved. A comparative and descriptive religious-philosophical approach was adopted to map the associated findings onto the presuppositions, problems, and perspectives in contemporary discussions of the Problem of Evil. Additional nuance and specificity were introduced via distinctions between evil as problem or argument, distinctions between different forms and versions of the problem, between different kinds of evil and between differences between defenses, theodicies, and other matters usually not so specifically discerned. In doing so other themes in philosophy of religion were brought to bear to the extent that acknowledging differences and

---

34. Cf. Krüger, "Qoh 2:24–26 und die Frage nach dem 'Guten' im Qohelet-Buch."

similarities between these variables and Qoheleth's associated assumptions are necessary for any holistic, historically conscious attempt at minimizing the fallacies associated with philosophical interpretations of this kind.

A holistic historically conscious considerations of background assumptions showed both similarities and differences in Qoheleth's spirituality in terms of what is it about poverty that is problematic, here with reference to different forms evil and versions of the problem, as well as what does and does not count as arguments, defenses, and theodicies and for who, how, why, when, and where. By highlighting those aspects as summarized above, one may conclude that a comparative religious philosophical clarification of this type is therefore invaluable also to the extent that they might lead us to speak with more appreciation, reservation, nuance, and awareness of the contingencies of how poverty and spirituality are constructed in and supervened on by the entire web of background assumptions practically related to other concepts, concerns, and categories. Not only in Qoheleth but also any other biblical text discussed with reference to poverty and spirituality requires both the additional reconstruction of religious-philosophically related matters, otherwise not made explicit.

BIBLIOGRAPHY

Angier, Tom P. S., ed. *The History of Evil in Antiquity: 2000 BCE—450 CE*. History of Evil 1. London: Routledge, 2018.

Calder, Todd. "The Concept of Evil." *Stanford Encyclopedia of Philosophy*. Edited by Edward N. Zalta and Uri Nodelman. Last updated October 3, 2022. https://plato.stanford.edu/archives/win2022/entries/concept-evil/.

Carny, Peter. "Theodicy in the Book of Qoheleth." In *Justice and Righteousness in Israel and the Nations: Equality and Freedom in Ancient Israel in Light of Social Justice in Ancient Near East*, edited by Moshe Weinfeld, 71–81. Jerusalem: Magnes, 1985.

Christianson, Eric S. *Ecclesiastes through the Centuries*. London: Wiley-Blackwell, 2007.

Coakley, Sarah. "Feminism and Analytic Philosophy of Religion." In *The Oxford Handbook in Philosophy of Religion*, edited by William W. Wainwright, 495–525. Oxford: Oxford University Press, 2005.

———. *Powers and Submissions: Spirituality, Philosophy, and Gender*. Oxford: Blackwell, 2002.

Crenshaw, James L. *Defending God: Biblical Responses to the Problem of Evil*. Oxford: Oxford University Press, 2005.

———. "Sipping from the Cup of Wisdom." In *Jesus and Philosophy*, edited by Paul D. Moser, 41–62. Cambridge: Cambridge University Press, 2009.

———. *A Whirlpool of Torment: Israelite Traditions of God as an Oppressive Presence*. Philadelphia: Fortress, 1984.

Davidson, Robert. *The Courage to Doubt: Exploring an Old Testament Theme*. London: SCM, 1983.

Forti, Tova. "'Yet, No One Remembered That Poor Man': Qoheleth and Ben Sira on the Wisdom of the Poor." In *Ben Sira in Conversation with Traditions: A Festschrift for Prof. Núria Calduch-Benages on the Occasion of Her 65th Birthday*, edited by Francis M. Macatangay and Francisco-Javier Ruiz-Ortiz, together with Renate Egger-Wenzel, 149–64. Berlin: de Gruyter, 2022.

Fox, Michael V. *A Time to Tear Down and a Time to Build Up: A Rereading of Ecclesiastes*. Grand Rapids: Eerdmans, 1999.

———. "On הבל in Qoheleth: A Reply to Mark Sneed." *Journal of Biblical Literature* 138 (2019) 559–63.

Gellman, Jerome, ed. *The History of Evil from the Mid-Twentieth Century to Today: 1950–2018*. History of Evil 6. London: Routledge, 2018

Gericke, Jaco. "Axiological Assumptions in Qohelet: A Historical-Philosophical Clarification." *Verbum et Ecclesia* (2012) 1–6.

———. "A Comprehensive Typology of Philosophical Perspectives on Qoheleth." *Verbum et Ecclesia* 36 (2015) 1–7.

———. "Injustice under the Sun? A New Perspective on Possible Allusions to Ancient Near Eastern Solar Mythology in Qohelet." *Old Testament Essays* 16 (2003) 244–58.

———. "Qohelet's Concept of Deity: A Comparative Philosophical Perspective." *Verbum et Ecclesia* 34 (2013) 1–7.

Gese, Hartmut. "The Crisis of Wisdom in Koheleth." In *Theodicy in the Old Testament*, edited by James L. Crenshaw, 141–53. Issues in Religion and Theology 4. Philadelphia: Fortress/SPCK, 1983.

Griffiths-Dickson, Gwen. *The Philosophy of Religion*. London: SCM, 2005.

Holter, Knut. "The 'Poor' in Ancient Israel—And in Contemporary African Biblical Studies." *Mission Studies* 33 (2016) 209–21.

Imray, Kathryn. "Qohelet's Philosophies of Death." PhD diss, Murdoch University, 2009.

Jones, Scott C. "The Values and Limits of Qoheleth's Sub-Celestial Economy." *Vetus Testamentum* 64 (2014) 21–33.

Kaiser, Otto. *Anweisungen zum gelingenden, gesegneten und ewigen Leben. Eine Einführung in die spätbiblischen Weisheitsbücher*. Forum Theologische Literaturzeitung 9. Leipzig: de Gruyter, 2003.

Keefer, Arthur Jan. "The Meaning of Life in the Book of Ecclesiastes: Coherence, Purpose and Significance from a Psychological Perspective." *Harvard Theological Review* 112 (2019) 447–66.

Krüger, Thomas. "'And They Have No Comforter': Job and Ecclesiastes in Dialogue." In *Reading Ecclesiastes Intertextually*, edited by Katharine Dell and Will Kynes, 94–105. Library of Hebrew Bible/Old Testament Studies 587. London: Bloomsbury, 2014.

———. "Leiden und Tod." In *Die Welt der Hebräischen Bibel*, edited by Walter Dietrich, 369–81. Stuttgart: Kohlhammer, 2017.

———. *Qoheleth: A Commentary*. Hermeneia. Philadelphia: Fortress, 2004.

———. "Qoh 2:24–26 und die Frage nach dem 'Guten' im Qohelet-Buch." *Biblische Notizen* 72 (1994) 70–84.

Levin, Christoph. "The Poor in the Old Testament: Some Observations." *Religion and Theology* 8 (2001) 253–73.

Lombaard, Christo. *The Old Testament and Christian Spirituality: Theoretical and Practical Essays from a South African Perspective*. International Voices in Biblical Studies 2. Atlanta: Society of Biblical Literature, 2012.

Meister, Chad, and Charles Taliaferro, eds. *History of Evil.* 6 vols. London: Routledge, 2018.
Meister, Chad, and Paul Moser, eds. *The Cambridge Companion to the Problem of Evil.* Cambridge: Cambridge University Press, 2017.
Müller, Hans-Peter. *Mensch—Umwelt—Eigenwelt. Gesammelte Aufsätze zur Weisheit Israels.* Stuttgart: Kohlhammer, 1992.
Murphy, Roland. *Ecclesiastes.* Word Biblical Commentary 23A. Dallas, TX: Word, 1992.
———. "The Faith of Qoheleth." *Word & World* 7 (1987) 253–60.
Nel, Philip J. "Trends in Wisdom Research: A Perspective from the African Continent: Old Testament Wisdom, Human Dignity and the Poor." *Scriptura* 111 (2012) 460–71.
Rubinstein, Ernest. *From Ecclesiastes to Simone Weil: Varieties of Philosophical Spirituality.* Fairleigh: Dickinson University Press, 2014.
Rudman, Dominic. *Determinism in the Book of Ecclesiastes.* Journal for the Study of the Old Testament Supplement 316. Sheffield, UK: Sheffield Academic, 2001.
Salazar, Heather, and Roderick Nicholls. *The Philosophy of Spirituality: Analytic, Continental, and Multicultural Approaches to a New Field of Philosophy.* Leiden: Brill-Rodopi, 2019.
Sanders, James T. "Wisdom, Theodicy, Death, and the Evolution of Intellectual Traditions." *Journal for the Study of Judaism in the Persian, Hellenistic and Roman Period* 36 (2005) 263–77.
Schoors, Antoon. *The Preacher Sought to Find Pleasing Words: A Study of the Language of Qoheleth.* Orientalia Lovaniensia Analecta 41. Leuven: Peeters, 1992.
———. *The Preacher Sought to Find Pleasing Words: A Study of the Language of Qoheleth, Part II, Vocabulary.* Orientalia Lovaniensia. Analecta 143. Leuven: Peeters, 2003.
———, ed. *Qoheleth in the Context of Wisdom.* Bibliotheca Ephemeridum theologicarum Lovaniensium 136. Leuven: Peeters, 1998.
———. "Theodicy in Qoheleth." In *Theodicy in the World of the Bible: The Goodness of God and the Problem of Evil,* edited by Antii Laato and Johannes de Moor, 375–409. Leiden: Brill, 2003.
Schwienhorst-Schönberger, Ludger. *Kohelet.* Herders theologischer Kommentar zum Alten Testament. Freiburg: Herder, 2011.
Sneed, Mark R. *The Politics of Pessimism in Ecclesiastes: A Social-Science Perspective.* Atlanta: Society of Biblical Literature, 2012.
———, ed. *Was There a Wisdom Tradition.* New Prospects in Israelite Wisdom Studies 23. Atlanta: Society of Biblical Literature, 2015.
Stump, Eleonore. *Wandering in Darkness: Narrative and the Problem of Suffering.* New York: Oxford University Press, 2010.
Tooley, Michael. "The Problem of Evil." *The Stanford Encyclopedia of Philosophy.* Edited by Edward N. Zalta. Last updated Mar 3, 2015. https://plato.stanford.edu/archives/win2021/entries/evil/.
Van Inwagen, Peter. *The Problem of Evil.* Oxford: Oxford University Press, 2008.
Walsh, Jerome T. "Despair as a Theological Virtue in the Spirituality of Ecclesiastes." *Biblical Theology Bulletin* 12 (1982) 46–49.
Weeks, Stuart. *A Critical and Exegetical Commentary on Ecclesiastes.* Vol. 1, *Introduction and Commentary on Ecclesiastes 1.1–5.6.* International Critical Commentary. London: T. & T. Clark, 2020.

Chapter 9

The Tension between Experiences of Nothingness and Hope in the Metaphorical Meaning of the Names of the Children (Isa 7–8) from a Perspective of Generational Imprinted Trauma and Resilience[1]

Elizabeth Esterhuizen and Alphonso Groenewald

INTRODUCTION

The American writer and poet Gertrude Stein's famous line a "Rose is a rose is a rose is a rose" comes from her poem "Sacred Emily" (published in 1913) and this line had a major impact on poetry and literary criticism in the twentieth century.[2] This line has often been interpreted meaning that all roses are the same; in other words, suggesting that things are what they

---

1. In this chapter we acknowledge our indebtedness to work that has already been done in a previous study, but our contribution represents a thoroughly reworked and updated version of material used. Cf. Esterhuizen, "Study of the Tension between Despair and Hope in Isaiah 7 and 8."

2. Ashton, "'Rose Is a Rose,'" 581; Fleissner, "Stein's Four Roses," 325.

are, or seem to be what one thinks they are or should be. If this is the case, it implies that if any noun or name is mentioned, it immediately calls to mind imagery, associations, and emotions which are related to this noun or word.³ However, according to Ashton, in lines like these the meaning of a word(s) become indeterminate, as "Rose" can refer to a person's name or "rose" can refer to a flower (which has many different forms, colors and aromas), thus implying that the same word can have completely different meanings, nuances, and even semantics.⁴ We thus have to learn to accept the ambiguity inherent in a word(s).

When shifting our focus from roses to people, and for our purpose in this contribution when we focus on individuals who were designated as prophets in the ancient Israelite and Judean society, we also have to accept the inherent ambiguity contained in the term "prophet," as well as the "prophetic roles" given to a specific person or individual. At this point in the discussion, we indeed have to ask ourselves the question whether Isaiah simply is "a prophet is a prophet is a prophet is a prophet," or is the prophet Isaiah maybe a thorn in the comparison, when referring to the original line by Gertrude Stein ("Rose is a rose is a rose is a rose")? Can we accept the ambiguity inherent in the portrayal of Isaiah as a prophet and the character Isaiah in the text? In other words, on the one hand he is depicted as a prophet who proclaims judgment, but on the other hand he is also a beacon of hope and resilience in the midst of feelings of nothingness as a result of the despair and overwhelming feelings of hopelessness that overwhelmed the people. The text oscillates the whole time between despair and nothingness, as well as hope, resilience, fullness, and the breadth of possibilities.

Furthermore, it is impossible to group any person(s) or individual(s) who were depicted as a prophet(s) together and to assert that the following saying applies to him/her/them as well, namely that "a prophet is a prophet is a prophet." Prophets and subsequently their respective prophetic roles would have been determined by the geographical as well as historical context in which they functioned; thus, implying we need to keep in mind several different contexts of understanding.⁵ The literary portrayal of a prophet or prophetic figure differed from book to book, as scribal activity

---

3. Ashton, "'Rose Is a Rose,'" 602, writes as follows: "If Stein can 'really caress' the noun by rendering it as a name, it is neither the material form—the petals and thorns—of the floral object it denotes nor the material form—the sound and shape—of the word that denotes it. What Stein caresses in caressing the 'rose' is the immaterial form—the very function of reference—belonging to the name itself." Cf. also Esterhuizen, "Study of the Tension between Despair and Hope," 1.

4. Ashton, "'Rose Is a Rose,'" 581–82.

5. Cook et al., *Prophets*, 29; Sharp, *Old Testament Prophets for Today*, 3.

also may have differed from time to time and from book to book—even within a prophetic book.[6] Berges therefore infers that in the book of Isaiah we first of all encounter the book[7] which is named after the prophet Isaiah, and subsequently we meet the prophet (figure) Isaiah who is *in* the literary testimony in this major piece of literature.[8] The book contains many other anonymous figures who are hiding behind the figure of Isaiah and subsequently it can be inferred that "he is the implied author who guides his readers through the historical vision that has now become a book (cf. Isaiah 7). These scribes have ascribed their work to the famous Jerusalem prophet, for they know that despite all discontinuities and new beginnings they are related to his body of thought."[9]

Therefore, the interpretation of any prophetic text (e.g., the book of Isaiah) is challenging as we need to break open the layers of historical interpretations inherent within these texts, i.e., how he was remembered by later communities. But most of all, we need to reinterpret and reformulate these "old truths" for new times and contexts within the current world in which we are living today.[10] The world is swaying on her axes because of the aftermath of a pandemic, which unfortunately is still prevalent and impacts most parts of the world.[11] Furthermore, we can mention socio-economic challenges and injustices, governmental instabilities, and major ecological crises which face the world. This uncertainty, fear, and anxiety caused by a

---

6. Cf. for example Sharp, *Old Testament Prophets for Today*, 13, who infers as follows: "The Hebrew Scriptures present us with two radically different views of the prophetic word. There is a striking difference between the prophetic word in the Deuteronomistic History and the prophetic word in the Latter prophets . . . . In Samuel and Kings, the prophetic word is always fulfilled. It is always an efficacious word: prophets predict the future, and God's word inevitably comes to pass. But in the Latter Prophets, the perspective is quite different. The prophets have pleaded with the people for generation after generation to no avail. For these prophets, the prophetic word is not something that is inevitably fulfilled. To the contrary, it is resisted and ignored for generations by those who hear it."

7. Cf. also Steck, *Prophetic Books and Their Theological Witness*, 7, who infers as follows: "This much is clear: The prophet is only provided in the superimposition of a relatively lengthy process of tradition that may have played a more or less active role. This process results in the prophetic writings. This situation means that the book stands in front of the prophet. Anyone wishing to find the prophet must first go through the book. In contrast to the long-dominant quest for the prophetic persons, the most pressing task now is an illuminating inquiry into the prophetic books."

8. Berges, *Isaiah*, 1; Berges, "Book of Isaiah as Isaiah's Book," 549–53.

9. Berges, *Isaiah*, 2.

10. Esterhuizen, "Study of the Tension between Despair and Hope," 1.

11. Cf. in this regard Esterhuizen and Groenewald, "'And It Shall Come to Pass on That Day.'"

lack of a future prospect creates traumatic feelings of nothingness for many people around the globe.

The book of Isaiah offers perspectives which enable us to dialogue with this monograph's overall question and theme. For the purpose of our analysis and contribution we have decided to focus on two central chapters in the book of Isaiah, namely chapters 7–8, as a recurring characteristic in these two chapters is the fluctuating tension between the experiences of nothingness (even despair) and moments of hope and resilience, that embodies the notion of everything. As the book of Isaiah constantly oscillates between prophecies of judgment and salvation, the verses of these two chapters abound with aspects of trauma and resilience, which are being highlighted by the symbols, imagery, and trauma specific metaphors which are all related to the trauma experienced by the prophet, King Ahaz, and the people of Judah.

Trauma is part of life, today and since the beginning of time. Questions of whether trauma in its broader sense is representable at all, and to use a more clarifying term "speakable," underline our inexplicable, sometimes impossible endeavor to explain and, most of the time, leave a verbal gap that plunges into a void of nothingness. The aim of this contribution therefore is to address the issue of nothingness (despair) and hope in these two chapters and, particularly, the role that *generational imprinted trauma*[12] and resilience played in this regard.

CHILDREN'S NAMES

The well-known expression "Children should be seen but not heard" has been around for many years, even centuries.[13] So much so, that it is sometimes quoted as if it is a command written in the Bible. The ambiguity of this expression in a sense underscores the nothingness of a child's validity, but it also amplifies the somethingness of their existence and symbolic meaning, because the "seen" becomes a loud visual noise that must be heard. This diminutive viewpoint of children also highlights the importance of children and the unspoken role that they played in the biblical world. Noting that children are integral in the text of the Hebrew Bible, it is almost ironic that they are so often invisible and therefore overlooked by scholars in their

---

12. According to us this term implies that past, present, and possible future trauma have an implicit impact on generations. Therefore, we would like to coin this *new term* in order to describe this process as *generational imprinted trauma*. Furthermore, for us this term implies "grief within grief."

13. Cf. also Nel, "'Children Must Be Seen and Heard.'"

search to understand the biblical text.[14] As with trauma related studies, research on the role that children play in biblical text is scarce and is only now coming to the forefront. As with trauma interpretation, a childhood lens could provide a new and interesting scope on biblical texts.[15]

The text of Isa 7 and 8 leaves one with a conundrum. The theme of both chapters centers around the three children and the symbolism of their respective names through their name-giving. However, almost nothing can be found in the text that portrays their significant roles as children per se, and the role they played in the prophecy of Isaiah, as it was intended for King Ahaz and the people of Judah. Even less is written about the perpetual trauma of the name-giving and how it shatters the sense of coherence and meaning for the prophet and the nation.[16] Meaning is patterned as an inner narrative or story, sometimes over generations, to give explanations and hope.

Isaiah's prophecy in chapters 7 and 8, through the name-giving of the children, metaphorically showcases the ruptures of possible suffering embedded in generational imprinted experiences of political violence, looming exile, pre-migration anxiety and desolation. All these traumatic circumstances encapsulated in the name-giving of the children were ancient traumas that formed part of the re-lived generational imprinted trauma of loss and fear. The remnant of traumas remains within the generational fiber with pieces of hope and resilience, and Elkins writes that "focusing on the survival that comes after trauma, means that the violence is acknowledged but so is the recovery and resilience."[17]

The metaphorical names of the children, namely *Shear-jashub*, *Immanuel*, and *Maher-shalal-hash-baz*, as it was embodied in their symbolic existence, had abstruse traumatic consequences on the Judean historical and cultural scene. The names of the children encapsulate a plethora of the despair and hope of the past, the turmoil of the present, and the possible hope of the future. Therefore, making the name-giving in a sense the notion that nothingness is everything and in everything lies nothingness. The name-giving in Isa 7 and 8 presents a pre-migration[18] text full of trauma and collective traumatic experiences which are contained in the symbolic names and embodiment of the children. Using a trauma perspective as well as a

14. Aasgaard, "History of Research on Children," 13–17.

15. Betsworth and Parker, "Introduction," 1–2; Aasgaard, "History of Research on Children," 16.

16. Cf. Esterhuizen, "Study of the Tension between Despair and Hope," 174.

17. Elkins, "Children and the Memory of Traumatic Violence," 188.

18. Cf. also in this regard Esterhuizen and Groenewald, "Towards a Theology of Migration."

pre-migration lens to read the text, an attempt will be made to address the onset and extension of trauma as nothingness and the possibility of hope within the name-giving of the children.

There is though no conclusive exegetical agreement whether "Immanuel" was the prophet's or another's child, as the narrator (scribe) does not state this fact clearly.[19] Childs, for example, infers as follows in this regard:

> One of the most significant features of this verse is the mysterious, even vague and indeterminate, tone that pervades the entire passage. The reader is simply not given information regarding the identity of the maiden, or how precisely the sign functions in relation to the giving of the name Immanuel. It is, therefore, idle to speculate on these matters; rather, the reader can determine if there are other avenues of understanding opened up by the larger context.[20]

Whatever the case may be regarding the child's parental identity, in this contribution we focus on the implications this name has for the narrative as a pre-migration text, as well as the specific trauma markers inherent in this text as well as in these names.

The central message of Isaiah's prophecy in chapters 7 and 8 is the giving of signs[21] to accentuate his prophetic intent. In these two chapters, three prominent signs are given to King Ahaz and the people of Judah to indicate YHWH's message and intentions. It is important to remember that these names are not merely symbolic in their prophetic nature in so far to convey Isaiah's prophetic message to a specific audience, but that the names were those of actual children. These children functioned and formed part of a household(s) within the community of Judah. Their lives, purpose, and meaning are intertwined in the prophetic history (and culture) of the time, rendering them and the community vulnerable to possible traumatic events. Yet the possible trauma implications and vestiges of survival, hope, and resilience of their names within the prophetic message has been largely overlooked by biblical scholars.

---

19. Beuken, *Jesaja 1-12*, 203-5; Roberts, *First Isaiah*, 119; Tull, *Isaiah 1-39*, 166.

20. Childs, *Isaiah*, 66.

21. Collins, "Sign of Immanuel," 228; Fohrer, *Symbolischen Handlungen der Propheten*, 29-31.

ISAIAH 7-8

During the latter half of the eighth century the modest kingdom of Judah found itself—once again—at the mercy of other nations due to larger political developments and events taking place in the ancient Near East. One of the major characteristics of this period was the instability on the larger political scene caused by the expansionistic policies of the neo-Assyrian king Tiglath-pileser III during his reign 745/744–727 BCE.[22] His rising to the throne once again marks a new beginning of Assyria's imperial phase and as a consequence it became a political and military powerhouse in the ancient Near East, dominating the political playfield as well as determining the rise and fall of many nations that crossed their path.[23] The Assyrians employed several tactics to keep the territories under their control, namely they destroyed cities, burdened the conquered nations with heavy tributes, and looted the economies of entire regions.[24]

The Assyrians threatened and harassed the vassal states to show their political power. Their independence was diminished step-by-step and finally they were incorporated into the provincial structures of the Assyrian Empire. These tactics created traumatic experiences, fear, and anxiety, not only for the people of Judah, but also for the other neighboring nations.[25] The political dynamics of this period heightened the looming danger and possible trauma that awaited them as the continuous exposure to the Assyrian threats to become a vassal state, caused distress, panic, and anxiety in many nations.

According to Dubovský,[26] the Levant saw a number of shifts in alliances during this time, and Syria and Palestine were no exception to the rule. Israel's alliance with Aram caused tension and hostility between the previous partners Judah-Israel to the point that they became enemies. This alliance between Aram and Israel is referred to as the Syro-Ephraimite coalition (734–732 BCE),[27] and this event is the historical setting for the significance

22. Dubovský, "Tiglath-Pileser III's Campaigns in 734–732 B.C.," 153, 164.

23. Hom, *Characterization of the Assyrians in Isaiah*, 1; Frahm, "Neo-Assyrian Period," 161; cf. also Esterhuizen, "Study of the Tension between Despair and Hope," 50.

24. Dubovský, "Tiglath-Pileser III's Campaigns in 734–732 B.C.," 168.

25. Esterhuizen, "Study of the Tension between Despair and Hope," 51.

26. Dubovský, "Tiglath-Pileser III's Campaigns in 734–732 B.C.," 154.

27. Cf. Dubovský, "Tiglath-Pileser III's Campaigns in 734–732 B.C.," 154–55, who infers as follows regarding this alliance and its threat to Judah: "The result of this shift of allegiance was that Judah lost some territories and was even invaded by Aram, Israel, Edom and Philistia (2 Kgs 15–16; 2 Chr 28; Isa 7). In scholarly literature several theories about the nature and the goals of the Syro-Ephraimite league and their invasion of Judah have been advanced. B. Oded, whose opinion has been followed by most modern scholars,

of the name-giving of Isaiah's children.[28] The first seventeen verses of chapter 7 narrates the encounter(s) between Isaiah and King Ahaz during a time when the royal family and Jerusalem were threatened by this Aram-Israel coalition.[29] According to this narrative Rezin, the Aramean king of Damascus, and Pekah, the king of Israel (probably with support from Philistine and Phoenicia), threatened to attack Judah and Jerusalem in order to overthrow Ahaz and to replace him with the son of Tabeel; the logic being that he probably would have been more submissive to their alliance policies.[30]

Subsequently Tiglath-pileser III launched a campaign in this area to dismantle the alliance consisting of Tyre, Damascus, and the Northern Kingdom of Israel.[31] According to the Assyrian Annals they were tribute bearers to the Assyrians during the years 740–738 BCE, and therefore any political aspirations of these nations would have been regarded as political pride which needed to be punished. Tiglath-pileser III undertook military

---

convincingly argued that the main reason for the Aram-Israel attack against Judah was control over Transjordan. Thus, the coalition Aram-Israel was primarily interested in territorial expansion and not in forming an anti-Assyrian league as was thought earlier. C. S. Ehrlich applied this logic to Phoenicia and Philistia. Thus, both Phoenicia and Philistia, even though presented as Assyrian enemies, were primarily interested in controlling the lucrative Levantine trade routes and ports along the Mediterranean coast. However, even though from the modern historians' point of view the Levantine states were not primarily interested in forming an anti-Assyrian league, from the Assyrian point of view the aspirations of the Levantine states for economic independence and their attempt to expand their territories were perceived as an anti-Assyrian activity. At the heart of this movement was Damascus (Aramean tribes) and Samaria (tribes in Northern Israel)."

28. Williamson, *Critical and Exegetical Commentary on Isaiah 1–27*, 108–10, infers as follows in this regard: "One particular historical question, where again an overwhelming consensus has occasionally been challenged, concerns the historical setting of the passage as a whole. The usual view, often dubbed the Syro-Ephraimite war (or crisis), assumes that the purpose of the coalition was to force Judah into their anti-Assyrian partnership, even though this is not directly mentioned in the passage. The broad outline of events during these crucial years (734–732 BCE) and their historical background is reasonably well known from other biblical as well as Assyrian sources and need not, perhaps, be rehearsed again here . . . . Thus, while I accept that the historical setting of this chapter cannot be finally determined, I believe that the usual scenario provides the most satisfying possibility. Nevertheless, the very fact that there is less certainty than is usually implied needs to be borne in mind in interpreting the purpose of the present narrative on its own terms, not in terms imposed from some hypothetical external source of knowledge." Cf. also Dubovský, "Tiglath-Pileser III's Campaigns in 734–732 B.C.," 153–70; Siddall, "Tiglath-Pileser III's Aid to Ahaz."

29. Tull, *Isaiah 1–39*, 157–58.

30. Cf. also Roberts, *First Isaiah*, 107, who infers in this regard: "The identity of this Tabeel is uncertain, and the name itself may be garbled. One suggestion is that the allies' candidate for the throne was a son of king Ittobaal of Tyre."

31. Siddall, "Tiglath-Pileser III's Aid to Ahaz," 94.

action against this alliance resulting in the defeat of Damascus, as well as the occupation of large parts of the Northern Kingdom and Tyre, which de facto meant they were turned into Assyrian provinces. This imperial policy meant that

> during the reign of Tiglath-pileser, Assyria exercised her control over the other nations of the Near East with a system of varying degrees of domination, depending on the subordinate nation's obedience. If, at the outset, a city submitted to Assyria, the local ruler would retain their throne, accept the Assyrian king as their overlord, and become a vassal . . . . If the local ruler fought or defied the Assyrian king once vassaldom was accepted, they would be replaced by a puppet ruler and suffer the burden of heavier annual tribute and more restricting treaty or oath conditions. The replacement of Peka with Hoshea is an example of this. Often acts of rebellion would then draw the punishment of a territory being annexed and transformed into an Assyrian province. This meant a total loss of autonomy, as Assyrian governors replaced the local leaders, a high chance of deportation occurring and loss of control over the local economy. An example of this is the provincialism of Damascus after the Syro-Ephraimite war.[32]

This crisis—in spite of the fact that the historical background cannot be determined with certainty[33]—forms the setting for the narrative which unfolds in these two chapters. The names of the children are significant for the theme of these chapters, namely that a message of encouragement and hope was given to King Ahaz and the people of Judah by the prophet Isaiah.[34] An encounter (possibly two—cf. 7:3, 10) takes place between the two men and the prophet's message is quite clear: as king of Judah you have to put your trust in YHWH. Ahaz decides against this advice and puts his hopes on Assyria;[35] in other words, he chooses the path of politics and not of faith (cf. "If you do not stand firm in faith, you shall not stand at all"—Isa 7:9).

Chapters 7 and 8 describe the prophet's and the other role players' thoughts in this persisting threat.[36] Ahaz panics and chapter 7:2 highlights both his as well as the people's overwhelming feelings of fear: "The heart of Ahaz and the heart of his people shook as the trees of the forest shake

---

32. Siddall, "Tiglath-Pileser III's Aid to Ahaz," 99–100.

33. Williamson, *Isaiah 6–12*, 109: "The coalition did not intend actually to fight at all but to achieve their goal through a major and overwhelming show of force . . ."

34. Grey, "Embodiment and the Prophetic Message in Isaiah's Memoir," 437; De Jong, *Isaiah among the Ancient Near Eastern Prophets*, 57.

35. Siddall, "Tiglath-Pileser III's Aid to Ahaz," 103.

36. Irvine, *Isaiah, Ahaz, and the Syro-Ephraimitic Crisis*, 2–3.

before the wind."³⁷ Isaiah's prophetic utterances to have faith and hope in YHWH also carries a silent judgment and warning what would happen if the king had a lack of faith. Despair would follow and, when the Assyrian threats were fulfilled, the people of Judah would suffer immensely. However, the king and the people of Judah become deaf and blind—as is written in Isa 6—and they become unmoved in their acceptance of Isaiah's prophetic words and encouragement. Even though Isaiah's prophetic messages are laced with judgment and feelings of desolation, they also carry messages in equal measures of expectation and hope.³⁸

As a result of this political crisis Isaiah not only gave verbal prophetic utterances to Ahaz and the people of Judah, but he also uses sign-acts to emphasize his message to the people, as the "symbolic naming of a prophet's child is also a form of sign-act," given that a sign-act reinforces the divine message to an audience.³⁹ In Isa 7 and 8 the prophet uses children from *inter alia* his own family as signs.⁴⁰ It has already been mentioned that the parental identity of the "Immanuel"-child is a matter of debate.

Although it may seem, at first glance, as if the children are background figures, the children and the significance of their names come to the fore when the texts are read in detail. In this regard Parker fittingly writes that "children help to shape the stories of the text, even when they play minor roles."⁴¹ Three children appear in Isa 7 and 8: *Shear-jashub* (שְׁאָר יָשׁוּב), meaning "a remnant shall return" (Isa 7:3ff: "And the Lord said to Isaiah: 'Go out to meet Ahaz, you and your son Shear-jashub'"), *Immanuel* (עִמָּנוּ אֵל), "God with us" (Isa 7:14: "Therefore the Lord himself will give you a sign. Look, the young woman is with child and shall bear a son, and shall call him Immanuel") and *Maher-shalal-hash-baz* (מַהֵר שָׁלָל חָשׁ בַּז) meaning "the spoil speeds, the prey hastens" (Isa 8:1: "Then the Lord said to me, Take a large tablet and write on it in common characters, 'For Maher-shalal-hash-baz'").

These three sign-names accentuate YHWH's message to the reluctant Judean audience, as these names indeed can be described as "visible evidence

---

37. Cf. also Esterhuizen, "Study of the Tension between Despair and Hope," 61.

38. Hammershaimb, "Immanuel Sign," 135; Weissflog, *Zeichen und Sinnbilder*, 513.

39. Lapsley, "'Look! The Children and I,'" 83. Cf. also Collins, "Sign of Immanuel," 226–38; Weissflog, *Zeichen und Sinnbilder*, 31–33; Wegner, *Examination of Kingship and Messianic Expectation*, 84–85; Williamson, "Messianic Texts in Isaiah 1–39," 253–54.

40. Cf. Isa 8:18: "See, I and the children whom the LORD has given me are signs and portents in Israel from the LORD of hosts, who dwells on Mount Zion."

41. Parker, *Valuable and Vulnerable*, 10.

of the presence and purpose of God."[42] The names function symbolically as signs, and their function is to authenticate YHWH's words to the Judean nation, that is to say, confirm that these words were from YHWH and directed to the people of Judah.[43] Although these names symbolize the word of YHWH to the nation, the children are much more than simply a name written on a tablet (or papyrus) to convey a message, because YHWH's message encapsulates both a message of judgment and despair, as well hope and resilience, and this message comes in the form of children.[44]

The events in Isa 7 and 8 therefore create a dialectic construct, where the signs and symbols which are inherent within the names of the children, permutates a plethora of trauma responses and experiences. Against this background, it is therefore understandable that these symbolic messages embedded in the names of the children can have a traumatic knock-on effect on the people, as it starts with an individual blow which ripples through the core of the community where even the social fiber of the community is put into question. The signs and symbols spark trauma responses where it entrenches the trauma in the scaffolds of the physical and psychological well-being of the individual and the collective society. Poser postulates that even a "historical framework acquires meaning for identity."[45] This framework within the sign-names of the children encircles the experiences of both the individual and the collective social group.

If we take the possible trauma implications of the sign-names of the children in chapters 7 and 8 into cognizance, then the affected within this historical scope would be King Ahaz, Isaiah, and the people of Judah. Therefore, we can assume that the traumatic implications increase from the individual exposure to the collective experience of the collective group.

A comprehensive study of the three named children of Isaiah as found in Isa 7 and 8 provides us with the research opportunity to assess this specific name-giving text as pre-traumatic experiences and possible *generational imprinted trauma*, because of the imminent and constant threat of war that was scourging their existence. This threat entailed the Syro-Ephraimite coalition as well as the Assyrian campaign where Judah was under the threat of beleaguering to become a vassal state for the Assyrians. In this regard Aster justly infers as follows: "The connection between the Syro-Ephraimite

---

42. Anderson, *Understanding the Old Testament*, 65.

43. Schutzius II, *Hebrew Word for "Sign,"* 121–24.

44. Motyer, *Prophecy of Isaiah*, 81–82; Esterhuizen, "Study of the Tension between Despair and Hope," 154.

45. Poser, "Embodied Memories," 338.

threat and the threat of an impending Assyrian invasion, which lie in the background of Isa 7, are explicit in 8:5–8."[46]

Up until now, our knowledge on migration is based on the post-exilic perspective as references to migration usually made after the fact. Pre-migration stressors personifies anticipation, possible devastating events, survival, and adjustment.[47] The name-giving texts in Isa 7 and 8 are encumbered with images of looming migration and possible destruction. In the metaphorical layers of "what is not said," the pre-migration stressors are screaming to be heard through the name-giving of the children. The metaphorical voices emblematically prophecy the relived experiences that form part of the *generational imprinted trauma*, but also through the relived sharing that creates a picture that offers glimmers of hope, resilience, and restitution for the people of Judah, as the children embody hope rather than judgment. Within the nothingness lies the everything of resilience and salvation.

Reading prophetic literature with a sensitivity to the effects that trauma has on individuals and communities at large, Stulman and Kim assert that biblical prophecy tries to find meaning in overwhelming suffering and to create a way for hope in the trauma-stricken communities.[48]

Shear-jashub (שְׁאָר יָשׁוּב)

The historical drama referring to the three significant children's names in Isa 7 and 8 contains all the elements of a real drama where there is a character, a plot, themes, and dialogue. With each reference the plot thickens, making the text more complex and puzzling with metaphorical meaning. The first name of a child that we read about is *Shear-jashub* (שְׁאָר יָשׁוּב—"a remnant shall return"). This child is physically present to embody the message from YHWH to the king and the nation. This child's metaphorical name forms part of the prophetic practice of Isa 7 where the symbolism underlines the message and character of the passage. Scholars such as Watts,[49] as well as McEntire,[50] state the notion that the boy must have been old enough to go with his father, Isaiah, to meet King Ahaz.

The physical presence of *Shear-jashub* becomes a very loud silent witness to the prophecy through his name-bearing at this historical point.

46. Aster, *Reflections of Empire in Isaiah 1–39*, 106.
47. Esterhuizen and Groenewald, "Towards a Theology of Migration," 34–41.
48. Stulman and Kim, *You Are My People*, 7.
49. Watts, *Isaiah 1–33*, 91.
50. McEntire, *Chorus of Prophetic Voices*, 37.

This charged moment of silent prophecy becomes even more resolved and tangible in the symbolic actions. Motyer postulates that the name embodies sound as well as sight and therefore could infer trauma elements of disaster and war.[51] Grammatically the name *Shear-jashub* is a short sentence, and Irvine explains that it consists of a subject, *Shear* (שְׁאָר), and a predicate *jashub* (יָשׁוּב), where the first part of the name *Shear* stems from the Hebrew root שאר, meaning "remain" or "left over";[52] in general this means "remnant," and יָשׁוּב comes from the stem שׁוּב which generally means "to return, go back."[53] It can also suggest a "turning back" to YHWH. According to Williamson, the verb can also be used in its military sense and would then mean "a return from battle" and the "survival in war."[54]

The historical plot of chapter 7 narrates a fearful King Ahaz who was shaking like a tree in the wind. Grey writes that the name of *Shear-jashub* hypothesizes that a remnant will return; even if the tree is to be cut down to a stump, the promise that it will survive is evident in the remnant that is left.[55] The metaphorical message that is given through the sign-name is that history will show that the threat from the north will not succeed, but that they will be cut down. In this context the name *Shear-jashub* embodies hope, comfort, and survival. The dichotomy in the name denotes that there is hope, but that the nothingness of despair is also just a breath away.

The complexity embedded in the name also predicts the possibility of future exile if King Ahaz chooses not to trust in YHWH through his lack of faith (7:9). The hesitancy of the king topples the equipoise into a dystopia of great suffering and trauma turbulence. The prophetic message of the sign-name *Shear-jashub* also prophesies something of the character of YHWH, that even in the midst of suffering and disaster, he will not abandon his people. Irvine cites that the dualistic meaning of the name could also imply a further two possible dissimilar reasons, namely, that the emphasis might suggest the smallest of remnant as "only a remnant" or "a remnant" and secondly, as an alternative it might intend an assertive meaning as "a remnant indeed" or less strongly "at least a remnant."[56] To synopsize Irvine's remarks, it suggests that the first and the second meaning are statements full of possible hope and resilience where the remnant repents and have faith

---

51. Motyer, *Prophecy of Isaiah*, 81.
52. Irvine, *Isaiah, Ahaz, and the Syro-Ephraimitic Crisis*, 142.
53. Willis, "Symbolic Names and Theological Themes," 74–75.
54. Williamson, *Isaiah 6–12*, 121.
55. Grey, "Embodiment and the Prophetic Message in Isaiah's Memoir," 439.
56. Irvine, *Isaiah, Ahaz, and the Syro-Ephraimitic Crisis*, 144.

THE TENSION BETWEEN EXPERIENCES OF NOTHINGNESS AND HOPE

and political survival is certain.[57] The tone of the third and the fourth translations are intertwined with negativity and hopelessness. These, however, differ from one another based on their response, either as a faithful turning back to YHWH or as "political survival."

The name *Shear-jashub* conveys a double implication pertaining to an appraising expression as well as a performative countenance. There are deluges of traumatic imagery in the name *Shear-jashub* in the text of Isa 7:2: "the heart of Ahaz and the heart of the people shook as the trees of the forest shake before the wind." These metaphorical images paint a dramatic opening scene of fear, tension, and anxiety, highlighting the overwhelming trauma markers and propensities within the text. The threat of war and the possibility of an Assyrian invasion on Judah from the northern borders elevate the trauma responses and experiences for all the role players concerned. The anxiety is palpable for King Ahaz and the people of Judah but more so for the prophet Isaiah who is anxious that the king would place his faith in Yahweh.

The name *Shear-jashub* holds a psychological stronghold for King Ahaz. The prophetic message in the name declares that a remnant shall return, but for the king in his struggle to grapple the meaning, a trauma offset point will be a reaction of disbelief and disillusion of the concept. The individual trauma trigger point of the king encompasses inner turmoil and conflict with himself, the reliving of past generational imprinted trauma and thought paralyses. Esterhuizen is of the opinion that the symptoms of a re-experienced trauma as pre-migration markers (*generational imprinted trauma*) "are the inability to make healthy choices and it is clearly visible in the choices that King Ahaz made in not trusting Yahweh but to place his fate in the hands of the Assyrians. King Ahaz's inability to choose faith has major ramifications for the people of Judah who will later experience the physical Assyrian threat of a looming war, and relentless exposure to the emotional stressors of fear and anxiety."[58]

The name *Shear-jashub* as an exemplar holds a double meaning as a trauma marker and indicator, because it promises within the sign-name fragments of hope and resilience. It also warns that despair will follow if the king displays a lack of faith in YHWH.[59] The whole impact of the name rests on the axes of faith even though despair lies embedded in the notion

---

57. Irvine, *Isaiah, Ahaz, and the Syro-Ephraimitic Crisis*, 144.
58. Esterhuizen, "Study of the Tension between Despair and Hope," 160.
59. Wegner, *Isaiah*, 105, infers in this regard as follows: "The child's name may be either a positive sign ('at least a remnant will return') or a negative one ('only a remnant will return'). The ambiguity could have been intentional and dependent on Ahaz's response."

that only *a* remnant will return *if* King Ahaz turns to YHWH in faith.[60] The returning remnant will only be experienced at a later stage within the historical drama of Judah, therefore impacting generational imprinted trauma and prolonging the culminating trauma symptoms for the king, Isaiah, and the people of Judah.

The name as a trauma marker creates a spontaneous visual picture,[61] and the young boy *Shear-jashub*, through his physical presence, visually embodied and portrayed the symbols of misery and hopefulness through his innocence. The intricacy of all these possible traumatic implications makes it possible to read the metaphorical name *Shear-jashub* through a lens of trauma and resilience.

Immanuel (עִמָּנוּ אֵל)

The Immanuel (עִמָּנוּ אֵל) name in Isa 7:14 is a very well-known passage in the book of Isaiah and many scholars have written an array of papers and commentaries about the meaning and interpretation of the name. For us, this specific sign-name is of extreme importance in the study of trauma and the symbolic trauma implications the name holds as part of the Isaiah prophecy and as an indicator of nothingness on the one hand, and hope and resilience on the other hand. It is of interest to note that this name reference does not appear anywhere else in the Hebrew Bible, but Childs writes in this regard that it has a close parallel with Ps 46:8, 12, which makes it clear that it is a close expression of trust in YHWH and the essential devotion he has towards Israel.[62] The dramatic plot in Isa 7:10–16 narrates the traumatic facts that King Ahaz presents with symbolic deafness and blindness to the message contained in the sign-name of *Shear-jashub*. This obstinate attitude of King Ahaz does not deter the prophet, and Isaiah persists through his prophetic utterances that the king should "ask a sign from YHWH your God" (7:11).

According to Motyer, the sign is no longer a matter of invitation or a sign of hope, but of prediction.[63] It topples the scale and becomes a sign of judgment and despair, as it displays the displeasure YHWH has with this stubborn king as well as with the Judean people. There is another sentiment offered by Hibbard which offers, in our opinion, a more ameliorate observation, namely that *Immanuel* as a sign-name is reused in Isaiah 8:8 and 8:10,

---

60. Esterhuizen, "Study of the Tension between Despair and Hope," 160.
61. Wilson and Lindy, *Trauma, Culture, and Metaphor*, 6.
62. Childs, *Isaiah*, 66.
63. Motyer, *Prophecy of Isaiah*, 84.

where in both verses reference is made to "God with us."[64] The verse in Isa 8:8, "it will sweep on into Judah as a flood, and, pouring over, it will reach up to the neck; and its outspread wings will fill the breadth of your land, O Immanuel," encompasses a threatening connection to the looming Assyrian invasion. This specific reference holds a glimmer of hope for Judah but an almost unenviable defeat for Samaria and Damascus. Chapter 8:10 reads: "Take counsel together, but it shall be brought to naught; speak a word, but it will not stand, for God is with us." The core message of this verse is to forewarn all the enemies that are threatening Judah that their wicked plans will not succeed against Jerusalem because "God is with us" (עִמָּנוּ אֵל).

The child-sign of *Immanuel* was later taken up in the Gospel of Matthew, but Grey makes a valid assumption that many scholars "miss the value and the importance"[65] of this passage within the background of the Syro-Ephraimite crisis and the traumatic events it pertains. Within research circles, much speculation and debates are given to clarify the possible identity of the father and mother of the child *Immanuel*. Whereas many scholars are of the opinion that the first child (*Shear-jashub*) and the third child (*Maher-shalal-hash-baz*) are Isaiah's sons, the identity of the second child (*Immanuel*) has often been discussed, and there is no final conclusion in this regard (e.g., whether it was Isaiah's son or Ahaz's son—as two of the possible options mentioned).[66] Although Roberts explains that Isaiah never openly recognized *Immanuel* as his son as it was in the case with *Shear-jashub* and *Maher-Shalal-Hash-Baz*, he is of the opinion that all three of these children with symbolic names were Isaiah's children.[67] The text, however, does not indicate to us who the child's father or mother is, and in spite of this the biological identity of the child is of lesser importance for the significance of the name which the child bears within the development of the narrative, as well as regarding the trauma indicators inherent in the name of this child. If the identity of the mother and child was important to the scribes, they would have made it known to the reader of this text.[68]

King Ahaz becomes the catalyst of the traumatic events to follow when he makes the fatal decision to place his trust in a precarious political scenario with a distrustful human king, rather than the steadfast promise of

64. Hibbard, "From Name to Book," 138.

65. Grey, "Embodiment and the Prophetic Message in Isaiah's Memoir," 442.

66. Cf. *inter alia* Beuken, *Jesaja 1–12*, 203–5; Childs, *Isaiah*, 66; Collins, "Sign of Immanuel," 231; Clements, "Immanuel Prophecy of Isaiah 7:10–17," 70; Roberts, *First Isaiah*, 119; Roberts, "Isaiah and His Children," 193–203; Tull, *Isaiah 1–39*, 166; Wildberger, *Isaiah 1–12*, 308–10; Williamson, *Isaiah 6–12*, 155–62.

67. Roberts, *First Isaiah*, 107.

68. Tull, *Isaiah 1–39*, 166.

salvation that YHWH offers through the prophetic utterances of Isaiah.[69] This will eventually lead to the traumatic devastation of his household and the people Judah (cf. the prediction in 8:5–10). The special imagery is used in a defined and precise way, and therefore Motyer writes, as already has been stated, that the sign of the name *Immanuel* is no longer a persuasion to have faith anymore, but rather a prediction of a disaster that will befall Judah.[70] It also underlines all that YHWH said to King Ahaz through the prophetic words of Isaiah—that this was the precipitant, where cause and effect collided, and the result would be divine retribution for this non-belief.

The metaphorical sign-name of *Immanuel* encapsulated trauma tendencies of destruction, fear, and possible death as an outcome of divine retribution for the people of Judah. The disillusionment and thought paralysis on the anticipation of loss of identity and becoming a vassal state must have triggered trauma responses of fear and anxiety in the minds of King Ahaz, Isaiah, and the Judean people. The stark reality of looming war and devastation created a trauma platform of fear as the prolonged exposure to these stressors impacted the social core and well-being of the people of Judah. A traumatic void is unfolding where nothingness, despair, and disaster occur together in a paradoxical sphere of hope, somethingness, redemption, and resilience, as is written in verses 14–16. Wilson and Lindy write that trauma markers or indicators contain facets that portray values, beliefs, and a social way of living.[71] To identify the trauma markers in the sign-name *Immanuel*, one needs to take the historical background of the time as narrated in Isa 7 into consideration. It is set against the milieu and turmoil of the Syro-Ephraimite threat, and YHWH offers King Ahaz a sign to defeat the political threat.

The wonder of hope and resilience in the sign-name *Immanuel* reaches further than a promise to the individual but encompasses the nation of Judah as a whole. The promise in the name "God with us" pervades the social fiber and functional breadths of the community, rendering possible future hope and growth through resilience and endurance.

---

69. Wegner, *Isaiah*, 110, infers in this regard as follows: "The syntax of verse 17, which places the direct object as far as possible from the verb, highlights the dread that the coming of the Assyrian king should instill. Thus, Ahaz is warned that the very instrument he will call upon for protection will instead bring destruction."

70. Motyer, *Isaiah by the Day*, 84.

71. Wilson and Lindy, *Trauma, Culture, and Metaphor*, 6.

Maher-shalal-hash-baz (מַהֵר שָׁלָל חָשׁ בַּז)

Chapter 8 tells the story of another child—a third child—who is present in the narrative which has commenced in chapter 7. Although the narrative style in chapter 8 differs from the style in chapter 7 (first-person versus third-person),[72] it is more important for our discussion that this child will also be a sign (אוֹת) to the nation during the tumultuous times they are experiencing during the Syro-Ephraimite crisis.[73] In spite of the blindness and deafness of Ahaz and the Judean community (cf. 6:10), Isaiah persists to embody his message to the king and the nation.[74] This third name, which is a child-sign, is indicated as *Maher-shalal-hash-baz* (מַהֵר שָׁלָל חָשׁ בַּז), with the meaning of "speedy plunder, swift pillage" or "the spoil speeds, the prey hastens" (Isa 8:1–4). In the development of the narrative the prophet was instructed to write this name in large characters on a tablet (גִּלָּיוֹן),[75] and only afterwards the name had to be given as a metaphorical name to his son who was born to symbolize the sudden attack by the Assyrian army.[76]

Childs infers that the sign is a form of symbolic action indicating that a prophecy of judgment will be fulfilled soon.[77] In this instance (Isa 8), the symbolic name of the child *Maher-shalal-hash-baz* functions as the sign and is preceded by a symbolic inscription on a tablet of the name which is to be given to the child. The presence of the well-known and reliable witnesses in this narrative could be an indication that YHWH has already decided upon the judgment which will be executed, namely before the child could say his first words, the two coalition partners of Damascus and Samaria will be attacked. This attack does not necessarily imply their final defeat or destruction, as it is plausible to see the context of this narrative during the Syro-Ephraimite crisis, and as Williamson infers, the "implications of the present verse of victory for the Assyrians without the necessary personal

---

72. Chapter 7 is written in the third-person style and chapter 8 is written in the first-person narrative style in which chapter 6 was also written. This is, however, not the aim of this contribution to elaborate in more detail on the difference in style. Cf. Beuken, *Jesaja 1–12*, 214; Williamson, *Isaiah 6–12*, 208.

73. Beuken, *Jesaja 1–12*, 219; Roberts, *First Isaiah*, 129; Smith, *Isaiah 1–39*, 219; Williamson, *Isaiah 6–12*, 208.

74. Grey, "Embodiment and the Prophetic Message in Isaiah's Memoir," 445.

75. Tull, *Isaiah 1–39*, 179, infers that a גִּלָּיוֹן was translated in the ancient translations in varied ways, namely as a "papyrus sheet; tanned skin; tablet; book. While the NIV calls it a 'large scroll,' others have suggested it may be of clay, stone, or wood covered with wax."

76. Esterhuizen, "Study of the Tension between Despair and Hope," 156.

77. Childs, *Isaiah*, 72.

involvement of the king and of payments made to him seem reasonably to have been fulfilled, therefore."[78]

Grey emphasizes the following three aspects in this pericope, namely the instruction from YHWH (8:1), the fulfilment of the particular instruction by Isaiah (8:2–3a), and lastly the interpretation given by YHWH himself (8:3b–4).[79] Each one of these aspects entails the sign-name of the child: the meaning of his name containing two comparable verbs, namely "quick; swift" and "spoil; plunder." According to YHWH's interpretation (8:4), the cities of Samaria and Damascus will be plundered by the Assyrians. The text thus unmistakably indicates who will fall victim to the Assyrians' plundering.[80]

According to Esterhuizen the name *Maher-shalal-hash-baz* implicates several trauma symptoms which were of particular concern to Judah and are therefore relevant for our discussion here.[81] As the name indicates, the enemy will come swiftly and speedily, will leave behind devastation and plunder, and will depart with the spoils of war.[82] Although Isaiah announces judgment for Judah's enemies, there is not much reason to celebrate, as we see in the following section (8:5–8).[83] As a consequence of Assyria's attack on Samaria and Damascus, Judah's vulnerability will be exposed even more and it indeed will become an easy target for a possible Assyrian threat.

The following section remembers the warning Isaiah gave to Judah not to celebrate the Assyrians as YHWH's instrument of liberation, but to be warned that Judah, like Samaria and Damascus, will be punished by the Assyrians as well (cf. 10:5—"the rod of my anger"). Once again, we hear ominous language in this section, which is described in vivid poetic language, namely that the Assyrians will come like the "mighty flood waters of the River" (8:7). The flood waters of this mighty river (i.e., the Euphrates) will sweep over the country and as a consequence will leave it devastated. As is the case with a flood, the people will be overwhelmed when the Assyrians enter their land ("it will sweep on into Judah as a flood, and, pouring over, it will reach up to the neck; and its outspread wings will fill the breadth of your land, O Immanuel"—Isa 8:8).[84]

---

78. Williamson, *Isaiah 6–12*, 223.
79. Grey, "Embodiment and the Prophetic Message in Isaiah's Memoir," 445–46.
80. Esterhuizen, "Study of the Tension between Despair and Hope," 166.
81. Esterhuizen, "Study of the Tension between Despair and Hope," 166.
82. Everson, *Vision of the Prophet Isaiah*, 39.
83. Wildberger, *Isaiah 1–12*, 339.
84. Everson, *Vision of the Prophet Isaiah*, 39–40.

Continuous exposure to traumatic events heightens the whole trauma episode, as we have seen in these two chapters. The trauma events, such as war, devastation, threats, subsequent fears and anxiety, to which King Ahaz, the prophet Isaiah, and the people of Judah have been exposed, can cause emotional desensitization where feelings of numbness[85] and hopelessness are present and have an effect on either the individual or the collective's emotional responses and rational behavior or thinking.[86] According to O'Connor, the above is a normal defence mechanism which protects "people from feeling unbearable violence, hurt, and loss."[87] If people lose all hope, it is as if they are in a state of shutdown; they are no longer alive in this world. This lack of emotional responsiveness is a coping mechanism in order to live through the trauma and to survive the trauma. Although the name *Maher-shalal-has-baz* would have caused a sigh of relief for the current moment, it is not a neutral term and inherent in the name is the indication of a forthcoming threat to Judah as well. The trauma implications of "speedy plunder, swift pillage" would have caused numbness as they had been threatened for a prolonged period already.

In this narrative YHWH's judgment and his displeasure with the king and the people are tangible. Because of their lack of faith, the nation is pushed into despair and nothingness, with apparently no hope of a new dawn at all. The question can rightfully be asked if any hope, in the midst of nothingness, is possible when we take the metaphorical meaning of the name *Maher-shalal-hash-baz* into consideration. Although the name may not indicate any immediate promise of salvation, it on the other hand provides the hope that in a few years Samaria and Damascus would not be a threat to Judah anymore. The little flame of hope, burning in the midst of feelings of nothingness, may be that Isaiah's prophetic utterances indicate to the nation, and the reader of the narrative as well, the promise that "God is with us" (8:8—עִמָּנוּ אֵל).[88]

CONCLUSION

The sign-names of the children in Isa 7 and 8 can leave the reader perplexed as the text narrates not only the metaphorical name meaning, but provides numerous trauma nuances and opacity in reference to these names. The complexity of the metaphorical meaning of the names embodies the possible

---

85. Visser, "Trauma and Power in Postcolonial Literary Studies," 115.
86. Esterhuizen, "Study of the Tension between Despair and Hope," 166.
87. O'Connor, *Jeremiah: Pain and Promise*, 25.
88. Esterhuizen, "Study of the Tension between Despair and Hope," 168.

traumatic outcome that not only King Ahaz had to face, but also forewarned the nation of Judah of their possible fate if they disobeyed YHWH. The names in a way included the traumatic consequences of the individual and the collective in a culminative manner.

The historical setting of Isa 7 and 8 sets the dramatic scene for tension, trauma, and threats. The major event that permutated the historical landscape of the time was the Syro-Ephraimite crisis that took place between 734–732 BCE. A scenario of looming war and destruction was set and the foreboding invasion by the Assyrians intensified the trauma levels to new heights for both the individual as well as the collective group. The relationship between King Ahaz and the prophet Isaiah came to the fore during the Syro-Ephraimite war where the possibility of war and suppression became a stark reality.

In the Judean history, the text in Isa 7 and 8 became the everyday epoch of imminent war, suppression, constant fear, hopelessness, and loss. The reaction and behavior of King Ahaz represented a king's and a nation's response to the oracles spoken by Isaiah. The king's callous reactions reverberate with the overall sense of nothingness and despair. However, the hope and restoration for a king and a nation was found within the inner fibers of the sign-names of the children. Children, though they sometimes might be in the background in the Hebrew text, do form an integral part of the prophetic message as attested in Isa 7 and 8. The symbolic sign-names not only embody the physical presence of these children but also emphasize that YHWH had a message for both King Ahaz and the nation of Judah. The names are not merely sign-acts but also symbols of despair and hope for the people of Judah. Faith and belief in YHWH would result in hope and restitution, but the lack of faith and trust would result in despair and suffering. The symbolism in the names exposed the trauma markers experienced by the king, the prophet, and the people of Judah as individuals but also as a collective group.

The prophecy of Isaiah cuts like a two-sided sword as it oscillates between prophecies of judgment and salvation. On the same continuum, these prophecies also signify messages of hope and despair that expose the possible tension and trauma tendencies within the layers of the text. The names of the children, *Shear-jashub*, *Immanuel*, and *Maher-shalal-hash-baz*, give the scope to use text correlated trauma markers as pre-migration trauma. This can then be read and understood as generational imprinted trauma, which is rooted in historical collective memories that draws the historical collective trauma into the imagined impending threat of reality. Out of the nothingness of despair, a profusion of the collective having everything is created. The names as signs as embodied in the children became barometers for the hope and salvation that YHWH would have for Judah if they believe, and by extension, for all humankind.

BIBLIOGRAPHY

Aasgaard, Reidar. "History of Research on Children in the Bible and the Biblical World: Past Developments, Present State—and Future Potential." In *T&T Clark Handbook of Children in the Bible and the Biblical World*, edited by Sharon Betsworth and Julie F Parker, 13–38. London: T. & T. Clark, 2019.

Anderson, Bernhard W. *Understanding the Old Testament*. 3rd ed. Englewood Cliffs, NJ: Prentice-Hall, 1975.

Ashton, Jennifer. "'Rose Is a Rose': Gertrude Stein and the Critique of Indeterminacy." *Modernism/Modernity* 9 (2002) 581–604.

Aster, Shawn Z. *Reflections of Empire in Isaiah 1–39: Responses to Assyrian Ideology*. Ancient Near Eastern Monographs 19. Atlanta: Society of Biblical Literature, 2017.

Berges, Ulrich. "The Book of Isaiah as Isaiah's Book: The Latest Developments in the Research of the Prophets." *Old Testament Essays* 23.3 (2010) 549–73.

———. *Isaiah: The Prophet and His Book*. Translated by P. Sumpter. Sheffield, UK: Sheffield Phoenix, 2012.

Betsworth, Sharon, and Julie F. Parker. "Introduction." In *T&T Clark Handbook of Children in the Bible and the Biblical World*, edited by Sharon Betsworth and Julie F Parker, 1–10. London: T. & T. Clark, 2019.

Beuken, Willem A. M. *Jesaja 1–12*. Translated by Ulrich F. Berges. Herders Theologischer Kommentar Zum Alten Testament. Freiburg i.Br.: Herder, 2003.

Childs, Brevard S. *Isaiah*. Old Testament Library. Louisville, KY: Westminster John Knox, 2001.

Clements, Ronald E. "The Immanuel Prophecy of Isaiah 7:10–17 and Its Messianic Interpretation." In *Old Testament Prophecy: From Oracles to Canon*, edited by Ronald E. Clements, 65–77. Louisville, KY: Westminster John Knox, 1996.

Collins, John J. "The Sign of Immanuel." In *Prophecy and Prophets in Ancient Israel: Proceedings of the Oxford Old Testament Seminar*, edited by John Day, 225–44. Library of Hebrew Bible/Old Testament Studies 531. London: T. & T. Clark, 2010.

Cook, Stephen L., et al. *The Prophets: Introducing Israel's Prophetic Writings*. Minneapolis: Fortress, 2022.

De Jong, Matthijs J. *Isaiah among the Ancient Near Eastern Prophets: A Comparative Study of the Earliest Stages of the Isaiah Tradition and the Neo-Assyrian Prophecies*. Supplements to Vetus Testamentum 117. Leiden: Brill, 2007.

Dubovský, Peter. "Tiglath-Pileser III's Campaigns in 734–732 B.C.: Historical Background of Isa 7; 2 Kgs 15–16 and 2 Chr 27–28." *Biblica* 87 (2006) 153–70.

Elkins, Kathleen G. "Children and the Memory of Traumatic Violence." In *T&T Clark Handbook of Children in the Bible and the Biblical World*, edited by Sharon Betsworth and Julie F Parker, 181–98. London: T. & T. Clark, 2019.

Esterhuizen, Elizabeth. "A Study of the Tension between Despair and Hope in Isaiah 7 and 8 from a Perspective of Trauma and Posttraumatic Growth." PhD diss., Unisa, Pretoria, 2016.

Esterhuizen, Elizabeth, and Alphonso Groenewald. "'And It Shall Come to Pass on That Day, the Lord Will Whistle for the Fly Which Is at the End of the Water Channels of Egypt, and for the Bee Which Is in the Land of Assyria' (Is 7:18): Traumatic Impact of the Covid-19 Virus as a Lens to Read Isaiah 7:18–25." *HTS Theological Studies* 77 (2021) 1–7. https://doi.org/10.4102/hts.v77i3.6333.

———. "Towards a Theology of Migration: A Survival Perspective from Isaiah 1–12." *Transilvania* 10 (2021) 34–41.

Everson, A. Joseph. *The Vision of the Prophet Isaiah: Hope in a War-Weary World—A Commentary*. Eugene, OR: Wipf & Stock, 2019.

Fleissner, Robert F. "Stein's Four Roses." *Journal of Modern Literature* 6 (1977) 325–28.

Fohrer, Georg. *Die symbolischen Handlungen der Propheten*. 2, Überarb. und erweitert. Abhandlungen zur Theologie des Alten und Neuen Testaments 54. Zürich: Zwingli, 1968.

Frahm, Eckart. "The Neo-Assyrian Period (ca. 1000–609 BCE)." In *Companion to Assyria*, edited by Eckart Frahm, 161–208. Hoboken, NJ: Wiley, 2017.

Grey, Jacqueline. "Embodiment and the Prophetic Message in Isaiah's Memoir." *Pneuma* 39 (2017) 431–56.

Hammershaimb, Erling. "The Immanuel Sign." *Studia Theologica—Nordic Journal of Theology* 3 (1949) 124–42.

Hibbard, J. Todd. "From Name to Book: Another Look at the Composition of the Book of Isaiah with Special Reference to Isaiah 56–66." In *A Teacher for All Generations: Essays in Honor of James C. Vanderkam, vol. 1*, edited by Eric F. Mason et al., 133–49. Supplements to the Journal for the Study of Judaism 153.1. Leiden: Brill, 2012.

Hom, Mary K. Y. H. *The Characterization of the Assyrians in Isaiah: Synchronic and Diachronic Perspectives*. Library of Hebrew Bible/Old Testament Studies 559. London: T. & T. Clark, 2012.

Irvine, Stuart A. *Isaiah, Ahaz, and the Syro-Ephraimitic Crisis*. Society of Biblical Literature Dissertation Series 123. Atlanta: Scholars, 1990.

Lapsley, Jacqueline E. "'Look! The Children and I Are as Signs and Portents in Israel': Children in Isaiah." In *The Child in the Bible*, edited by Marcia J. Bunge et al., 82–102. Grand Rapids: Eerdmans, 2008.

McEntire, Mark. *A Chorus of Prophetic Voices: Introducing the Prophetic Literature of Ancient Israel*. Louisville, KY: Presbyterian, 2015.

Motyer, J. Alec. *Isaiah by the Day: A New Devotional Translation*. Rossshire, UK: Christian Focus, 2011.

———. *The Prophecy of Isaiah*. Leicester: InterVarsity, 1993.

Nel, Reggie. "Children Must Be Seen and Heard"—Doing Postcolonial Theology with Children in a (Southern) African Reformed Church. *HTS Theological Studies* 72 (2016) 1–7.

O'Connor, Kathleen M. *Jeremiah: Pain and Promise*. Minneapolis: Fortress, 2011.

Parker, Julie F. *Valuable and Vulnerable: Children in the Hebrew Bible, Especially the Elisha Cycle*. Brown Judaic Studies 355. Providence, RI: Brown University Press, 2013.

Poser, Ruth. "Embodied Memories: Gender-Specific Aspects of Prophecy as Trauma Literature." In *Prophecy and Gender in the Hebrew Bible*, edited by L. Juliana M. Claassens and Irmtraud Fischer, 333–57. The Bible and Women: An Encyclopaedia of Exegesis and Cultural History 1.2. Atlanta: Society of Biblical Literature, 2021.

Roberts, Jimmy J. M. *First Isaiah: A Commentary*. Hermeneia. Minneapolis: Fortress, 2015.

———. "Isaiah and His Children." In *Biblical and Related Studies Presented to Samuel Iwry*, edited by Scott Morschauser and Ann Kort, 193-203. Winona Lake, IN: Eisenbrauns, 1985.

Schutzius, Mark D., II. *The Hebrew Word for "Sign" and Its Impact on Isaiah 7:14*. Eugene, OR: Wipf & Stock, 2015.

Sharp, Carolyn J. *Old Testament Prophets for Today*. Louisville, KY: Westminster John Knox, 2009.

Siddall, Luis R. "Tiglath-Pileser III's Aid to Ahaz: A New Look at the Problems of the Biblical Accounts in Light of the Assyrian Sources." *Ancient Near Eastern Studies* 46 (2009) 93-106.

Smith, Gary V. *Isaiah 1-39*. New American Commentary 15A. Nashville: Broadman & Holman, 2007.

Steck, Odil H. *The Prophetic Books and Their Theological Witness*. St. Louis, MO: Chalice, 2000.

Stulman, Louis, and Hyun C. P. Kim. *You Are My People: An Introduction to Prophetic Literature*. Nashville: Abingdon, 2010.

Tull, Patricia K. *Isaiah 1-39*. Smyth and Helwys Bible Commentary. Macon, GA: Smyth & Helwys, 2010.

Visser, Irene. "Trauma and Power in Postcolonial Literary Studies." In *Contemporary Approaches in Literary Trauma Theory*, edited by Michelle Balaev, 106-29. Hampshire, UK: Palgrave Macmillan, 2014.

Watts, John D. W. *Isaiah 1-33*. Rev. ed. Word Biblical Commentary 24. Nashville: Thomas Nelson, 2005.

Wegner, Paul D. *An Examination of Kingship and Messianic Expectation in Isaiah 1-35*. Lewiston: Mellen Biblical, 1992.

———. *Isaiah: An Introduction and Commentary*. Tyndale Old Testament Commentaries 20. Downers Grove: InterVarsity Press Academic, 2021.

Weissflog, Kay. *Zeichen und Sinnbilder: die Kinder der Propheten Jesaja und Hosea*. Leipzig: Evangelische Verlagsanstalt, 2011.

Wildberger, Hans. *Isaiah 1-12: A Commentary*. Translated by Thomas H. Trapp. Continental Commentaries. Minneapolis: Fortress, 1991.

Williamson, Hugh G. M. *A Critical and Exegetical Commentary on Isaiah 1-27*. Vol. 2, *Commentary on Isaiah 6-12*. International Critical Commentary. London: Bloomsbury T. & T. Clark, 2018.

———. "The Messianic Texts in Isaiah 1-39." In *King and Messiah in Israel and the Ancient Near East: Proceedings of the Oxford Old Testament Seminar*, edited by John Day, 238-70. Journal for the Study of the Old Testament Supplement 270. Sheffield, UK: Sheffield Academic, 1998.

Willis, John T. "Symbolic Names and Theological Themes in the Book of Isaiah." *Horizons in Biblical Theology* 23 (2001) 72-92.

Wilson, John P., and Jacob D. Lindy. *Trauma, Culture, and Metaphor: Pathways of Transformation and Integration*. Routledge Psychosocial Stress Series 47. New York: Routledge, 2013.

Chapter 10

Using Biblical Trauma-Texts to Help Pain-Bearers Find Hope

June F. Dickie

INTRODUCTION

Many people today live in situations of extreme difficulty, whether it be their physical or financial situations (for example, living in an informal settlement or township in South Africa, plagued with violence and poverty), or facing seemingly hopeless vulnerability (as experienced by those suffering chronic illness, loneliness, or family estrangements). Although the particular problem might seem related to modern life, there are many biblical narratives and poems which touch on the same emotional issues. Thus, in this study, trauma-bearers were invited to physically enter into the world of the text through oral performance (drama and song), thereby coming closer to the emotional world of the characters. Apart from facilitating a meaningful engagement with the text on an affective level, they could also bring cultural nuances into the story/poem, thereby "owning" the text.

The participants in this study included adults and grade 7 learners from townships in Cape Town, and three different groups of "burden-bearers" (refugees, HIV+ women, and members of the LGBT community) from two provinces in South Africa. The former engaged with the story of Ruth and performed the narrative before an audience. The latter used the form of biblical lament to write and perform their own laments, either individually or as a group. In all cases, the participants enjoyed the activities, and found them helpful and healing.

Trauma-theory is well established, and the study makes use of the work of the psychiatrist Judith Herman[1] as well as pastoral theologians who address "soul abuse." Further, literary trauma theory (with specific reference to biblical literature) is introduced, as well as the theory underlying biblical lament. Once this foundation has been laid, the empirical studies are briefly described along with the results which emerged. A conclusion compares this approach to other "trauma-healing" programs which also use biblical literature, and suggests some advantages achieved by this non-invasive, indirect methodology.

THEORETICAL BASIS

Herman's Three Steps towards Emotional Healing

Judith Herman lists three factors that are essential for a traumatized person to begin to heal.[2] First, the person must know that she is safe (physically and emotionally); second, she must reclaim the memory, bringing it back to consciousness with the emotional and bodily sensations that attach to it. Herman calls this "remembering and mourning." And third, connection must be restored between the survivor and her community, in order for her to be able to move positively into the future.

A common problem is that the neurological impact of trauma often results in the trauma-survivor battling to find the words to express her pain.[3] Nevertheless, it is essential that the traumatic experience be reactivated if she is to gain dominance over the emotions and cognitive processes connected with the trauma.[4] As noted, it is important that care be taken to ensure that the former victim feels safe when being re-exposed to the trauma trigger. Towards this end, the emotional load must be "contained."[5] In the words of Herman: "There is a need to constantly maintain a balance between preserving safety and facing the past."[6]

---

1. Herman, *Trauma and Recovery*.
2. Herman, *Trauma and Recovery*, 155, 175–77.
3. Sölle, *Suffering*, 71–72.
4. Allen, *Coping with Trauma*, 262. Also, Ringel and Brandel, *Trauma*, 22.
5. Allen, *Coping with Trauma*, 250.
6. Herman, *Trauma and Recovery*, 176.

The third step in trauma-healing requires the burden-bearer to establish social connections with others in order to be able to move forward in her life. However, "traumatic events destroy the sustaining bonds between the individual and community,"[7] leaving a former victim feeling isolated. This is a major obstacle for, as Sweeney notes, "One of the greatest of human pains is the loneliness of being alone."[8] Thus, establishing a support group for those who have endured a similar trauma can be very helpful. Participants often report the comfort they experience being with fellow-sufferers. As Herman notes, their sense of worth is restored.[9] Indeed, having others listen empathically to her story gives an abused person the gift of *being heard*, which greatly reduces her sense of social isolation.[10] Further, having experienced similar pain, the fellow-sufferers *validate* what the burden-bearer shares, a "vital component [of the healing process]."[11] They also can serve as "dialogue partners,"[12] helping the former-victim reinterpret her experience. The presence of others who are supportive, in an environment that is safe, helps the sufferer overcome the "freezing of an ability to plan" that follows trauma, and she is slowly enabled, once again, to make decisions.

This approach to healing is slow and "never complete,"[13] but if the memory can be processed and stored as a "past" event, the survivor can focus on the present and the future, with renewed hope and enthusiasm.

Literary Trauma Theory

Scholars working with "trauma literature" in the Bible[14] have been exploring the role and function of such biblical texts. An understanding of the processes that support healing, in particular "remembering and mourning,"[15] has alerted them to the possibility of using literature to help a sufferer take these steps. First, a recognition that linguistic symbols facilitate the confrontation of difficult memories "at a distance" means they can be safely processed,[16]

---

7. Herman, *Trauma and Recovery*, 214.
8. Sweeney, "Group Play Therapy," 227.
9. Herman, *Trauma and Recovery*, 215.
10. Allen, *Coping with Trauma*, 252, 266.
11. West, "Between Text and Trauma," 220.
12. Frechette and Boase, "Defining 'Trauma' as a Useful Lens for Biblical Interpretation," 7.
13. Herman, *Trauma and Recovery*, 195.
14. E.g., Frechette and Boase, "Defining 'Trauma.'"
15. Herman, *Trauma and Recovery*.
16. Granofsky, *Trauma Novel*, 6–7.

thereby addressing the first two criteria for emotional healing. The "trauma trigger" can be introduced, but its impact contained, thereby facilitating the vital balance (between exposure and safety) needed for healing to occur.

Further, the expression of the trauma story within an empathetic context, to fellow-sufferers or good listeners, provides for the third criterion, connecting with others.[17] Thus, given a supportive audience, literature can play a significant role in helping both individuals and communities recover and build resilience.[18]

In this chapter, two ways of using biblical literature for trauma-healing are introduced. First, a carefully selected biblical text (which includes aspects of trauma) can help readers (or hearers) engage with the emotions of the characters in a story. If they can identify with some of the struggles the characters experience, and further, note how God intervenes in the situation, this can give them hope in their own context. Such texts often show characters revealing a "capacity for resistance, survival, and recovery,"[19] which can help readers/hearers think about how to preserve agency or develop initiative in their own situations. Thus, such texts have within them a "restorative capacity."[20]

Many biblical texts can be used in this way. Those which have been found to be particularly helpful are the narratives of Ruth and Job,[21] and the rape of Tamar in 2 Sam 13.[22] Esala has used the experience of Ruth having to go down to the threshing floor at night to meet with her boss (Ruth 3) as a means to talk about the fears of young girls in Ghana, where "sugar-daddies" are prevalent.[23] Similarly, Job is filled with traumatic experiences (such as the loss of children in 2:9, or Job's confusion as seen in his lament in chapter 30). Another well-known text with which many might identify is Christ's cry on the cross: "My God, my God, why have you forsaken me!" Miller believes that the inclusion in the biblical text of such a deep lament from Christ validates all our laments (they being included in that profound lament) and gives sufferers a sense of Christ "being with them" in their agony.[24]

A second way in which biblical texts can help a "burden-bearer" revisit her trauma is through either providing the words which express her

---

17. Rahim, "Reflections on Contemporary Christian Theologies of Suffering," 90.
18. Frechette and Boase, "Defining 'Trauma,'" 10–11.
19. Claassens, "Trauma and Recovery," 20.
20. Strawn, "Trauma, Psalmic Disclosure, and Authentic Happiness."
21. Frechette and Boase, "Defining 'Trauma,'" 14.
22. West, "Between Text and Trauma," 216.
23. Esala, "Translation as Invasion in Post-Colonial Northern Ghana."
24. Miller, "Heaven's Prisoners," 22.

emotion (as in reading a lament psalm) or by modeling the "form" of a lament, to enable her to compose her own prayer. One psalm that is very useful in the latter case is Ps 13 as it includes all[25] the elements of a typical biblical lament. The empirical work will give examples of how various participants used the form of this psalm to express their own unique pain. First, the theory underlying this approach is discussed.

Lament Theory

Two features make biblical lament unique, and different from "whining" (or "grumbling" as seen in Exod 15:24 or Phil 2:14). First, the lament is a prayer, *addressed to God*. It is not the same as complaining to someone else, or even complaining *about* God. It is a bringing of one's pain *to* God, trusting that God can do something about it. Second, a biblical lament includes complaint arising from deep distress, as is apparent in a pouring forth of emotion. The cause of the lamenter's pain may be enemies, or even God, but the sufferer is not just requesting God's help, but is expressing a depth of negative emotion. In many cases, the lamenter's frustration is occasioned by God's apparent inaction or lack of care in the face of the lamenter's difficulty. At such times, the lamenter seems to be more upset with God than with the enemy (if there is an enemy), feeling that God is not holding to God's covenant promises. As Herman observes, deep trauma is often caused by someone who has power but does not appear to prevent the suffering the victim endures.[26]

Expressing lament satisfies the second criterion of trauma-healing (restoring agency to the former victim) and is recognized by modern psychotherapy to be part of healing.[27] Moreover, as biblical laments are not just complaints, they also point to a way to deal with the problem.[28]

Apart from personal lament, there is also a need for communal lament in the case of groups of people who together suffer a common problem. The empirical work includes both personal and communal laments, with participants generally first composing their own personal lament, and then together combining their thoughts, where they overlapped, into a communal prayer.

---

25. The one element not found in Ps 13 (but apparent in many lament psalms) is the request for justice (as in Ps 3:7; cf. Ps 3:2).
26. Herman, *Trauma and Recovery*, 94–95.
27. Westermann, *Lamentations*, 91.
28. Mandolfo, *God in the Dock*, 3–5.

The need for public lament is important not only for the sufferers to be able to express their pain and be heard,[29] but also for the other members of the community to hear the pain, and if necessary, be convicted by it. As many researchers have noted,[30] many abusers were themselves abused: the one victimized against becomes the perpetrator. Thus, in the church community, those who need to lament may at other times need to *hear* the lament of others and accept their own culpability. Further, in order to cultivate a caring community, all need to hear and give attention to the pain of others in their midst.

Thus far, we have considered the *content* of biblical literature which is helpful for trauma-healing. Other elements are also important in the restoring process, two of which are discussed next. Performance is a powerful means whereby the literature is engaged, and liturgy or ritual actions can be very helpful in dealing with "soul abuse."

Performance and Ritual Acts to Help Heal "Soul Abuse"

Oral Expression of Laments

Biblical psalms were composed for oral performance (not to be read silently), and thus a lament (personal or communal) needs to be expressed vocally to achieve its full potential. Careful reading of psalms will indicate they often include several voices.[31] There may be different speakers and/or different addressees. Attention to these voices brings a new understanding to the dialogue occurring in the psalm. Indeed, even a lament psalm often includes not only the words of the lamenter, and sometimes enemies (as the lamenter quotes their derision), but also the voice of God (often apparently in the "space" preceding a sudden change of mood in the psalmist). The inclusion of various voices in the prayer (particularly that of God, heard in various ways[32]) helps the lamenter see her situation in a new perspective.

Such attention to the voices becomes very apparent in liturgical reading of the psalm, or in performance. Both of these expressions become "ritual acts," along with various others that also engage movement, as in dance or symbolical expression (an example of which follows).

---

29. Grand, *Reproduction of Evil*, 5.
30. E.g., Seto, *Pedophilia and Sexual Offending against Children*.
31. Mandolfo, *God in the Dock*, 5.
32. See Dickie, "Performing Psalms of Lament."

Ritual Acts

Ritual acts are actions, such as the public expression of lament, the engagement with a biblical text through performance, or an expression of emotion (or prayer) through dance or symbolism. It is necessary that a special time and place be established for a ritual to take place to indicate that it is a *sacred* event, engaging with God. Further, there must be a sense of "safety" for all participants (with confidentiality a key element) and one of "solidarity."[33] Towards this latter goal, the expression of rituals in a public setting, within the regular worship of the church, can be very helpful. This has been proven to be the case in terms of communal lament prayers.[34] Indeed, this has been found to bring about "a change in the persons praying and the audience."[35]

Presenting a lament as a "sacramental action" (in the company of others who care) can lead to stronger relationships within the church community and a place of "safety" within the liturgy for all those battling various issues. This suggests the value of lament becoming a regular ritual within the weekly worship service, thereby providing a "liturgical" opportunity (in the company of the believing community) for pain-bearers to unload their burden as *part of their worship*, an expression of trust in God. Indeed, Lyon argues for *new liturgies* in church-worship which include sacramental actions "involving reparative relationships." In particular, Lyon emphasizes that attention should be given to an abused person's sense of shame and injustice. As she points out, "soul damage" is caused by "interpersonal evil, a theological problem which only the church is equipped to address."[36]

One element of soul damage is a "collapse of the survivor's self, a kind of extinction, an internal space of catastrophic loneliness imbued with hate and fear and shame and despair."[37] The person's sense of identity, and of having a personal history, is fragmented or confused.[38] Indeed, a sense of trust and safety has been shattered, resulting in "a mangling of the soul."[39] Lyon suggests that rituals to deal with such soul damage should take place within a "transcendent and transformative spiritual experience." Lament, expressed in a context of public worship, and including the notion of justice (explicitly included in many biblical laments, e.g., Ps 3) can meet these conditions.

33. Frechette and Boase, "Defining 'Trauma,'" 16.
34. Mandolfo, *God in the Dock*.
35. Dickie, "Building Community in the Church." Also, Corvin, "Stylistic and Functional Study of the Prose Prayers," 145.
36. Lyon, "Spiritual Implications of Interpersonal Abuse," 240–41.
37. Grand, *Reproduction of Evil*, 4–5.
38. Lyon, "Spiritual Implications," 236.
39. Becker "'Trauma Studies,'" 22.

Apart from laments, performances of biblical texts (such as the story of Ruth), enacted in spaces and times set apart from the ordinary, can also serve as powerful rituals, opening people emotionally in a way not experienced in the general reading of a text. Significant attention is given to these approaches in the empirical section.

Ritual acts many also include movement of the body (be it through gestures, mime, or dance) as well as through song and rhythm. The physical stimulation adds to the healing power of a lament performance,[40] and the rhythm serves to unite an audience with both the singers and one another.[41] An example of a communal dance of lament (performed annually) is that developed by an oppressed group in Korea. This ritual dance provided opportunity for the women to comfort one another, and to encourage one another to resist injustice and not give in to resignation.[42] Lyon suggests that such rituals could also be very helpful for oppressed and abused men and women today.[43] In addition to the emotional release, the new and energetic patterns of movement, and the crying out of anger and grief, would provide the neural *stimulation* needed to break old habits and form new avenues for free expression.

Another example of "body lament" was part of a communal response by a Cape Town church to the spate of domestic violence in August 2019. Congregation members were invited to get out of their seats and move to the front where they could take a pinch of salt and add it to a bucket of saltwater, representing the tears of God[44] and those of the people. As they added their tears to the "communal pain," they could express the particular burden on their heart, aloud or silently, as a prayer accompanying their symbolic action.[45]

Thus, rituals and various expressions of performance can contribute to the social, emotional, and spiritual healing of an individual in pain.[46] Further, the moderate level of stimulation involved could also well promote neural development, bringing about biological healing too.[47] This is next described.

40. See the next section.
41. Sacks, *Musicophilia*, 244.
42. Choi, *Ancient Korean Woman's Hanpuri (Healing) Spirituality*, 8.
43. Lyon, "Spiritual Implications," 239.
44. See Ps 56:8.
45. Dickie, "Translating Psalms for Performance."
46. Dickie, "Translating Psalms for Performance."
47. See Dickie, "Intersection of Biblical Lament and Psychotherapy," 888–91.

Biochemical Healing as a Result of Performance and Liturgical Expression

The human response to stress is handled largely by the right hemisphere of the brain,[48] which is also responsible for integrating unconscious emotions into a sense of the "implicit self."[49] Thus when the right brain no longer functions properly (as a result of over-secretion of biochemicals during trauma), the "implicit self" disintegrates, leaving the person to feel unsafe and unable to trust others.[50] Moreover, the over-production of certain hormones causes the amygdala to show hyper-activity which impedes the normal processing activity of the hippocampus.[51] Consequently, new experiences are not processed,[52] leaving the (trauma) memories to be stored as raw, poisonous sensory fragments. As a result, if the trauma trigger occurs (reactivating the former trauma event), unconscious and upsetting "flashbacks" will intrude into consciousness.

However, good news in the past fifteen years is that the brain has great "plasticity," and is able to heal itself.[53] If conditions are right, hormones can be released which will stimulate neural development, replacing those neurons destroyed during the trauma. The "right conditions" include "moderate levels of stress such as that involved in new learning" in a positive interpersonal environment.[54] This finding has been replicated by other scholars,[55] showing that an optimum level of stimulation can lead to the successful processing of memories into the hippocampus.[56] I argue that the creative stimulation and "moderate learning" involved in composing and/or performing a "biblical lament" (within a positive social context) can promote such biological healing. Further, Hug maintains that the right brain is associated with religious experience.[57] Thus, engaging in biblical lament can be expected to not only heal memories, but also heal the soul.[58]

---

48. Wittling, "Right Hemisphere and the Human Stress Response," 55–59.
49. Schore, "Right-Brain Affect Regulation," 144.
50. Schore, "Right-Brain Affect Regulation," 126.
51. McNally, *Remembering Trauma*, 137.
52. Hug, "Neuroscience Perspective on Psychodrama," 232.
53. E.g., Doidge, *Brain That Changes Itself*; Schore, "Right-Brain Affect Regulation," 142.
54. Cozolino, *Neuroscience of Psychotherapy*, 24.
55. E.g., Van der Kolk et al., *Traumatic Stress*, 225; Hug "Neuroscience Perspective," 232.
56. Schore, "Right-Brain Affect Regulation," 140.
57. Hug, "Neuroscience Perspective," 234.
58. Lyon, "Spiritual Implications," 238.

Application of This Theory in the Empirical Work

The theory we have considered points to the following being important for a person to heal from a trauma experience: First, the person must transform from a victim into an *agent*, able to tell his/her story and feel safe doing so. Second, the context must encourage and enable the person to build *social relationships*. Third, the person's *sense of justice* must be restored. And fourth, the person needs to *experience God* in his/her situation. The two empirical approaches described next both address these various needs, either by helping the former victims to compose their own laments, or by facilitating them to express themselves creatively (including the characters' emotions) as they recount a biblical story.

As noted in trauma literature theory, the use of literature (in this case, the biblical story of Ruth and psalms of lament) enables participants to engage with their pain but in a contained[59] way. Consequently, they experience the safety that enables healing to begin. Then they need to recover their voice in order to become an agent[60] and to express their account of what happened (using language and/or nonverbal and paralingual means). If this is done in the presence of empathic others (either fellow-sufferers or good listeners), the person is freed from the burden of isolation and enabled to build social relationships for the future.

Biblical lament can be particularly helpful in furthering the healing process in that it provides for the abused person's need of justice. As noted, biblical laments typically include a request for God to bring about justice against the perpetrator. By handing over their need for recompense to God, those who have been burdened with the injustice of abuse levied against them are free to get on with their lives. Further, lament (being a form of prayer) is two-directional and thus facilitates the opportunity for sufferers to hear God respond to their cries of pain.[61]

EMPIRICAL STUDIES

Engaging with the Story of Naomi and Ruth

Those living in townships in the Cape Town area experience many traumatic situations which are similar to those described in the biblical story of

---

59. Pain is "contained" in that (initially) it is the pain of another person in focus, either Naomi/Ruth or the lamenting psalmist.

60. Herman, *Trauma and Recovery*, 155.

61. Dickie, "Performing Psalms of Lament."

Naomi and Ruth. Adults would identify with the loss of a spouse or breadwinner, the death of sons, hunger, vulnerability (without a man to provide for, and protect, them) or being a foreigner. Younger people would resonate with feeling hungry or vulnerable, and girls might identify with Ruth's fear especially when she is instructed to go down to the threshing-floor at night. To test these ideas, and the possibility of the approach facilitating healing, two groups were invited to learn to enact the story of Ruth.

The first group consisted of five grade 7 learners from a local township school.[62] The other group were six adults from a township Bible-study fellowship.[63] Each group met weekly for an hour to go through the story and discuss the emotions of the characters in each situation. The hope was that the performers would internalize the events to the extent that they could enact the story from memory. However, this proved not possible, and thus the performance was a "dramatic reading." However, short, poetic sections (such as Ruth's commitment to Naomi) had been memorized and were performed without paper.

One important advantage of using performance in the arena of trauma-healing is that, on stage, *gaps* in the text must be filled. Inter-personal reactions must be indicated in some way; even a "blank" response indicates passivity and non-engagement. For example, the person playing the role of Naomi must show some response to Ruth's strong commitment in chapter 1. The text gives no indication of how Naomi responded. But the actor must decide whether she might consider Ruth's decision as a burden for her (increasing her responsibility, to care for a foreigner in Bethlehem) or whether she might be grateful (to have a younger woman help her). In turn, the person playing the role of Ruth must show some facial indication as to how she feels in this situation. The possible tension in this "mother-in-law situation" could be something with which many young African women would identify. To facilitate discussion about such traumatic events, a jester was introduced into the cast, to interrupt the narrative with pertinent questions. Thus, a question such as "How do you think Ruth felt in this context?" might provoke audience members to respond and discuss their fears and views.

The jester's questions not only give former victims the opportunity to be agents and voice their opinion, but also they enable audience members to hear the views of others, thereby possibly enlarging their own perception of the situation and suggesting solutions. For example, after Naomi instructs Ruth to go down to the threshing-floor at night and meet her former boss, the jester asked the audience "How do you think Ruth felt?" The males in

---

62. Westlake Primary School, Cape Town.

63. The adults were from Capricorn Township, Cape Town.

the audience (both schoolboys and adult men) responded "Excited." But when the girls and women were asked, their response was "Frightened." But as the story progressed, the female audience members noted how God cared for Ruth in that difficult situation. Hopefully the male audience members would also learn to see things from a different perspective and to recognize the traumatic feelings females may have in some situations.

Thus, as various traumatic events were brought to the fore (through the narrative and the jester's questions), audience members were given opportunity to think about, and discuss, situations with which they were familiar, such as death of family members, hunger, vulnerability, and being a foreigner. Fears were expressed, but also comfort received, as audience members realized they were not alone in their pain (seeing it evident in the situations of the biblical characters, but also in the responses of fellow audience members).

A variation on this approach of using performance in trauma healing was successfully carried out with a group of women in Ivory Coast. All of these women had experienced decades of war with the associated traumas of bereavement, hunger, displacement, and vulnerability in a male-dominated society. In this empirical study, the women used either drama or song to tell the story of Ruth and Naomi. After having internalized the story, through listening to it being told several times, then telling it to one another in small groups, and finally by studying the translated biblical text in their own language, they then chose to either retell the story through song or drama. The story was divided into five sections to facilitate easier remembrance, and the women were repeatedly exposed to the contents of each section as they explored ways to represent the events in song or drama. As the traumas endured by the story characters drew resonance from them, they entered deeply into the various emotions connected to the difficulties. However, they also were struck by how God cared for the women in various ways, and this heartened them in their own situations. Several women later testified: "I am Naomi!" I have experienced what she suffered, and I can see how God cared for her. Likewise, I must be alert to see how he is caring for me.

Composing One's Own Lament (Based On the Form of Biblical Laments)

Over the past five years, I have conducted many lament workshops in both KwaZulu-Natal (KZN) and Cape Town. In KZN, participants included HIV+ women, refugees (from DRC and Burundi), and the LGBT community, and in Cape Town, refugees as well as in Cape Town, refugees as well as youth and adults youth and adults from Capricorn Township. In each workshop, Pss 3 and 13 were first studied to identify the typical elements in a biblical lament. These were noted to be an address to God, a complaint (often using accusatory language against God or the enemies), request(s) including for justice against the enemies, and an affirmation of trust. Moreover, it was clear that the lamenting psalmist did not restrain his emotions, but presented them to God, raw and uncensored. It became clear to the workshop participants that God accepts a lament-prayer as an act of faith, and is not judgmental of their deep negative emotions, even when directed to God. Surprisingly too, the psalmist usually revealed a sudden change in mood, from negative to positive, with hope and a sense that his dilemma had been addressed. Indeed, the sudden change in mood seemed to represent something the psalmist had heard from God, speaking to him in his situation.[64]

For example, Ps 3 has the psalmist crying out to the Lord and complaining about his many enemies (vv. 1–2). However, in v. 3, there is an extraordinary change in his mood, with him using three strong metaphors of confidence in the Lord. The change from fear and discouragement to one of confident hope seems to come from something he has been reminded of (e.g., concerning God's character, or God's former interventions on his behalf), or heard (from a theophany or a community member). For the participants, it is important that they are able to reflect on their former experience of God, or what they have been taught, so that they can affirm something about God which will give them confidence that God might respond to their prayers.

To help participants apply in their own lives these four elements of a biblical lament, they were asked to consider the following questions:

1. What one main burden would you like to express to God (something that worries you, or some unjust situation you are dealing with)?
2. What is the main thing you would like to ask God to do in your situation?
3. How would you like God to bring justice into your situation?
4. What truth or experience of God gives you assurance that God might act in your situation?

After answering the questions above, participants then composed their own lament, incorporating these ideas. Below is an example written by a woman in the HIV+ support-group. It indicates her response to these

---

64. Dickie, "Practice of Biblical Lament."

questions incorporated into her lament prayer (with a translation into English following):

> Nkosi, kanti ngiyohlupheka kuze kube inini?
> Ngiyodlala abantu kuze kube inini bengenza imoto engadumi emile engen msebenzi, kuyoze kube inini?
> Ngisabathe ngizama ukuhlanganisa impila kodwa qyhlangane.
> Wena ukhona uyabukela njekanti kwalangoshiwo yini kuthi wena uwumaphendula asabele kodwa uyaphuza ukuphendula, kuti kuyoze kube inini.
> Kanti kuyoza kube inini Nkosi mina ngiphila impilo yokuhluphela adanye bayasizakala kodwa mina.
> Ngiyazi Nkosi kuyanele ngilinde kodwa akuvami ngizohlalela ethembeni ngoba wena uwukhukhonya wami.

1. Lord, till when will I suffer? For how long will people play me?
2. They make me like a car that won't start, a useless one. Till when?
3. Every time I try to put things together, life is not coming together. And you are there, just looking.
4. Didn't they say that you listen when you are called?
5. But you are taking long to answer, But . . . till when? Till when, my Lord—me leaving my poverty?
6. Others do get help, but me—I'm not.
7. I know my Lord, I have to wait, but it's hard.
8. I will stay in the hope, and you are my light.

The English translation shows how she has included the four elements of a biblical lament: First, her poem is addressed to God (line 1). Second, her poem includes deeply felt complaints (lines 1–6); some of these accusations take the form of rhetorical questions. Third, a lament usually has at least one request but, in this poem, the requests are veiled in the writer's rhetorical questions (lines 1–2, 4–5) implying that she is asking God to relieve her of her poverty. The fourth element of a biblical lament, an affirmation of faith, is seen in lines 7 and 8 (although line 7 also includes a note of complaint).

BENEFITS OF THIS APPROACH

Using (biblical) trauma literature as a means towards trauma-healing is an indirect approach, and consequently has several advantages over other methods in use today. A significant strength is that it facilitates a review of the trauma but within a contained context. Participants find resonance at a deep (emotional) level with the trauma experienced by the story characters, but it is not directly their pain and thus is manageable. Also, the focus on *emotions* differs from some approaches to trauma-healing which are more "content-based," dealing with *ideas* which only address the mind but not the soul or the body.[65] The method also allows a modern burden-bearer to see how God orchestrates circumstances to help Ruth, and so be encouraged to also have a "transformational experience with God," and appropriate for herself the help that God might be providing for her in her situation.

Another advantage of this approach is that it avoids a "didactic" approach which often appears condescending.[66] Moreover, the fact that questions are open-ended, not seeking a pre-determined (content-based) answer, allows people to bring their own rich insights. Further, the methodology is playful and fun, and avoids confrontational "soul searching" that often is a part of traditional "trauma-healing," requiring people to confront difficult memories before they are ready to do so. As noted, the story serves as a container, but more than that, it also serves as a bridge. When the person is ready to explore the painful emotions of her traumatic experience, the story provides a way in, gently and without threat. Further, drama, song, and dance are creative means which most Africans particularly enjoy, and which sometimes reveal hidden talents, particularly in the case of young people, developing a new level of self-confidence.

With regard to the lament-prayers, a particular benefit is that it encourages participants to develop a greater "spiritual authenticity."[67] Also, the fact that laments include the critical feature of dealing with the "justice problem" means that they enable participants to put recompense into the hands of God, and thus be free to forgive the perpetrator. This then enables them to proceed without hindrance in their lives, confident that justice will be done.

CONCLUSION

The empirical work described in this chapter makes use of performance as a means to enter into the emotions of characters in the biblical text. Two cases were described: first, drama was used to present the story of Ruth

---

65. Some approaches to trauma-healing are story-based but the focus is on remembering and retelling the events in the story, rather than entering into the emotions of the characters.

66. A didactic approach (to storytelling) asks "What happened next?" and gives affirmation when the person responds as the questioner wants them to (with an expected "correct answer").

67. Dickie, "Practice of Biblical Lament."

and Naomi, and second, psalms of lament provided a helpful form to help people create their own personal laments. In both cases, participants were able to find a new level of hope as they recognized God's hand in their lives and brought their pain to God.

The methodology does not require finances or advanced training, and so can be used in many situations to help those who have suffered (or are suffering) some trauma. It is hoped, then, that the examples described will encourage those seeking to help those facing difficult circumstances in their communities. There are many narratives in the Scriptures that can speak into the various problematic situations facing people today. Even those not able to read the biblical stories can quickly internalize the message of these narratives and find application in them to their own lives. Consequently, those who feel they have no resources can find a treasure that will transform their lives. As they realize that others before them have experienced a similar pain, they too can discover God transforming their situations and providing wisdom and strength for the way ahead.

BIBLIOGRAPHY

Allen, Jon G. *Coping with Trauma: Hope through Understanding*. Washington, DC: American Psychiatric, 2005.

Bauman, R. *Folklore, Cultural Performance and Popular Entertainments*. New York: Oxford University Press, 1992.

Becker, Eve-Marie. "'Trauma Studies' and Exegesis: Challenges, Limits and Prospects." In *Trauma and Traumatization in Individual and Collective Dimensions: Insights from Biblical Studies and Beyond*, edited by Eve-Marie Becker et al., 15–29. Göttingen: Vandenhoeck and Ruprecht, 2014.

Choi, Jae Haeng. *Ancient Korean Woman's Hanpuri (Healing) Spirituality: Kanggangsulae Dance*. Comprehensive Examination II, Interdisciplinary Studies. Berkeley: Graduate Theological Union, 2007.

Claassens, L. Juliana. "Trauma and Recovery: A New Hermeneutical Framework for the Rape of Tamar (2 Samuel 13)." In *Bible through the Lens of Trauma*, edited by Elizabeth Boase and Christopher G. Frechette, 177–92. Atlanta: Society of Biblical Literature, 2016.

Corvin, J. "A Stylistic and Functional Study of the Prose Prayers in the Historical Narratives of the Old Testament." PhD diss., Atlanta, GA, Emory University, 1972.

Cozolino, Louis L. *The Neuroscience of Psychotherapy*. New York: Norton, 2002.

Doidge, N. *The Brain That Changes Itself: Stories of Personal Triumph from the Frontiers of Brain Science*. New York: Penguin, 2007.

Dickie, June F. "Building Community in the Church between 'Insiders' and 'Outsiders.'" *Acta Theologica* 40 (2020) 49–67.

———. "The Intersection of Biblical Lament and Psychotherapy in the Healing of Trauma Memories." *Old Testament Essays* 32 (2019) 885–907.

———. "Lament as a Contributor to the Healing of Trauma: An Application of Poetry in the Form of Biblical Lament." *Pastoral Psychology* 68 (2019) 145–56.

———. "Performing Psalms of Lament: Does God (Off-Stage) Respond to the Complainant's Cry?" *Scriptura* 119 (2020) 1–17.

———. "The Practice of Biblical Lament as a Means towards Facilitating Authenticity and Psychological Well-Being." *Pastoral Psychology* 69 (2020) 523–37.

———. "Translating Psalms for Performance and Their Use in Various Ministries within the Church: Examples from South Africa." *Bible Translator* 73 (2022) 6–25.

Dickie, June F., and Lynell Zogbo. "Interacting with and Performing the Book of Ruth as a Pathway towards Trauma Healing: An Empirical Study from Côte D'Ivoire." *Ethnodoxology: Global Forum on Arts and Christian Faith* (2022) 18–31.

Esala, Nathan. "Translation as Invasion in Post-Colonial Northern Ghana." PhD diss., University of KwaZulu-Natal, South Africa, 2020.

Frechette, Christopher G., and Elizabeth Boase. "Defining 'Trauma' as a Useful Lens for Biblical Interpretation." In *Bible through the Lens of Trauma*, edited by Elizabeth Boase and Christopher G. Frechette, 1–23. Atlanta: Society of Biblical Literature, 2016.

Grand, Sue. *The Reproduction of Evil: A Clinical and Cultural Perspective.* Hillsdale, NJ: Analytic, 2000.

Granofsky, Ronald. *The Trauma Novel: Contemporary Symbolic Depictions of Collective Disaster.* New York: Lang, 1995.

Herman, Judith L. *Trauma and Recovery. The Aftermath of Violence—From Domestic Abuse to Political Terror.* New York: Basic, 1992.

Hug, Edward. "A Neuroscience Perspective on Psychodrama." In *Psychodrama: Advances in Theory and Practice*, edited by Clark Baim et al., 227–38. London: Routledge, 2007.

LeDoux, Joseph. "Cellular and System Reconsolidation in the Hippocampus." *Neuron* 36 (2002) 527–38.

Lyon, Emily. "The Spiritual Implications of Interpersonal Abuse: Speaking of the Soul." *Pastoral Psychology* 59 (2010) 233–47.

Mandolfo, Carleen. *God in the Dock: Dialogic Tension in the Psalms of Lament.* Sheffield, UK: Sheffield Academic, 2002.

McCann, J. "The Psalms as Instruction." *Interpretation* 46 (1992) 117–28.

McNally, Richard J. *Remembering Trauma.* Cambridge: Harvard University Press, 2003.

Miller, Patrick D. "Heaven's Prisoners: The Lament as Christian Prayer." In *Lament: Reclaiming Practices in Pulpit, Pew and Public Square*, edited by S. Brown and P. D. Miller, 15–26. Louisville, KY: Westminster John Knox, 2005.

Rahim, Jennifer A. "Reflections on Contemporary Christian Theologies of Suffering and the Value of Trauma Literature." MA diss., Toronto School of Theology, 2016.

Ringel, Shoshana, and Jerrold R. Brandel. *Trauma: Contemporary Directions in Theory, Practice, and Research.* California: Sage, 2012.

Sacks, Oliver. *Musicophilia—Tales of Music and the Brain.* Britain: Picador, 2007.

Schore, Allan N. "Right-Brain Affect Regulation." In *The Healing Power of Emotion*, edited by Diana Fosha et al., 112–44. New York: Norton, 2009.

Seto, Michael C. *Pedophilia and Sexual Offending against Children.* Washington, DC: American Psychological Association, 2008.

Sölle, Dorothee. *Suffering.* Translated by Everett R. Kalin. Philadelphia: Fortress, 1975.

Strawn, Brent. "Trauma, Psalmic Disclosure, and Authentic Happiness." In *Bible through the Lens of Trauma*, edited by Elizabeth Boase and Christopher G. Frechette, 143–60. Atlanta: Society of Biblical Literature, 2016.

Sweeney, Daniel S. "Group Play Therapy." In *Foundations of Play Therapy*. Edited by Charles Schaefer, 227–52. New Jersey: Wiley, 2011.

Van der Kolk, Bessel A., et al., eds. *Traumatic Stress: The Effects of Overwhelming Experience on Mind, Body, and Society*. New York: Guilford, 1996, 2006.

Weil, Simone. *Gravity and Grace*. Translated by Arthur Wills. New York: Putnam, 1952.

West, Gerald O. "Between Text and Trauma: Reading Job with People Living with HIV." In *Bible through the Lens of Trauma*, edited by Elizabeth Boase and Christopher G. Frechette, 209–30. Atlanta: Society of Biblical Literature, 2016.

Westermann, Claus. *Lamentations: Issues and Interpretation*. Edinburgh: T. & T. Clark, 1994.

Wittling, W. "The Right Hemisphere and the Human Stress Response." *Acta Physiologica Scandinavica* 161 Suppl. 640 (1997) 55–59.

Chapter 11

Hope in the Midst of Death?
A Reading of the Book of Job in the Time of Despair

Hassan Musa

INTRODUCTION: CONTEXT AND APPROACH

This essay intends to present a reading of the book of Job in African contexts. This is a reading in postcolonial Africa with the quest for dialogic discourse with regards to human suffering in the midst of despair and death. This is a reading in search of hope amid despair and death by means of a creative spirituality from the book of Job. The recent sociopolitical events in Nigeria are so traumatic and, more often than not, push people more into places and moments of despair rather than hope. The human condition in the Nigerian context has been that of deep distress and suffering. The presence of suffering in many aspects of life has been the major challenge in Nigeria today. We live amidst human inhumanity against one another in the quest for human domination and control. The Islamic extremists' campaigns around us have left many people like the victim of banditry on the road to Jericho, in the pool of blood—just for death. Many women have lost their husbands and children, many children have lost their parents and friends. The reality of the human sense of being has been jeopardized and bastardized.

The African context has been a context of hope in the midst of human injustice and segregation. The need for inclusive justice and growing love and righteousness is quite urgent. The need for creative vision for the reconstruction of the new Africa that embraces and cares for all people on the streets, in various homes and public places as those who suffer, groan, and die in silence, is an alarming situation. The cases of murder, suicide, social and political marginalization, identity crises, and the quest for human dignity and freedom for all remains an ongoing cry and movement.

It is my hope that reading the Scripture anew, like the book of Job, would be helpful in order to point people in the midst of despair and dehumanization to a sense of having a companion in Job. The words of Job in his despair and his hope may be useful in our attempt to help ourselves survive the tragedies of our time. My approach in this contribution is polyphonic, as seen in the works of Carol A. Newsom.[1] In Newsom's reading of the book of Job as a "moral imagination," she points us to the presence and function of the polyphonic texture of the book. In this case I would try to point to the presence of polyphony in Job not by means of repeating Newsom's theory of interpretation but from my own perspective as an aspect of reception of the text. The reading of the book of Job as a polyphonic text helps us to have time and deep sense of interest and possible respect to the many voices that are found and heard within it. There is no need to jump into any quick conclusion on the function of the voices, but rather than being arbitrary we would be more intentional in allowing the voices to address us in their intentional complexity. This intentional complexity is not an attempt at simplifying the sense of intentionality within the text, but rather it is more of an invitation to the close engagement with it as something that is there but not under any of our categorical control. The polyphonic texture of the book of Job continually leaves it open to be used in any given conversation. This is more fitting in life situations that may be related to that experienced by Job, namely, the situations of suffering, disaster, loss, and pains. This is suffering in the world before death and away from an expected comfort. This is what led to the despair of Job to the extent that he felt being broken to pieces in which he too broke words in pieces.

One of the serious and strange turns of Job's experiences and expressions from the depth of his suffering was his question of theodicy. Theodicy is the existential and moral struggle with the goodness, love, and justice of God. This problem raises the questions, If God is good and loving why is there evil in the world and even the suffering and death of the innocent? If God is all powerful why can't God stop all forms of evil and suffering at once? If God knows then why can't God help here and now? etc. Theodicy struggle is the human, ultimate search for God amid pain and sorrow. This is the search for God during one's sad situation. This is the search for light

1. Newsom, "Considering Job"; Newsom, "Job," 317–638; Newsom, *Book of Job*.

in the thickness of the darkness of the soul. This is the feeling of being lost in the midst of life. Job struggled with theodicy from the beginning to the end of his utterances. Until he was confronted by God; then he had another new turn and his voice changed from that of a despairing person in search for God to a person in need of an inner sense of quietness from the torment of God. It was so strange and challenging that Job was drawn to know God more in his suffering than in his joy. Job did not only suffer the problem of injustice in the world, but he equally suffered the reality of God. God became his problem; God was his suffering and at the end God was his blessing. For it was God who finally vindicated him from the accusations of his friends and gave him a fulfilled end of life (42:9–17).

JOB, HUMAN SUFFERING, AND THE SEARCH FOR GOD

"Where is God?" This question has been a common question amid despair and death. Many people are moved to ask this question when they are faced with the evil of the age. The evil of our time today is the ongoing human inhumanity against one another. The death of the innocent, men, women, and children. The death of people in great needs as could be seen in many African contexts today. Many people are suffering from the evil that led to the wars and political upheavals that render them homeless and impoverished. These people often have mixed feelings about the reality of God in the midst of their lives. Young children in Nigeria often ask their parents if God really sees, and if God really loves them. Some have asked why did God create their enemies? Why can't they live in a new world without an enemy who wants to kill them? etc. These realities are all part of the kind of theodicy that Job had to struggle with. Right from Job 3 his words have been those of a despairing sufferer in the world. Job 3 is a text that demonstrates the power of human suffering and the ugliness of evil. The feelings and fears of Job came together and became a dreadful utterance. Job in his words broke to pieces the history of his life. Job cursed the day and night of his conception and birth and left himself as vulnerable as he felt himself. The vulnerability of Job was not just a sense of presentation of how he felt and where he was in his life, but rather it was a lament, a protest against the status quo. It was a quest and a movement into something better than what he felt and where he was. His early life of great affluence was indeed a depiction of a blessed life (1:1–5). Job was a great man of wealth, integrity, and wisdom. He has been portrayed as an ideal patriarch of his time. Yet, he was confronted with deep sadness and sorrow that left him utterly vulnerable.

One of the first reactions of Job amid his tragedy and suffering was sheer silence. He was silent in the midst of his tragedy, and his friends came also in silence with him for seven days (2:11–13). The solidarity of his friends in silence could be seen as a direct loss of speech in the face of an immeasurable sorrow and the unimaginable suffering. This kind of suffering went beyond human description. Job was so lost in the tragedy that his friends could not even recognize him. The silence of Job could be seen as another voice of wisdom or the voice of silence in itself. This could be the end of the polyphonic discourse as an exchange in human wisdom. Silence here is felt as the only possible situation or response when there is no other way to use speech in controlling or even countering the tragedy.

In their "sitting with Job" his friends, namely, Eliphaz, Bildad, and Zophar, each in his turn confronted Job with the wisdom of his time and from his perspective tried all they could to explain the situation as a retributive action on Job that definitely required Job's humility and repentance.[2] The friends of Job like many African friends of today often believe in the retributive reality of their time. Whatever happens must be explained with reference to who caused it and why. The tragedy of Job was discussed beyond an accident of life to a definite move in the reality of action. This must be the reaction of the gods in order to correct the misconduct of Job. Bildad asked a penetrating rhetorical question, whether Job has ever heard of an innocent person suffering or God perverting justice (8:1–3). This kind of confrontation is in a way a sure way of pinning Job to the thickness of the tragedy.

Job's response to his friends continued as an ongoing "dispute" and not even a "dialogue" as many scholars have seen it.[3] Contributions of scholars like Norman C. Habel,[4] J. E. Hartley,[5] and Samuel Balentine[6] have critically interpreted Job from the vantage point of his personal piety and how that has been critically confronted with indescribable horror in the midst of his misfortune. From the perspective of his inner sense of piety Job's life was seen as exemplary in his time not only of wisdom that knows God but also of wisdom that seeks God. Job's search for God was surely for his own sense of justification during his suffering, but also it goes beyond a mere sense of justification to a new sense of encounter.

---

2. Zuck, *Sitting With Job*.
3. Brueggemann, *Introduction to the Old Testament*.
4. Habel, *Book of Job*.
5. Hartley, *Book of Job*.
6. Balentine, *Job*.

Mark Sheldon has given attention to the book of Job from three main Jewish perspectives.[7] The problem of theodicy has been closely examined within that exploration and assessment. The theodicy questions were discussed from philosophical perspectives of the Jewish scholars, namely, Solomon B. Freehof, Martin Buber, and Robert Gordis. This was done by closely reading their selected contributions in order to see how they approached and interpreted the book of Job. In this reflection I shall draw some of their thoughts from Sheldon's reception as representative interpretations of the book of Job from a traditional Jewish critical perspective.

Firstly, we shall begin with Freehof in his work *The Book of Job: A Commentary*;[8] Freehof reflected on the book of Job and concluded that "the book is not offered as a clear analysis of the problem of underserved suffering."[9] The theme of innocent suffering has been one of the most important themes of the book of Job. Job has been portrayed as an innocent sufferer even in some of the earlier versions of his or similar stories in the ancient Near East. This calls attention to the kind of reality of life that must be considered in the world in which we live today.

In Freehof's analysis as reflected in Sheldon, "Job must be guilty of something."[10] This critical analysis of Job as somehow guilty agrees with the ancient tradition of retribution theory on the cause and effect. This means that nothing happens for nothing. Job cannot suffer without a cause. But even Job is totally unclear whether his guilt is substantial or not. This remains his own quest for God: that he might be vindicated. If Job is truly guilty then the theme of an innocent sufferer does not hold substantial ground in his case. But if he is not guilty and appears to be actually innocent, then the burden remains on the meaning and purpose of the justice of God. This question must remain open and critically engaging.

Like Elihu in the book of Job (32–37), Freehof does not focus really on the cause of Job's suffering but on its purpose, namely, that "suffering is education."[11] Job was said to have suffered to gain wisdom. This must be new wisdom beyond what he might have gotten traditionally. But it still remains an enigma what kind of wisdom he must have gotten from that experience of tragedy and grave loss. "Precisely to what wisdom leads is unspecified."[12] At best, the suffering of Job then and now remains a mystery. Sheldon

---

7. Sheldon, "Job, Human Suffering and Knowledge," 229 and thereafter.
8. Freehof, *Book of Job*.
9. Sheldon, "Job, Human Suffering and Knowledge," 229.
10. Sheldon, "Job, Human Suffering and Knowledge," 230.
11. Sheldon, "Job, Human Suffering and Knowledge," 231.
12. Sheldon, "Job, Human Suffering and Knowledge," 231.

rightly argues that "mystery is everywhere,"[13] which may be revelatory or even remain enigmatic only for the purpose of further contemplation.

The second Jewish scholar that Sheldon examined was Martin Buber from his contribution on *Dimensions on Job*,[14] which has also been reflected in his magnum opus of biblical literature, *The Prophetic Faith*. Buber presented four views which have been represented also by Sheldon about which we shall here only briefly comment in passing. Sheldon explains that "according to Buber, Job offers an inner dialectic, presenting four views of the relationship between God and the suffering of human beings."[15] Firstly, "God allows a creature, Satan, to wander around the world."[16] It is quite enigmatic here that Buber and Sheldon have concluded the Satan in Job to be more than an adversary. Yet, that is not the main concern, but rather the gift of freedom to wander about in the world and even have the freedom to confront, contest, and afflict a human being (Job 2:1–8). The general idea of God putting Job to test is still clear and open, namely, that "God wants to know whether Job serves him gratuitously or for a reward."[17] This test was not in the presence and even with the help of the Satan to satisfy its suspicion and hopefully use Job to prove the truth of Yahweh and Job's gratuitous faithfulness.

Secondly, "the view of the friends."[18] The friends come from a very typical worldview of retributive justice from which they all concluded that "Job's sufferings testify to his guilt."[19] "The friends bring him religion, reasonable and rational, but he clings to the cruel and living God, not the God of his friends whom he cannot accept."[20] It is so ironic that Job and his three friends argue from the dark side of the spectrum. None of them actually knew the truth of the story nor the actual purpose of it. They were only guessing from their traditional philosophy and general observations. Their voices appeared to add a lot of colors to the polyphony, but they collapsed on the way to being the final voices of truth that should comfort Job. Instead of helping to alleviate his suffering they added to it by condemning him to be a guilty person suffering the wrath of God.

---

13. Sheldon, "Job, Human Suffering and Knowledge," 231.
14. Buber, *Dimensions of Job*.
15. Sheldon, "Job, Human Suffering and Knowledge," 232.
16. Sheldon, "Job, Human Suffering and Knowledge," 232.
17. Sheldon, "Job, Human Suffering and Knowledge," 232.
18. Sheldon, "Job, Human Suffering and Knowledge," 232.
19. Sheldon, "Job, Human Suffering and Knowledge," 232.
20. Sheldon, "Job, Human Suffering and Knowledge," 232.

Thirdly, a God who hides his face. "Job is caught between his truth, God's view of him, and his friend's view of him."[21] "It is true that he experiences God in suffering and contradiction but even in this way he does experience God."[22] The being of God revealed the so-called "dark side" of God in this book of Job as possibly mirroring the role of God in the world universal.[23] The being and role of God in Job oscillated from being cruel and dark to being patient and wise. Many interpreters of Job have been disturbed and even put off by the silence of God as the element of God's dark side in the face of suffering. Hardly do we have the patience today to watch the tale until sunset.

Fourthly, Buber in Sheldon turns to the expression of God.[24] "The speech out of the whirlwind is intended to do more than teach the impossibility of understanding the mystery of creation. The whole concern comes back to a question of justice."[25] What does God mean by speaking out of the whirlwind? Does that mean the gift of justice or further enigma? David Clines sees the speech from the whirlwind more as the problem than the solution. In that speech God does not address Job's problem but God merely bypassed it to other complexities of life in creation.[26]

Third on the Jewish scholars is Robert Gordis in his work *The Book of God and Man*[27] in which he put *two* arguments forward, namely, complexity and ambiguity in creation[28] and secondly, the acknowledgment of beauty and order in the complexity of nature. Nature is not only mystery but also miracle.[29] Gordis argues from the point of view that God used nature to teach Job a new sense of wisdom in a practical sense. It is worthy of note from Sheldon that, "just as there is order and harmony in the natural world, though imperfectly grasped by man, so there is order and meaning in the moral sphere, though often incomprehensible to man."[30] Thus to him the book of Job is an experiential journey from the sense of chaos to order in the complex world of God. This cannot be the world under human control

21. Sheldon, "Job, Human Suffering and Knowledge," 232.
22. Sheldon, "Job, Human Suffering and Knowledge," 232.
23. Cf. Boorer, "Dark Side of God?"
24. Sheldon, "Job, Human Suffering and Knowledge," 233.
25. Sheldon, "Job, Human Suffering and Knowledge," 233.
26. Clines, "Putting Elihu in His Place"; Clines, *Job 21–37*; Clines, *Job 1–20*; Clines, "Job 5.1–8: A New Exegesis," 185–94; Clines, "In Search of an Indian Job"; cf. Brenner, "God's Answer to Job"; Williams, "You Have Not Spoken Truth of Me."
27. Gordis, *Book of God and Man*.
28. Sheldon, "Job, Human Suffering and Knowledge," 233–34.
29. Sheldon, "Job, Human Suffering and Knowledge," 234.
30. Sheldon, "Job, Human Suffering and Knowledge," 234.

but rather beyond it. This calls for the spirituality of wisdom and humility in the world.

Job was awakened into a new search for spiritual encounter with God in his sorrow. Job was moved in his responses to his friends to reflect critically on who he was and who he has become in the presence of God. Job's reflection on the limitation of being human in the sight of God remains instructive (7:1–10). Job thought of his being human in the midst of the trouble of the life and feared to know himself directly. He asked who is human that God's eyes were always on him? The gaze of the Almighty became the nightmare of Job. He thought deeply on the possibility of moving away not only from the troubles of his time but also from the trouble of God. Job sought for peace and quietness in a new place of silence and loneliness.

Job further used his words to speak out his mind in his search for God in chapters 9 and 10. These two chapters remain quite controversial and contested especially within traditional readings of the text. Some may see the movement of Job and his demand to meet with God and challenge God with words as the manifestation of human sheer arrogance before God. Job in chapter 9 did not actually dismiss the possibility of God's involvement in human tragedy, he even pushed all the blame to God as the major actor in such cases (9:21–24). Job was not blaming God for injustice, but like one who has come to the last point of his contemplation he had no way of explaining his tragedy away from God. In other words, his words in chapter 10 are words of deep contestation, confrontation, and resistance. Job was resisting the possibility of death even from the hands of God. He asked new questions to God to make God rethink what God was doing. Why would a good God of creation suddenly turn to be the sad god of destruction? Job could not believe that the purpose of his creation was destruction, but rather he moved his thoughts to the possibility of life in the midst of his suffering. The exchange of wisdom with his friends moved the idea of retribution to a bear minimal especially with Job's new insight and quest for life amid suffering. Job made a vow to himself that until he died he would not relinquish his integrity or accept the accusations of his friends (27:6). Job continued to be a man of integrity even though his vulnerability is seen as clearly as possible in his humanity. We shall now briefly turn to Job's thoughts on hope to see how to build a new spirituality of hope in the midst of tragedy.

THE MYSTERY OF SUFFERING IN THE BOOK OF JOB

One of the golden threads that runs through the book of Job is that of mystery. As Sheldon earlier observed as mentioned above, "Mystery is everywhere."[31] The book of Job itself is mystery. Human beings are mystery even to themselves.[32] And above all the world and God are mystery that we cannot fully grasp. The mystery in the book of Job appears in very ironic ways. In the ways of God's actions and speeches and the way that Job is portrayed in the presence of God and his personal experience through the book. There is a creative connection and tension between the fear of the Lord and the worldview of wisdom in Job.[33]

There is irony of wisdom and fear of the Lord especially in the life of Job as the main character. It is a general divine requirement that wisdom comes as a blessing from the fear of the Lord. Job was portrayed as a man who feared God and turns away from evil (1:1–5). Job is portrayed as an "ideal example" of a man of wisdom in the ancient Near East.[34] The ironic mystery here is that even though Job feared God, he still suffered a great deal of tragedy and sorrow.

It is remarkable that "Job affirms a central teaching of traditional wisdom, even if he questions the usual assumption of order and consequence on which that tradition was based."[35] Job's affirmation of the tradition of retribution justice has three main phases. Firstly, he affirms its possibility only "if" he can be proven as guilty by being pointed to any of his wrongdoings even before God. Secondly, he affirms its efficacy on himself if he is truly guilty. But then finally he confronted it and even seeks to reject it for the fact that he did not commit anything wrong before God and humanity. This leaves the book of Job as unique in its rhetorical texture and purpose but then still calls for a spirituality of hope even amid tragedy, darkness, and the mystery of life in the world.

It is ironic that Job even from the beginning of his tragic experience wished and even hoped for death. Job's hope for death remains as enigmatic move from hope to hopelessness (Job 3–8, 11).[36] This is the revealing pattern of Job's brokenness and how he too was ready to break what stood on his way. This he will do even by being taken away in death. That is why he may mock and even say that, when God looks for him later probably to

---

31. Sheldon, "Job, Human Suffering and Knowledge," 231.

32. Ackermann, "Metaphor, Mystery and Paradox," 25–36.

33. Barre, "'Fear of God' and the World View of Wisdom," 41–43; Blocher, "Fear of the Lord as the 'Principle' of Wisdom"; Cox, "Fear or Conscience?"; Wilson, "Book of Job and the Fear of God."

34. Bosman, "Being Wise betwixt Order and Mystery," 437.

35. Bosman, "Being Wise betwixt Order and Mystery," 437.

36. Boorer, "Job's Hope," 104.

further afflict him with more troubles, he (Job) would not be found (7:21). Job gave a laughter of resistance of the tragedy he was experiencing.[37]

It is through Job's resilience and his polyphonic confrontation to his tragic experience that we further notice the "emergence of Job's hope for vindication in relation to the motif of death." This is his further move "from Hope to Hopelessness" (Job 13–14).[38] The more Job spoke about his tragedy the angrier he became and the deeper he sank in them. His move into hopelessness remains the tragedy of his words. This shows Job's weakness in his strength. The strength of his words could not vindicate him but only made him feel his sadness and meaninglessness in life. Job's thought led him to the thought of death as the final destiny without hope of any liberation. In the book of Job, "death" is portrayed "as the symbol of hopelessness" (cf. 17:13, 15; 19:10; 27:8).[39]

From Job's experience and his polyphonic discourses, we see only the emergence of more darkness and sorrow into his mind and from his mouth. What we need to learn from this is the spirituality of faith and resilient hope that cannot take death as the final option, but rather even through death the hope of life and life is possible. This is the given wisdom of God beyond the ugliness of life in the world as we see it today. It is ironically interesting to note that all hope is not lost. Even Job who seemed to have given up all hope returned to it. This is what leads up to Job's hope. Not really the hope of justification as to the actual cause of his suffering but rather liberation and then vindication from his suffering.[40]

JOB'S HOPE

Job's suffering has been a historic example of the suffering of the innocent. This happens all over the world which often takes away the joy of life from human beings. In the face of the suffering of the innocent, women, children, old people, the handicapped and disabled, we are found amidst the wilderness of life. We are found with only few words to survive. We are found stripped of our dancing abilities, just like the Israelites cried over their misfortune amid the Babylonian exile and said, How can we sing the Lord's song in a strange land? (Ps 137). So it is today with us in Africa and in Nigeria in particular, during incessant violence against innocent human beings we find it truly difficult to sing and dance as free people, for we find

37. Cf. Claassens, "Tragic Laughter," 143–55.
38. Boorer, "Job's Hope," 108.
39. Boorer, "Job's Hope," 111.
40. Cf. Gutierrez, *On Job: God-Talk and the Suffering of the Innocent*.

ourselves more in the strange land of human injustice and evil than in the free land of love and justice and human dignity.

Suzanne Boorer further discussed the possibility and the reality of "Job's vindication." This idea of vindication is what I would take as liberation. Job in the end was not justified but liberated. He was vindicated from the suspicion of his friends and the chaos of his heart. He was liberated from the pains he was suffering and the alienation from family and friends (Job 42).

There are two important moves worth our consideration in this section. Firstly was "Job's hope for vindication vis a vis an unjust God (19:23–27; 23:3–4; chaps. 29–31)."[41] Job summoned courage to confront God for his vindication. This was a very radical aspect of Job's experience and engagement with God. This man grew larger and stronger than he used to be. He presented his quest to God and left it with God; unless God is unjust, Job asked for vindication from his suffering. This is the radical demonstration of faith and hope beyond any conventional tradition. This is possible only in the kind of condition that Job found himself. The second move followed the first which was "the Divine Response to Job's Hope for Vindication—Job is Vindicated but God is not Unjust."[42] God's final verdict in 42:9–11 shows Job as innocent all through the drama. God vindicated or liberated Job from the retributive fixity of his friends and even family and, on the other hand, God liberated God's self from the natural human suspicions of Divine cruelty and the darkness of God. The book of Job then ends as a book of liberation and the restoration of human dignity even when justice and justification remain very enigmatic and somewhat elusive.

Like Job in his suffering, we do not see the big picture. We do not know the actual role of God in the entire drama but like Job the only sure way of building our spirituality is in hope. Job built his spirituality of hope through his sense of integrity. In our own case we do not even have any sense of personal integrity that we must hold on to, but rather we stand in the righteousness of God as God's gift to us. The new sense of hope that emerged in Job was another step in the miracle of *creatio ex nihilo*. It was created out of nothing. Job lost everything that he could own and boast about. Job lost even his personal health and all sense of comfort. He was utterly cast into the depth of darkness in his tragedy. Job remained alive with the taste of death on his lips. This is how many people today live in the Nigerian context; they live always with the taste of death on their lips. This is the height of the misfortune and tragedy of our time. In God's active and creative love for

---

41. Boorer, "Job's Hope," 113.
42. Boorer, "Job's Hope," 118.

us as human beings we believe God's grace is always sufficient for us amidst all kinds of suffering. God participates in our suffering through his love. The suffering of the innocent has become the suffering of God. This calls into question the reality of God in the midst of our suffering. God was with Job and Job was constantly in search of God. This is ironic in itself nevertheless; the force of the irony remains the beauty of the event. Job vowed to insist on seeing God to dialogue on this matter of his tragic experience; even if God would slay Job, he promised to still hope in him. He promised to still await God's last words, for the suffering that he had experienced does not have the last words. Suffering is not an end in itself. This was what kept Job hopeful not in himself or in his possessions or the traditional verdict of his friends but rather in God. Job's hope has always been a hope of meeting with God, of seeing God and of receiving justice from God. The classic phrase "I know that my redeemer lives" (19:25) calls the attention of many scholars over the years to try to decipher Job's focus on movement in his thought. I think it may be a revelation that came beyond Job and goes far away. This is why some could see it as a messianic vision, etc. Job only uttered his voice of hope amidst his tragedy that even death does not have the last word in his case.

CONCLUSION

As we live today in the world of deep troubles and incessant attacks on our humanity and freedom to be, it is time for us think of hope, justice, and truth in these troubled times. These are surely the end times in which we experience the apocalyptic turns of events in the history of the world. For us this may or may not be the history of the end. It is always the history of the beginning for "in the end is always the beginning" of the new actions of God (cf. Moltmann). We may be suffering immensely like Job even without knowing why we actually suffer. We may witness the killings of people by unknown gunmen who rejoice in dehumanizing and destroying others in the name of their gods. This is the new religious idolatry of our time. The killings and destruction of humanity in the name of God cannot be anything more than the worship of self and death.[43] This is truly a move away from the God of life, love, and justice. This may render us homeless but not hopeless. This may expose us more to our vulnerability than affluence and strength. Nevertheless, amidst all this tragedy the light of hope is always possible. The words of people whether family or friends do not define our future. The actions of men who do evil do not seal our future. Our future

---

43. Moltmann, "Living God, Renew and Transform Us."

is in God and God is our future. In the polyphony of Job, we hear different voices. Some are voices of pride and arrogance, voices of certainty and judgmentalism, voices of hope seeking justice and rest. In these last set of voices, we must be found amidst tragedy and suffering. Not to think we are certain of what befalls us but to always seek justice, and rest in the hope that remains our courage and sustaining grace.

BIBLIOGRAPHY

Ackermann, Denise M. "Metaphor, Mystery and Paradox: Orientations for Christian Spirituality." In *Discerning God's Justice in Church, Society and Academy: Festschrift for Jaap Durand*, edited by Ernst Conradie and Christo Lombard, 25–36. Stellenbosch: SUN, 2009.

Balentine, S. E. *Job*. Smyth & Helwys Bible Commentary. Macon, GA: Smyth & Helwys, 2006.

Barre, M. "'Fear of God' and the World View of Wisdom." *Biblical Theology Bulletin* 11 (1981) 41–43.

Blocher, H. "The Fear of the Lord as the 'Principle' of Wisdom." *Tyndale Bulletin* 28 (1977) 3–28.

Boorer, S. "The Dark Side of God? A Dialogue with Jung's Interpretation of the Book of Job." *Pacifica* 10 (1997) 277–97.

———. "Job's Hope: A Reading of the Book of Job from the Perspective of Hope." *Colloquium* 30.2 (1998) 101–22.

Bosman, Hendrik. "Being Wise betwixt Order and Mystery: Keeping the Commandments and Fearing the LORD." *Scriptura* 111 (2012) 433–39.

Brenner, A. "God's Answer to Job." *Vetus Testamentum* 31 (1981) 129–37.

Brueggemann, Walter. *An Introduction to the Old Testament: The Canon and Christian Imagination*. Louisville, KY: Westminster John Knox, 2003.

Buber, Martin. *The Dimensions of Job*. Edited by Nahum Glatzer. New York: Schocken, 1969.

Claassens, L. Juliana. "Tragic Laughter: Laughter as Resistance in the Book of Job." *Interpretation: A Journal of Bible and Theology* 69 (2015) 143–55.

Clines, D. J. A. "In Search of an Indian Job." *Vestus Testamentum* 33 (1983) 398–418.

———. *Job 1–20*. Dallas, TX: Word, 1989.

———. "Job 5.1–8: A New Exegesis." *Biblica* 62 (1981) 185–94.

———. *Job 21–37*. Nashville: Thomas Nelson, 2006.

———. "Putting Elihu in His Place: A Proposal for the Relocation of Job 32–37." *JSOT* 29 (2004) 115–29.

Cox, D. "Fear or Conscience? Yir'at YHWH in Proverbs 1–9." *Studia Hierosolymitana* 3 (1982) 83–90.

Freehof, Solomon B. *The Book of Job: A Commentary*. New York: Union of American Hebrew Congregation, 1958.

Gordis, Robert. *The Book of God and Man*. Chicago: University of Chicago Press, 1965.

Gutierrez, Gustavo. *On Job: God-Talk and the Suffering of the Innocent*. Maryknoll, NY: Orbis, 1987.

Habel, N. *The Book of Job*. London: SCM, 1985.

Hartley, J. E. *The Book of Job*. Grand Rapids: Eerdmans, 1988.
Moltmann, Jürgen. "Living God, Renew and Transform Us—26th General Council of the World Communion of Reformed Churches, in Leipzig, Germany, 29 June to 07 July 2017." *HTS Theological Studies* 73 (2017) 1–8.
Newsom, C. A. *The Book of Job: A Contest of Moral Imagination*. Oxford: Oxford University Press, 2003.
———. "Considering Job." *Currents in Research* 1 (1993) 97–131.
———. "Job." In *The New Interpreter's Bible, vol 4*, edited by L. E. Keck, 317–638. Nashville: Abingdon, 1996.
Sheldon, Mark. "Job, Human Suffering and Knowledge: Some Contemporary Jewish Perspectives." *Encounter* 41 (1980) 229–35.
Williams, J. G. "You Have Not Spoken Truth of Me: Mystery and Irony in Job." *Zeitschrift für Altentestamentliche Wissenschaft* 83 (1971) 231–55.
Wilson, L. "The Book of Job and the Fear of God." *Tyndale Bulletin* 46 (1995) 59–79.
Zuck, R. B., ed. *Sitting with Job: Selected Studies on the Book of Job*. Grand Rapids: Baker, 1992.

Chapter 12

Bible, Spirituality, and Method
Continuing the Debate

Christo Lombaard

BIBLE-HISTORY-FAITH

The relationship between the *Bible*, *history*, and *faith* in the broad Judeo-Christian—and in a different, though related sense, Islamic—religious streams goes back as far as the earliest days of the youngest of these three phenomena, which together constitute this stream of religiosity: namely, the Bible. A mere two millennia old, the Bible is a youngster when compared to history and faith, even as its Hebrew opening two-thirds traditions, particularly in its oral form, reach further into history by another millennium or so.[1] The existence of our species, from some three hundred millennia ago, and its earliest expressions of religiosity some fifty millennia ago, significantly pre-date the coming into existence of the traditions and texts that we find in the Bible. The processes of the canonizations of these texts into religiously authoritative collections of relative stability by the fourth century CE,[2] combined in distinctive ways the three aspects of Bible, history, and faith. From then on, first Christianity, then Judaism, and later Islam—the so-called three Religions of the Book—would not understand themselves outside of

---

1. Accurately dating the origins of the oldest literary heritage retained in the Hebrew Bible, the wisdom traditions, are only sometimes somewhat possible.
2. Cf., however, Lombaard, "Spirituality and Culture in Interaction," 6–30.

the perimeters of this combination, Bible-history-faith. From then onwards, within these faith circles themselves as much, as with outsiders' perspectives on them, the very act of naming these three phenomena—as separate matters—as was just done portray a distinction that would be experienced as contrived. The distinction is not false (which would mean that it bore no resemblance to what is referred to), but it remains a true artefact of Modernity, namely, of the Enlightenment; only in our rarified academic circles can such a characterization be upheld.

Briefly to explain the latter position, restricting the rest of the argument here to Christian precincts over recent centuries: within historical pre-Modernity (and hence, in contemporary situations, within a-Modernist contexts), and always in pre-critical religious suppositioning, the distinction Scripture-history-faith hardly arises: these three "entities" (or their parallels) form a kind of unified trinity, a ternion. The religious experience of by far the greater part of humanity, with all its variance and with the exception—in some respects only—of Western/ized intelligentsia, relates (implicitly understood or sensed) to this ternion as a whole. The insightfulness of Rationality (here counted among the corollaries of Modernity and the Enlightenment) rendered great advantages in the depth of comprehension gained on these and on all other matters that we encounter as humans. It may in various circles of late have become a kind of habit to denigrate these "advances." However, our scholarly understanding and hence our human condition (despite their respective limitations and predicaments) would have been much the poorer, had it not been for the penetrating analyses offered, from within this frame of reference, on our world and for our lives. These advantages include deepening our grasp of the Bible, of historiography, and of faith.

As merely some instances of this deepening (and as preparation for what follows below):

1. On the *Bible*, we now know that for the greater part of the Hebrew Bible, there had never been an original text to which to return[3] as there had indeed been for most of the New Testament texts; that for both these Bible anthologies (the Hebrew-Aramaic and the Greek), the underlying primary oralities were unavoidably altered by the enscripting processes; that in all such cases, however, not the earlier or later versions nor the various persons or processes involved can be placed on a (most often unacknowledged) scale of reliability or authenticity or holiness, since *living traditions* are involved, the life of which is extended every time those texts are read.

3. Deist, *Witnesses to the Old Testament*.

2. On *history*, we have seen that naïveties implode on their self-assurednesses, as much when high correlationality between text (biblical or other) and the event or person or idea (etc.) recounted is assumed, as when no such correspondence is posited; that is: as much when full referentiality as when no external referentiality of a text is presumed; that is: as much when author or text or reader is one-sidedly taken to be the seat of meaning (usually when distinguishing, respectively, between historical analyses, literary approaches, and readers' responses as constituting more valid exegesis); historiography too implies (overtly and inadvertently) participating in a *given heritage*.

3. On *faith* observed: whether this observance is the existentially committed participation in a faith tradition or the (somewhat) detached observation of the dynamics of (a) faith, the conclusion continually presents itself that faith is alive and active, both as experienced interiority and in the effects it has on human reality. Whether as a religiously sensed depth-meaning or as a phenomenological given, whether on individual or on social plane, the experienced presence of God in the history of Israel and, differently, in the life and works of Jesus of Nazareth, play out as histories that continuously have concrete effects (from positive to negative). Faith remains as something *sensed-in-living*, in assorted forms (acts, words, symbols, awarenesses) of affirmation, and, importantly, just as much in doubt and in disavowal. All these possibilities are *faith experienced*.

Each of these instances of deepening of insight that resulted from Modernism/the Enlightenment/Rationality, can of course be much expanded; what has been rendered here are of necessity but cryptic summaries. Yet, the abridgments here serve to illustrate that we who stand in the wake of such a major turn in manner of being (as Modernism/the Enlightenment/Rationality had been) have gained much therefrom. Criticisms of these contributions will always be valuable; outright rejection (which are found from various religious, cultural and—to be sure—also intellectual fronts) constitutes a loss of these precious intellectual gains since the 1700s.

Among these valid criticisms are that the atomism inherent to Modernism/the Enlightenment/Rationality also, and quite naturally, lead us away from foundationally meaning-giving relationalities—even as atomism is often seen precisely as the source of its strength.[4] The value of gaining the ever-smaller picture, the details and *minutiae*, has meant that we have

---

4. Danie Goosen's works make this point soundly: Goosen, *Nihilisme*; *Oor gemeenskap en plek*.

at times become oblivious of the ever-present bigger picture;[5] that is, of the sacred canopy or the re-enchanted world, in the influential language of Berger[6] or of the metaphysical dimension implicit in any and all human acts (of commission and omission) and cognitions.[7]

In the era in which we find ourselves, the world when taken as a whole[8] has been becoming more religious, and more conservatively religious, and will continue along these trends, according to the influential Pew Trust surveys.[9] Such quantitative demographics, along with the large body of sociological literature in the wake of Berger's insights and philosophical works on for instance post-secularism, mean in practice that within Christianity (as the focus here) the questions on the relationship between Bible and faith are not set to diminish, but to increase. Not only through the more usual revivalisms in some contexts, but in qualitatively morphed and morphing expressions of faith that lie outside of the usual scope of churchly circles, and hence often remain unobserved, Christianity grows.[10] The vagaries of proof-texting, biblicism, and (in many respects phenomenologically parallel though confessionally contrasting) a- or anti-historical readings of the Bible are set to continue. When the validity of such Bible interpretations is put to question, the surprised reactions often include the claim that one does not hold to the continued relevance of the Bible for our time, current matters, and the continued Christian faith.

Such surprised reactions spring from assumptions that the Bible can and must be understood in only one way: the meaning ascribed to the texts concerned by the reader (with the implication, at times overtly stated, as led by the Holy Spirit). This, not with the theoretical sophistication of Reader Response theories (of most influentially French, Spanish—i.e., Latin American liberationist—and English origins) or of hermeneutics (of mostly German origin), but through direct, immediate application. As I tried elsewhere to drive this point home related to such unreflective readings in African contexts, it remains "*difficult to grasp how a continent* which understands itself as post-colonial, taking decoloniality ever more seriously, extending also to matters of engagement with Bible texts, *has to such a significant extent held*

---

5. Lombaard et al., "Faith, Society and the Post-Secular," 11.
6. Berger, *Sacred Canopy*.
7. Lowe, *Survey of Metaphysics*.
8. Here acknowledging the pockets of exception such as England.
9 Pew Research Center, "Changing Global Religious Landscape."
10. Cf. Lombaard, "Normal(ised) Christianity/Religiosity in the Public Arena," 330–43.

onto the most spiritually impairing of North Atlantic interpretative strategies on the Bible, fundamentalism (biblicism)."[11]

In order to move away from such a- or anti-historical readings of the Bible, a few strategies may be followed—one of which was indicated in the just-mentioned chapter;[12] another which is discussed in what follows.

BIBLICAL SPIRITUALITY CAN/NOT FUNCTION WITH A BIBLE HISTORICALLY READ?

Most overtly during the discussion times at specialist conferences on the discipline of biblical spirituality in Nijmegen, the Netherlands; University of Gloucestershire, UK; and the Carmelite Institute, Malta;[13] and between the proverbial lines in publications by especially South Africans when writing on the discipline of biblical spirituality, a perennial debate continues on the possibility of the religiously formative value of historical-critical exegesis. Such formative, "mystagogical" dimensions[14] of the engagement with the Bible is of central importance to the discipline of biblical spirituality. Put differently: the phenomenon of *biblical spirituality* which is studied in discipline of *biblical spirituality* relates to how faith and Bible texts relate to one another, both as faith (among other aspects) formed the Bible texts and as the Bible texts (among other aspects) form faith. The extant models for studying this dynamic have been reviewed by Huub Welzen.[15] The two schools of thought include that historical-critical methodologies, especially in their more mature forms in recent decades, do indeed contribute positively to fostering spiritual growth, versus the opposite position, that other methodologies are much more productive in this respect, with these methodologies then always contrasted with the assumed negative effects of historical-critical methodologies with regard to faith formation.

Recently, the latter position has again found express articulation in an article published on the Afrikaans language academic e-journal for religion sciences, *LitNet Akademies (Godsdienswetenskappe)*. The article was

11. Lombaard, "Proposal on the Bible and African Christian Spirituality, 2020 to 2050," 186, drawing on Van Deventer, "Did Someone Say 'History,'" 713–14, 717–20.

12. Lombaard, "Proposal on the Bible and African Christian Spirituality, 2020 to 2050," 181–91.

13. Kourie, "Weaving Colourful Threads," 4n9.

14. Cf. Lombaard, "Considering Mystagogy as Method in Biblical Spirituality," 1–8.

15. Welzen, "Contours of Biblical Spirituality as a Discipline," 37–60; more substantively in Welzen, *Biblical Spirituality*; for the newest perspectives on methodology in spirituality studies, cf. Cavazos-González and De Col, *Evolving Methodologies in the Study of Spirituality*.

titled "Die transformerende effek van 'n mistieke lees van die Skrif" ("The transforming/transformational effect of a mystical reading of Scripture"), published under the authorship of Celia Kourie.[16] This article contains some sections that are critical of the employment of historical-critical exegesis towards spiritually endearing engagements with or from the Bible text. For the sake of fairness of representation, where applicable the text is below given first in the Afrikaans as published, on which follows my translation into English.

It should be kept in mind here that the purpose of pointing out what I do below is nothing more than advancing the discussion on historical-critical exegesis and the relation thereof to Christian spiritual formation. As to the colleagues involved, namely, Celia Kourie and the editor of *LitNet Akademies (Godsdienswetenskappe)*, Pieter de Villiers, I hold them in the highest esteem. This is attested to by my frequent positive reference to their work, my involvement in publication projects in their honor, my writings on them, my cooperation with them on conference and other academic projects, as much as my positive relationships with them, which I have always deeply appreciated. In addition, I hold them to be the founding figures of spirituality studies on the South African university scene,[17] even though there had been precursors to their formal establishment of this academic discipline in South Africa.[18] These matters I point out here, lest my intentions with this contribution be misconstrued. The aim here is to help advance the case in favor of historical-critical exegesis as a positive impulse towards Christian spiritual formation, in its intellectual (i.e., biblical spirituality as an academic specialism) as much as its experiential (i.e., biblical spirituality as a religious phenomenon) dimensions.

ANALYZING THE TEXT OF "DIE TRANSFORMERENDE EFFEK VAN 'N MISTIEKE LEES VAN DIE SKRIF"

The first expression against historical exegetical methodologies in this article is found already in the initial Afrikaans summary of the article. Usually, the summary that introduces an article is not employed in academic discussions: the difficulties involved with summarizing in a few words only a longer writing does not render the abstract suitable material for analysis. In the case of *LitNet Akademies (Godsdienswetenskappe)* articles, however, a more substantive than usual English summary is required of authors, and in

16. Kourie, "Transformerende effek van 'n mistieke lees van die Skrif."
17. Kourie, "Spirituality and the University," 148–73.
18. Cf. Joubert and Lombaard, "Theology and Spirituality."

the case of this particular article, the two versions—the Afrikaans and the English—are not quite in accord with one another as far as the orientation towards historical criticism is concerned. This variation is quite noticeable. Although, still, not too much can ever be made of these differences, again given the nature of the genre of the introductory article abstract, at least these differences ought to be noted, because this divergence plays out in the argument that unfolds in that publication as much as here below.

The Afrikaans abstract[19] includes the following comment:

> Dit word algemeen aanvaar dat die dekades lange oorheersing van histories-kritiese benaderings in die Bybelwetenskappe nie langer volhoubaar is nie. As 'n metode wat die teks sien as 'n historiese artefak, wend dit 'n minimale, indien enige, poging aan om die *ervaring* te verstaan van diegene wat die teks geskryf het. Die benaderings bied voorts 'n interpretasie van die Skrif aan wat die veelvlakkige aard daarvan misken.

Translated:

> It is generally accepted that the decades-long dominance by historical-critical approaches in the Bible sciences is no longer sustainable. As a method that sees the text as a historical artifact, it makes minimal, if any, effort to understand the *experience* of those who had written the text. The approaches furthermore present an interpretation of Scripture that ignores its multifaceted nature.

As mentioned above, the English abstracts accompanying *LitNet Akademies (Godsdienswetenskappe)* articles are substantively longer than the usual abstracts published along with research journal articles, as an international norm. Presumably the reasons for this includes intentions also to communicate somewhat more fully than can be the case with the usual such summaries, to an international scholarly readership the contents of the Afrikaans language articles. The objective of this publication, as with the other specialist e-journals in the *LitNet Akademies* group, is that it has set itself the worthy goal of retaining and expanding the hard-won academic niveau of the Afrikaans language, language which senses itself to be under political and hence social pressure, given reflexive public and political attitudes to this language in particular (among the other eleven official languages of South Africa). In this English abstract accompanying "Die transformerende effek . . .," the expectation is therefore not that the contents would precisely match the Afrikaans abstract; rather, the longer summary would expand

---

19. Kourie, "Transformerende effek," 235.

the briefer Afrikaans version. The expectation is however that in contents the two versions would follow the same rhetorical thrust. The English text (hence therefore not translated here) reads:[20]

> ... the academy is freeing itself from the fetters of determinism. This is largely due to a major heterodox methodological explosion within the field of biblical hermeneutics within the last few decades. Without denying the value of historical-critical approaches, their hegemony has been challenged and the limitations of the positivistic framework within which the method operates have been brought to the fore. This is not to deny its validity. In spite of its shortcomings, it has been and continues to be of vital importance in determining the provenance of the text...
>
> The semantic autonomy of the text, while pointing to the fact that its meaning is not limited to the "intention" of the original author, nevertheless does not mean that authorial meaning has lost all significance...
>
> Scripture interpretation is freeing itself from the fetters of determinism, and the limits of rationalism are becoming more apparent... The semantic potential of the text, in which the possibility of multiple readings comes to the fore, elucidates the illuminatory and existential significance of a mystical interpretation.

When comparing these two summaries, or abstracts, it is particularly in relation to the topic of historical readings of the Bible texts, that the longer English version is more nuanced (which can be expected, given the greater allotted word count). However, where these two versions are at odds is that the longer English version does not carry the dismissive tone of the shorter Afrikaans version regarding the spiritual value of historical-critical exegesis. The English abstract, to be sure, notes the value of historical criticism too; the Afrikaans summary is, conversely, much firmer in its stance against historical Bible readings.

The question that presents itself is: Which of these two orientations towards historical criticism in Bible reading in its relationship to spiritual value is carried through in the rest of the "Die transformerende effek..." article? This can be easily traced through the paragraphs of "Die transformerende effek..."; the rest of the article under discussion includes a number of comments on historically oriented exegesis—noteworthy—especially in the framing introductory and the concluding sections of the article.

---

20. Kourie, "Transformerende effek," 236–38.

In the introductory section of the article,[21] we read:

> Dit is belangrik om aan te toon dat bykans alle opleiding in Bybelse hermeneutiek gedurende die laaste drie eeue, op 'n suiwer intellektuele benadering gekonsentreer het, teenoor die bestudering van die Skrif in die tydperk voor die Verligting wat intellektuele kennis met 'n geestelike sensitiwiteit gekombineer het en wat gevolglik tot 'n mistieke lees van die Skrif aanleiding gegee het.
>
> Die ernstige tekortkominge van histories-kritiese benaderings tot die Bybel is reeds bekend. Dit sluit onder andere in: sy atomistiese en fragmentariese aard, sy gebrekkige insig in die literêre eenheid en geheel van die dokumente; sy konsentrasie op die voorliterêre fase wat die tradisie fragmenteer en 'n meer holistiese betekenis van die teks in sy breër konteks verhinder; sy hantering van die Skrif as 'n voorwerp wat gedissekteer moet word eerder as 'n lewegewende openbaring wat ervaar moet word; en die positivistiese raamwerk waarbinne die metode sy beslag vind. Hierdie lys kan nog verder uitgebrei word. Weinig moeite word byvoorbeeld gedoen om die ervaring te verstaan van diegene wat die teks voortgebring het. Daarmee is die eintlike bestaansrede vir hierdie geskrifte van die vroeë Christengemeenskappe geïgnoreer . . .
>
> Histories-kritiese benaderings het voorts ook veral gefokus op die betekenis soos dit deur die outeur bedoel is, maar dan tot die nadeel van "meer as net" letterlike en allegoriese benaderings.

Translated:

> It is important to show that almost all training in biblical hermeneutics during the last three centuries concentrated on a purely intellectual approach, as opposed to the study of Scripture in the period before the Enlightenment, which combined intellectual knowledge with a spiritual sensitivity, which consequently led to a mystical reading of Scripture . . .
>
> The serious deficiencies of historical-critical approaches to the Bible are already known. These include, among other matters: their atomistic and fragmenting nature; their inadequate insight into the literary unity and coherence of these documents; its emphasis on the pre-literary phase, which fragments the tradition and precludes [understanding the] more holistic meaning of the text within its wider context; its treatment of

---

21. Kourie, "Transformerende effek," 238.

Scripture as an object to be dissected rather than experiencing Scripture as life-giving revelation; and the positivist framework within which the method is rooted. This list could be extended. Little effort is for instance made to understand the experience of those who produced the text. This means that the true reason for the coming into being of these writings of the early Christian communities, is ignored . . .

Historical-critical approaches have moreover focused especially on meaning as intended by the author, but then neglecting the "more than merely" literal and allegorical approaches.

Then, further explicit comments on historically oriented exegesis occur in the conclusion to the "Die transformerende effek . . ." article:[22]

> Moderniteit, en in die besonder 'n tipe akademiese meerderwaardigheid, het bygedra tot hierdie stand van sake, en tekste wat bedoel is om op vele vlakke van betekenis te resoneer, is tot hulle letterlike betekenis gereduseer . . .
>
> Gelukkig dan dat Skrifinterpretasie van die boeie van determinisme bevry word, en rasionalisme se beperkinge al duideliker blyk.

Translated:

> Modernity, and particularly a kind of academic superiority, has contributed to this state of affairs, and texts intended to resound with many levels of meaning, have been reduced to their literal meanings . . .
>
> It is fortunate, then, that the interpretation of Scripture is freed from the shackles of determinism, and the limitations of rationalism become clearer.

Lastly, in the footnotes section of the article,[23] the following is found:

> Hiermee word die geldigheid daarvan nie ontken nie; ten spyte van talle tekortkominge was en is histories-kritiese benaderings sekerlik van kardinale belang vir die verstaan van 'n teks.

Translated:

> This does not deny its validity [= the validity of historical methodology]; despite numerous shortcomings, historical-critical approaches were and are certainly of crucial importance for understanding a text.

22. Kourie, "Transformerende effek," 247.
23. Kourie, "Transformerende effek," 252n2.

LAYERS IN "DIE TRANSFORMERENDE EFFEK VAN 'N MISTIEKE LEES VAN DIE SKRIF"

By now, the unevenness within the article, indicated above, should be quite apparent. In the same way as when one's analytical skills have been trained into virtually reflexively seeing the editorial layers in Bible texts to be exegeted—the different "hands" at work in the creation of those writings, at different times, in different contexts, with different intentions—here too such an editorial layeredness seems evident.

This initial insight, as a methodological point of verification, was then put forward during an interview to the editor of the journal concerned, *LitNet Akademies (Godsdienswetenskappe)*, Pieter de Villiers, in January 2023, in Stellenbosch. During this discussion, De Villiers confirmed the editorial trajectory of the "Die transformerende effek . . ." article as having been, in broad outlines (which historical reconstructions are always safest), as follows:

1. The article was originally written by Celia Kourie, in English
2. An Afrikaans translation of the article was presented to *LitNet Akademies (Godsdienswetenskappe)*
3. During the subsequent editorial processes, the Afrikaans translation was edited by De Villiers, as part of the collegial duties that is often the selfless remit of the editors of academic journals.

One can therefore, from both the initial observation and then the oral confirmation, comfortably speak of three editorial layers in this article (that is, if the academic sources employed are not included as part of a more detailed study, the possibility of which lies beyond the intent). Moreover, this initial observation has been enriched by reading, over decades, the publications of these two colleagues, and by taking part in some of the conferences mentioned above, which gives one a deep sense of what the approaches and orientations are that endear these colleagues to one another, but also of where they differ. These are parts of the joys of sustained scholarship, which experience is unique among human relationships.

The two most significant of these layers for the purposes here, in "Die transformerende effek . . .," are Layers 1 and 3, as numbered immediately above. Naturally, it would be relatively easy to determine who had indeed been the initial translator of the English original piece into Afrikaans; though interesting, that would however not be an important contribution to what is being illustrated below. What the identification of Layers 1 and 3 here do demonstrate, is:

1. That it is indeed possible with reasonable accuracy to indicate editorial layers within the "finalized" (here, published) version of a text (and in a modern text, that is of course more straightforwardly personally verifiable than would be the case with ancient texts).
2. That the differences between these editorial layers show the active, that is, positive presence of different sensibilities during the coming-into-being of the finalized/published text.
3. That reconstructing these different (that is: diverging, which is to say: non-synonymous; but which does not necessarily mean: opposing) sensibilities, does not destroy the meaning that the finalized/published text may have for later readers, but in fact brings that meaning alive, further enhancing its already evocative worth.
4. The latter enhancement is effected by realizing that the finalized/published text is the product of historically discrete persons, of dissimilar (though not necessarily unalike) agency, whose distinct ideas and sentiments are inadvertently (meant here in a positive sense) captured in the final text, with—crucially—the trajectory of that inclusion that can still be judiciously retraced from the final text, and, thereby, that trajectory of meaning can, in a sense, be relived.
5. When these initially discrete ideas and sentiments are disentangled, it shows their respective value (their concretely historical importance in the minds of the original scribes), with, then, additional hermeneutic value to be gained by understanding how these sensibilities had been brought together into a new whole.
6. This "new whole," the finalized/published text, replaces none of its formational impulses, but adds to the tapestry[24] of the final text.
7. Reading this "tapestry" results in a more abundantly nuanced meaning that is to be gained by those of us who treasure this text (and others such as it), as part of the library of primary and secondary texts that keep us engaged in the study of spirituality.

To concretize these just-numbered points in relation to the two views on historical criticism taken up in the article, "Die transformerende effek" (and these details that follow were not verified during the interview mentioned above, which means a return here to the slightly more experimental methodological mode):

---

24. A term from Kourie, "Weaving Colourful Threads," 1–9.

1. The greater part by far of the text of the article is directly ascribable to Kourie, as Editorial Layer 1 of this writing—though we only have access to it in translation (with the translator's work indicated above as Editorial Layer 2).[25]

2. The Afrikaans abstract,[26] which starts (in my translation above) with "It is generally accepted that...," contains the thoughts more typical of Editorial Layer 3, i.e., De Villiers: the language is more strongly critical of historically oriented exegesis.

3. The English abstract,[27] which reads from "... the academy is freeing itself from ...," contains the thoughts more typical of Editorial Layer 1, i.e., Kourie: not uncritical of historically oriented exegesis, but not quite as strongly unsympathetic either, containing tones of appreciation too.

4. The introductory section of the article,[28] beginning (in my translation above) with "It is important to show that almost all training...," contains thoughts which in general amalgamates the two more or less disinclined views on historical criticism, but the more strongly worded tone of Layer 3/De Villiers certainly dominates.

5. Then, from in the conclusion to the article,[29] from "Modernity, and particularly a kind of academic superiority" onwards: here too, the De Villiers view is in the foreground.

6. Lastly, from the footnote text:[30] "This does not deny its validity..." contains the more conciliatory tone of Kourie. This footnote however relates to the "This list could be extended,"[31] which—interestingly—is a section ascribable to De Villiers, but with the footnote which thus softens the tone of the introductory article text that counters the historical exegetical approaches.

---

25. The allusion here to the older indications of the Pentateuchal sources as J-E, D, and P; in current theory generally indicated as P and non-P; or in New Testament studies to the Matthean and Lukan sources as Mark and Q, apart from the *Sondergut* in each, is playful, but with clear parallels, deliberately so.

26. Kourie, "Transformerende effek," 235.

27. Kourie, "Transformerende effek," 236–38.

28. Kourie, "Transformerende effek," 238.

29. Kourie, "Transformerende effek," 247.

30. Kourie, "Transformerende effek," 252n2.

31. Kourie, "Transformerende effek," 238; see my text in this regard, above.

"ALIVE WITH POSSIBILITIES"

From the above, three aspects of the article "Die transformerende effek . . ." emerge: the text is editorially (in more traditional exegetical language: redactionally) complex in its layeredness; the two identified main layers contains two differing ways of speaking on the spiritual worth of historical criticism;[32] neither of these two views are however advanced ideologically so strongly that the one drowns out the other; into oblivion, as it were. (This tolerance in compromise is illustrated most clearly by the relationship between footnote 2 and the text on which it comments.)[33]

The parallels of such a conclusion, here, to the findings of many historically-oriented exegetical studies, are noteworthy. The character of the "Die transformerende effek . . ." text as a compromise document, incorporating more than one central view, has to be taken seriously, if the nature of the document is to be acknowledged with any validity; that is: corresponding to reality. Ignoring this layeredness, and the divergence of thought that come along with this textual-historical reality, would be to deny what the document, in fact, is; that is, how it in fact had come into being. "Die transformerende effek . . ." is a composite document, with a redactional history. This much is demonstrable.

What is more, drawing here on my reading experience of "Die transformerende effek . . .," the final text has meaning not only because it is a finalized document—which a religious text would be its canonized form. This final text indeed has meaning, which significance is however constituted also by the differing views reconciled within it. The trajectory of meanings thus created, from Layer 1 to Layer 3, and the reception history it further creates in its wake, among us as subsequent readers, is in addition part of how meaning unfolds. The latter, not in an uncompromisingly linear fashion, but certainly in a manner now honed by a created tradition, which then shapes subsequent readings—be these subsequent readings in continuance with or divergent to the broad intent with the read text.

---

32. The differences may be ascribed to various causes: Kourie hails from a Roman Catholic background; De Villiers, from a Reformed background. Although both work professionally in South Africa, Kourie's formative theological years were in the United Kingdom, and in South Africa she worked exclusively in the northern part of the country, whereas De Villiers's career was located more in the southern part of South Africa (which in Afrikaans theological culture is significant). These are just the briefest indications of such influences on their respective views. For the purposes of this contribution, which simply seeks to make the point that the differences are noticeable, these causes and the differences do not have to be further explored.

33. Kourie, "Transformerende effek," 238; again with reference to my text, above, in this regard.

Such a process of the unfolding of meaning is positive, as it constitutes gain. It is therefore the opposite of the typically ascribed Derridean reflex, in which following meaning into the deeper regions of texts is said to render traces upon traces of meaning that eventually destroys any firm meaning/fulness.[34] What we see above is an experience contrary to the loss of meaning; the "gain" is namely a fuller meaning, a more encompassing meaning that may be taken from "Die transformerende effek . . ." We are enriched by this text—as much by how it (quite noticeably) came about as by what it does to us, as we read the text and as we notice how it came to say what it now, meaningfully, conveys.

This effect of the "Die transformerende effek . . ." text therefore includes reactions such as mine, here. This reaction, namely, goes against the grain of the argumentation in "Die transformerende effek . . .," which combines two strands of thought that are roughly in accordance with one another, being much less appreciative of historical criticism than my views are in this regard. These views have developed especially since the late 1980s, notably without the (at times) too harshly positivist earlier exegeses. In the latter respect, I thus concur with one or two of the sentiments along these lines expressed in "Die transformerende effek. . . ." I however also understand the apologetic intent of those studies, as they had to maintain Bible exegesis as a discipline in at times harshly logical-positivist climes, which would in at least some contexts bear hardly any existential, particularly theological, or spiritual insights that may have accompanied exegetical work.

The (in truth, repressive) naiveté of that particular cultural climate with its reflex against theology and spirituality has however long since passed. Some studies have indicated how faith dimensions had indeed been included, subtly (inadvertently, or subversively) in exegetical studies that in our time seem easily dismissible as perhaps spiritually dry. Such exegetes had to make do with the intellectual climate that made, ultimately, indefensible demands on them, as we have to too with other unsustainable demands. Moreover, many studies have in recent decades been published which, either by implication or directly, demonstrate the thoroughgoing religious worth of historically-oriented approaches to the Bible text.

It is in the post-1980s climate that I came of intellectual age; hence my criticisms of the then dominant a- and anti-historical exegetical approaches in South Africa as more destructive of spiritual nourishment than historical methodologies are. It is for that same reason, too, that I could not but with great appreciation enjoy the "Die transformerende effek . . ." article, not only

---

34. Cf., e.g., Derrida, *Of Grammatology*.

for what it says, but also for how it came about saying it. In every layer of the text there is meaning; something of worth—*much* of worth.

The very fact of this *enhanced richness* of "Die transformerende effek...," also because of its (now demonstrated) historical development, can be taken as proof that the same, in parallel, holds for Bible texts. In reading their layeredness, which is a historical given, the spiritual worth of those texts is increased—not diminished. For a moment to poach the marketing slogan of the official South African tourism authorities, we have in all such cases a text that is "alive with possibilities."

BIBLIOGRAPHY

Berger, Peter. *The Sacred Canopy: Elements of a Sociological Theory of Religion*. Garden City, NJ: Doubleday, 1967.
Cavazos-González, Gilberto, and Rossano Zas Friz De Col, eds. *Evolving Methodologies in the Study of Spirituality*. Rome: Mysterion, 2022.
Deist, Ferdinand. *Witnesses to the Old Testament*. Pretoria: NG Kerkboekhandel, 1988.
Derrida, Jacques. *Of Grammatology*. Baltimore: Johns Hopkins University Press, 1976.
Goosen, Danie. *Die nihilisme: Notas oor ons tyd*. Pretoria: Praag, 2007.
———. *Oor gemeenskap en plek. Anderkant die onbehae*. Pretoria: FAK, 2015.
Joubert, Lisel, and Christo Lombaard. "Theology and Spirituality." *Journal of Systematic Theology* (2023) 1–41. https://journalofsystematictheology.com.
Kourie, Celia. "The Historical-Critical Method in Roman Catholic Biblical Scholarship." *Theologia Evangelica* 18 (1985) 42–9.
———. "Spirituality and the University." *Verbum et Ecclesia* 30 (2009) 148–73.
———. "Die transformerende effek van 'n mistieke lees van die Skrif." *LitNet Akademies (Godsdienswetenskappe)* 16 (2019) 235–55. www.litnet.co.za/wp-content/uploads/2019/12/LitNet_Akademies_16-3_Kourie_235-255.pdf.
———. "Weaving Colourful Threads: A Tapestry of Spirituality and Mysticism." *HTS Theological Studies* 71 (2015) 1–9.
Lombaard, Christo. "Considering Mystagogy as Method in Biblical Spirituality." *HTS Theological Studies* 76 (2020) 1–8.
———. "Normal(ised) Christianity/Religiosity in the Public Arena—A Mission of the Mind." In *Mission—The "Labour Room" of Theology*, edited by Johannes Knoetze, 330–43. Wellington, South Africa: CLF, 2022.
———. "Proposal on the Bible and African Christian Spirituality, 2020 to 2050." In *What Is the Old Testament? Understanding the Hebrew Scriptures Anew*, edited by Obedben Mmesomachukwu Lumanze, 181–91. Aba, Nigeria: Centre of Biblical Studies, Research & Development: LIFE College of Theology, 2023.
———. "Spirituality and Culture in Interaction: The Illustrative Recurring Debate on the Role of the Oldest Testament in Christian Theology and Broader Culture." In *Proceedings of the Spirituality, Culture and Well-Being Conference: Inaugural Conference of the Lumen Research Institute, Excelsia College & Indiana Wesleyan University, 4th-5th October 2016*, edited by Maureen Miner and Martin Dowson, 6–30. Sydney: Lumen Research Institute/Centre for Human Interaction, Learning and Development, 2016.

Lombaard, Christo, et al. "Faith, Society and the Post-Secular: Private and Public Religion in Law and Theology." *HTS Theological Studies* 75 (2019) 1–12.

Lowe, Edward Jonathan. *A Survey of Metaphysics*. Oxford: Oxford University Press, 2002.

Pew Research Center. "The Changing Global Religious Landscape." Apr 5, 2017. www.pewresearch.org/religion/2017/04/05/the-changing-global-religious-landscape/.

Van Deventer, Hans. "Did Someone Say 'History'? In Africa We Say 'His Story'! A Study in African Biblical Hermeneutics with Reference to the Book of Daniel." *Old Testament Essays* 21 (2008) 713–28.

Welzen, Huub. *Biblical Spirituality: Contours of a Discipline*. Leuven: Peeters, 2017.

———. "Contours of Biblical Spirituality as a Discipline." In *The Spirit That Inspires: Perspectives on Biblical Spirituality*, edited by Pieter de Villiers and Lloyd Pietersen, 37–60. Acta Theologica Supplementum 15. Bloemfontein: University of the Free State Press, 2011.

Author Index

Aarde, Timothy van, 128
Aasgard, Reidar, 152
Ackermann, Denise, 91 198
Adams, Ellis A., 104
Adelana, Segun, 37
Agamben, Giorgio, 58
Aijian, Janelle, 56
Allen, Jon G., 173, 174
Anderson, Bernard W., 158
Angier, Tom, 137
Ankersmit, Franklin, 47
Anthony of the Desert, 23
Ashton, Jennifer, 148
Assmann, Aleida, 64–65
Assmann, Jan, 6, 64–67, 122, 123
Aster, Shawn Z., 159
Augustine of Hippo, 22

Badiou, Alain, 68, 69
Balentine, Samuel, 6
Barre, M., 198
Barth, Karl, 68
Battle, Michael, 90, 92
Baudrillard, Jean, 50
Bauer, Walter, 32
Beale, Greg, 111
Becker, Eve-Marie, 178
Beer, Stephan de, 37
Beller, Jonathan, 45
Berger, Peter, 207
Berges, Ulrich, 150
Berquist, Jon L., 27
Bessant, Judith, 100

Betsworth, Sharon, 152
Beuken, Willem A. M., 153, 163, 165
Beukes, Jacques, 7, 97, 99, 101, 102, 103
Bills, Neal, 123
Black, Antony, 113, 117
Black, Matthew, 33
Blocher, Henri, 198
Boase, Elizabeth, 174, 175, 178
Bonhoeffer, Dietrich, 79
Boorer, Suzanne, 196, 198, 199, 200
Booysen, Susan, 100
Bosman, Hendrik, 132, 198
Brandel, Jerrold R., 173
Bremner, Lindsay, 37, 38
Brenner, Athalya, 196
Breytenbach, Cilliers, 30, 31, 32, 34
Brueggemann, Walter, 193
Buber, Martin, 194, 195, 196
Bucher, Taina, 50
Bunge, Gabriel, 56

Calder, Todd, 137
Carny, Peter, 138
Carter, J. Kameron, 81,
Casiday, Augustine, 53, 56
Cavazos-González, Gilberto, 208
Certeau, Michel de, 39
Chawla, Louise, 104
Childs, Brevard, 153, 162, 163, 165
Chipkin, Ivor, 125, 126
Choi, Jae Haeng, 178
Christianson, Eric S., 135
Claassens, L. Juliana, 174, 199

Clements, Ronald E., 163
Clines, David, 196
Citton, Yves, 45, 52
Coakley, Sarah, 135
Collins, John J., 153, 157, 163
Corrigan, Terence, 101
Corvin, J., 178
Cox, Rory, 113, 115
Cozolino, Louis L., 180
Crary, Jonathan, 46
Crenshaw, James L., 138, 139, 140
Culp, Kristine, 69
Cushing, Debra Flanders, 104
Cezula, Simon, 132

Dahl, Nils, 30
Dalferth, Ingolf, 69
Davidson, Robert, 135
De Col, Rossano Zas Friz, 208
De Jong, Matthijs J., 156
Deist, Ferdinand, 205
Deleuze, Gilles, 50
Delport, Khegan, 6, 124
Derrida, Jacques, 21, 218
Deventer, Hans van, 208
Dickie, June F., 8, 177, 178, 179, 181, 184, 186
Diggle, James, 56
Doidge, N., 180
Dolan, Phoebe, 104
Downey, Michael, 29
Dubovský, Peter, 154, 155
Duffet, Rodney G., 48
Dumitrescu, Irina 57, 58

Edwards, Felicity, 4
Ekpo, Friday, 124
Eliade, Mircea, 39
Elkins, Kathleen G., 152
England, Frank, 16
Esala, Nathan, 132, 175
Eslinger, Lyle, 110, 128
Esterhuizen, Elisabeth, 8, 148, 149, 152, 154, 157, 159, 161, 162, 165, 166, 167
Evagrius Ponticus, 6, 46–47, 52–60, 89
Etzelmüller, Gregor, 74
Everson, A. Joseph., 166

Falque, Emmanuel, 6, 70–72, 74
Farley, Wendy, 10
Feffer, John, 118
Fernandes, Gavin, 7
Fleissner, Robert F., 148, 149
Fohrer, Georg, 153
Ford, William A., 116
Forster, Dion, 86
Forti, Tova, 143
Fox, Michael V., 132
Frahm, Eckart, 154
Franck, Georg, 49, 50
Franke, William, 12
Frechette, Christopher G., 174, 175, 178
Freehof, Solomon B., 194
Fretheim, Terence E., 113
Freud, Sigmund, 65
Frohlich, Mary, 18, 20, 21
Fung, Cadi, 104

Gadamer, Hans-Georg, 73
Gager, John G., 35, 36, 38
Gellman, Jerome, 137
Gericke, Jaco, 7, 133, 138, 139, 141, 142
Gese, Hartmut, 138
Gibbons, Kathleen, 56
Goldhaber, Michael, 48
Goosen, Danie, 206
Gordis, Robert, 194, 196
Gottlieb, Roger, 105, 106
Grand, Sue, 177, 178
Granofsky, Ronald, 174
Greijdanus, S., 33
Gregersen, Niels Henrik, 74
Gregory of Nazianzus, 22
Gregory of Nyssa, 13
Grey, Jacqueline, 156, 160, 163, 166
Griffin, D. R., 29
Griffiths-Dickson, Gwen, 140
Groenewald, Alphonso, 8, 132, 150, 152, 159
Gruchy, John de, 14, 36, 88, 89
Gruchy, Steve de, 36
Grønhøj, Alice, 103
Guattari, Félix, 50
Gunda, Masiiwa Ragies, 124
Gunn, David M., 110
Gurney, Oliver R., 115

AUTHOR INDEX

Gutierrez, Gustavo, 199

Habel, Norman C., 193
Hackett, Justin, 104
Hammershaimb, Erling, 157
Harrison, Kathryn, 21
Hartley, J. E., 193
Harvey, Barry, 90
Hayles, Katherine, 49
Heever, Gerhard van den, 28
Hendricks, Ashraf, 100
Heidegger, Martin, 70, 72, 73
Herman, Judith, 8, 173, 174, 176, 181
Hibbard, J. Todd., 163
Holdt, Karl von, 124
Holloway, Julian, 39
Holter, Knut, 132
Hom, Mary K. Y. H., 154
Houssay-Holzschuch, Myriam, 37
Houtman, Cornelis, 111
Hug, Edward, 180
Huizing, Klaas, 69
Human, Dirk, 132
Hunter, Shona, 82, 85, 86, 91
Husserl, Edmund, 72–73

Imray, Kathryn, 142
Irigaray, Luce, 73
Irvin, Aaron, 115
Irvine, Stuart A., 156, 160, 161
Isbell, Charles D., 121
Isherwood, Lisa, 35, 38

Jenkins, Jacqueline, 15
Jennings, Willie, 81, 91
John Chrysostom, 13
John of the Cross, 10, 16, 22, 89
Johnstone, William, 122
Jones, Scott C., 141
Joubert, Lisel, 1, 2, 4, 6
Julian of Norwich, 6, 11, 15–17, 22, 23

Kaiser, Otto, 135
Karenga, Maulana, 116
Käsemann, Ernst, 33
Keefer, Arthur Jan, 135
Kim, Hyun C. P., 159
Knoetze, Johannes, 101

Knott, Kim, 29, 30
Kobe, Sandiswa, 83
Kobo, Fundiswa, 5
Kolk, Bessel van der, 180
Konstantinovsky, Julia, 55
Kosciulek, Desirée, 101, 102
Kotva, Simone, 52
Kourie, Celia, 1, 2, 4, 5, 8, 29, 83, 209–19
Krašovec, Jože, 111
Kretzschmar, Louise, 1, 2, 4, 5, 29, 83
Kritzinger, J. N., 39, 87–88, 92
Krüger, Thomas, 133, 144

Lacoste, Jean-Yves, 71
Lampe, Geoffrey, 56
Lane, Belden, 10, 12, 13, 15, 16, 17, 22, 23, 24
Lanzetta, Beverly, 12, 17
Lapsley, Jacqueline E., 157
Lawrie, Douglas, 91
Lefebvre, Henri, 29–30
Lemanski, Christine, 37
Lemon, Anthony, 37
Lethoko, Mankolo, 97
Levin, Christoph, 134
Lichtheim, Miriam, 121
Lindy, Jacob D., 162, 164
Liverani, Mario, 118
Lohse, Eduard, 32, 33
Lombaard, Christo, 1, 2, 4, 5, 8, 135, 204, 207, 208
Louth, Andrew, 12, 13
Lovink, Geert, 47–48
Lowe, Edward Jonathan, 207
Lyon, Emily, 178, 179, 180

Magome, Mogomotsi, 128
Makoena, Lerato, 132
Maimonides, 112
Malina, Bruce, 40
Mandolofo, Carleen, 176, 177
Marcus, George E., 50
Marion, Jean-Luc, 71
Marquart-Pyatt, Sandra, 104
Masango, Maake, 38
Maseko, Nomsa, 126
Masenya, Madipoane, 132

Matthews, Victor, 30
Matter, E. Anne, 12
Maximus the Confessor, 14
Mayekiso, Theo, 88
McAffee, Matthew, 111, 114
McEntire, Mark. A, 159
McFarland, Ian, 14, 17, 23, 24
McGinnis, Claire Mathews, 111
McGrath, Alister, 12, 13, 22, 24, 83
McIntosh, Mark, 14
McKnight, Scot, 30, 35
McNally, Richard J., 180
Mechthild of Magdeburg, 10
Meister, Chad, 137
Meister Eckhart, 13, 15
Merleau-Ponty, Maurice, 73–74
Merton, Thomas, 10
Michel, Otto, 32
Milbank, John, 49
Miller, Patrick D., 175
Moltmann, Jürgen, 201
Moo, Douglas, 32
Moser, Paul, 137
Moss, Candida, 28, 40
Motyer, J. Alec, 158, 160, 162, 164
Moxnes, Halvor, 27, 38
Mtshiselwa, Ndikho, 132
Murphy, Roland, 134, 135
Musa, Hassan, 8

Nagel, Ramus, 68–69
Nakamura, Hajime, 18
Nancy, Jean-Luc, 65
Nault, Jean-Charles, 56, 57
Nel, Philip J., 132
Nel, Reggie, 98, 101, 151
Nell, Ian, 91
Newsom, Carol A., 191
Nicholls, Roderick, 135
Nisly, L. Lamar, 23
Niven, Thomas R., 18, 19, 20
Nkrumah, Bright, 97
Nongbri, Brent, 29

O'Connor, Kathleen M., 167
Odell, Jenny, 59
Olojede, Funlola, 132
O'Reilley, Mary Rose, 18, 19, 21

Oranje, M., 37
Origen of Alexandria, 89
Oswald, Wolfgang, 109

Pabst, Adrian, 49
Paintner, Christine, 23
Parker, Julie F., 157
Parkinson, R. B., 113, 117
Pernau, Margrit, 28
Pilling, David, 127
Plato, 72
Pseudo-Dionysius, 6, 13, 15, 89
Pope Pius XI, 18
Porter, Stanley, 23
Poser, Ruth, 158
Postman, Zoë, 100
Potgieter, Annette, 5, 6, 28, 132
Powell, Samuel, 29
Propp, William H. C., 112, 117
Punt, Jeremy, 38, 40

Rahim, Jennifer A., 174
Ramantswana, Hulisani, 132
Rancière, Jacques, 68
Ranft, Patricia, 18–19
Rendsburg, Gary, 118
Rensburg, Fika van, 4
Reysen, Stephen, 104
Riet, Louis van der, 7, 80, 92
Richter, Melvin, 125
Ricoeur, Paul, 65, 71, 73
Rieger, Anna-Katharina, 3
Riley, Greg, 56
Ringel, Shoshana, 173
Roberts, Jimmy J. M., 155, 163, 165
Robinson, Marilynne, 22
Rossouw, Fourie, 86, 92
Rubinstein, Ernest, 135
Rudman, Dominic, 143
Rugwiji, Temba, 132

Sacks, Oliver, 178
Saka, Erkan, 50
Salazar, Heather, 135
Sanders, James, 138
Sanders, Paul, 115, 138
Sartre, Jean-Paul, 73
Schoors, Antoon, 134, 135, 138

AUTHOR INDEX

Scheffler, Eben, 132
Schiffhorst, Gerald J., 24, 25
Schlier, Heinrich, 32, 33
Schmitt, Carl, 67–68
Schneiders, Sandra, 1, 2
Schore, Allan N., 180
Schutzius, Mark D., II, 158
Schwienhorst-Schönberger, Ludger, 133
Scott-Macnab, David, 56
Sebastian, C. D., 18
Seto, Michael C., 177
Seymour, Richard, 47
Sharp, Carolyn J., 149, 150
Shapshak, Toby, 125
Sheldon, Mark, 194, 195, 197–98
Sheldrake, Philip, 13, 27, 39
Siddall, Luis R., 155, 156
Singer, Itamar, 115
Signer, M., 64
Sigurdson, Ola, 74
Sivek, Daniel J., 103
Smith, Caleb, 57, 58
Smith, Caroline, 105
Smith, Gary V., 165
Sneed, Mark. R. 136
Soja, Edward, 29–30
Sölle, Dorothee, 173
Spearing, Elizabeth, 17
Spicq, Ceslas, 33
Spinoza, Benedict de, 75
Steck, Odil H., 150
Steinmetz-Jenkins, Daniel, 67
Stewart, Columba, 47, 54
Stewart, Eric C., 27, 30, 39
Steyn, Melissa, 59, 80, 90
Stiegler, Bernard, 45, 51
Stoecklin, Daniel, 99
Strawn, Brent, 174
Stuart, Elisabeth, 35, 38
Stulman, Louis, 159
Stump, Eleanore, 139
Sutton, Sharon Egretta, 101
Sweeney, Daniel S., 174
Swilling, Mark, 125

Taliaferro, Charles, 137
Taylor, Justin, 111
Teppo, Annika, 37

Terranova, Tiziana, 51
Thérèse of Lisieux, 6, 11, 15, 18–21, 22
Thøgersen, John, 103
Turchetti, Mario, 125
Tooley, Michael, 136, 138
Tull, Patricia K., 155, 163, 165
Turner, Denys, 15–16, 17
Tutu, Desmond, 90

Ullrich, Calvin, 6
Utzschneider, Helmut, 109

Vellem, Vuyani, 78–79, 87, 88
Verwoerd, Wilhelm, 80, 92
Vidojević, Jelena, 126
Villiers, Pieter de, 4, 5, 8, 86, 209–19
Visser, Irene, 167
Vogel, Jeffrey A. 58
Vosloo, Robert, 36, 37, 64
Vosloo, Wil, 4

Waaijman, Kees, 13, 35
Wakeham, Myles, 48
Wallace, James A., 23
Walsh, Jerome T., 135
Walsh, Zack, 46
Watson, Nicholas, 15
Watts, John D. W., 159
Weaver, Dorothy Jean, 32, 34
Weeks, Stuart T., 133
Wegner, Paul D., 157, 161, 163
Weissenrieder, Annette, 74
Weissflog, Kay, 157
Welzen, Huub, 208
Wepener, Cas, 91
West, Gerald, 124, 125, 132, 174, 175
Westbrook, Raymond, 115
Westermann, Claus, 176
Westhuizen, Christi van der, 82, 85, 86, 91
Wildberger, Hans, 163, 166
Williams, J. G., 196
Williams, Rowan, 2–3, 55
Williamson, Hugh G. M., 155, 156, 157, 160, 163, 165, 166
Willis, John T., 160
Wilson, John P., 162, 164
Wilson, Lindsay, 198

Wittgenstein, Ludwig, 73
Wittling, W., 180
Wolter, Michael, 33
Worrell, William, 56
Wyk, Tanya van, 5
Wyngaard, Cobus van, 80, 81–82, 83–84, 92

Zeller, Dieter, 33
Žižek, Slavoj, 68, 69
Zuck, R. B., 193

Scripture Index

Gen
25:21	115
31:7	118

Exod
1:10	112
1:11	113
3:14	13
3:19	112
4:6–9	113
4:22–23	116, 122
5:2	112, 114
5:5–9	112, 123
5:14–16	113
5:15	113
7:10	113
7:15–18	122
7:23–24	114
7:27	116
8–11	122
8:4	115, 116, 118
8:8	115
8:11	116
8:12	117
8:14	117
8:15	117
8:16–19	122
8:21	118
8:24	118
8:25	118
8:28	119
9:3	119
9:4	119
9:5	119
9:7	119
9:9	120
9:12	120
9:13–19	122
9:14	120
9:15	120
9:20	120
9:27	121
9:34	121
10:1	121
10:7	121
10:17	122
12:33–36	122
15:24	176
20:9	121
21:29	119
24–27	122
31:18	117

Deut
9:10	117

1 Sam
15:24	121

2 Sam
12:13	121

1 Kgs

1:52	119
2:22–23	119

2 Kgs

18:14	121
15–16	154

2 Chr

28	154

Ps

3	184
3:2	176
3:7	176
13	176, 184
13:1–3	184
46:8	162
46:12	162
51:7	85–86
56:8	179
137	199

Job

1:1–5	192, 198
2:1–8	195
2:4–6	120
2:11–13	193
3	192
3–8	198
11	198
7:1–10	197
7:21	199
8:1–3	193
9:21–24	197
13–14	199
17:3	116
17:13	199
17:15	199
19:10	199
19:23–27	200
19:25	201
23:3–4	200
27:6	197
27:8	199
29–31	200
32–37	194
33:26	115
42:9–11	200
42:9–17	192

Eccl

1:13	137
2:21	137
4:3	137
4:13	134
4:13–18	134
5:1	137
5:16	137
6:1	137
9:11–12	137
9:13–16	134
9:15	134
9:16	134
10:1	137
10:5	137
11:2	137
12:1	137

Isa

6:10	165
7–8	148–71
7:2	156, 161
7:3	156
7:9	156, 160
7:10	156
7:10–16	162
7:11	162
7:14	157, 162
7:14–16	164
8:1	157, 166
8:2–3	166
8:3–4	166
8:1–4	166
8:4	166
8:5–8	159, 166
8:5–10	163
8:7	166
8:8	162, 163, 166
8:10	162
8:18	157

10:5	166

Jonah
1:16	115

Luke
11:19	117

John
8:6	117

Rom
1–4	30
5–8	28, 30
5:1–5	30
5:2	30, 31
5:3–5	33
5:5	30
5:10	30
5:1–11	30
5:12–21	31
6:1–7:6	31
6:4	34
6:5	31
7:7—8:17	31
7:14—8:4	31
7:21	31
7:23	31
7:24	31
8:5–9	31
8:9–11	31
8:9–17	31
8:17	32
8:18	32
8:11	31, 34
8:18	32
8:18–21	32
8:18–30	27–43.
8:19	32
8:21	32
8:22	32
8:22–27	32
8:23	32, 33
8:24	33
8:24–25	33
8:25	33
8:26–27	34
8:28	34
8:29	31, 34, 35, 38
8:31–39	30
9:17–18	111
10:17–18	111

1 Cor
6:15	34
6:19	34
11:24	63
15:35–49	34

2 Cor
4:16	32
4:17	32
4:18	33
5:1–2	32
5:2	32
5:4	32
12:1–4	34

Eph
3:19	60

Phil
2:14	176

1 Pet
5:7	60

EARLY CHRISTIAN WRITINGS

Evagrius

Gnostikos
4	53–54
20	53
49	53

Kephalaia Gnostika

1.49	54
1.89	55
3.12	55
3.28	54
3.30	55
3.59	54

On the Eight Thoughts

6.5	58
6.12–13	58

Praktikos

1	53
8	53
12	56
86	55

Scholia on Ecclesiastes

1	53
8	53
15	53

Skemmata

2	56
4	56

To Eulogios

21	56
30	56

www.ingramcontent.com/pod-product-compliance
Lightning Source LLC
Chambersburg PA
CBHW051640230426
43669CB00013B/2375